MODERN ENGLISH STRUCTURE

IN MEMORIAM

F. A. C.

A. M. C.

Modern English Structure

SECOND EDITION

BARBARA M. H. STRANG

*Professor of English Language and General Linguistics
in the University of Newcastle upon Tyne*

EDWARD ARNOLD

© Barbara M. H. Strang, 1969

First published 1962 by
Edward Arnold (Publishers) Ltd
41 Maddox Street, London W1
Reprinted 1963
Reprinted 1964
Reprinted 1965
Second edition, revised, 1968
Reprinted 1969

Boards edition SBN : 7131 5414 4
Paper   edition SBN : 7131 5415 2

PRINTED IN GREAT BRITAIN BY
WILLIAM CLOWES AND SONS, LIMITED, LONDON AND BECCLES

Introduction

The need has long been felt for an introductory textbook on the study of English which shall be useful to elementary students without offending against the standards of professional linguists. Perhaps everyone who tries to teach on these lines feels the necessity of writing his own course and will be dissatisfied with anyone else's. At any rate, I know I am not alone in my discontent with anything currently available.

Some choice of method and terminology is always open to a grammarian, and I realise that what I have written is open to theoretical objection on the grounds of its conformity with tradition. I believe it is good for an elementary textbook of a student's own vernacular to bring out the distinctive character of the language not in terms solely applicable to it, but as far as possible in terms which will serve for, and enable him to effect comparisons with, at least those cognate languages he is most likely to be acquainted with. That is, I do not think it right, *for this purpose*, to discuss, for instance, whether English has nouns or not, but rather how the term *noun* can most revealingly be defined in the study of English. It is this principle which has guided my choice of methods and terms, and has even contributed to my notion of what is the available range of choice.

I have spoken of a particular purpose, and would like to define it more closely. It is to give the elementary student an awareness of the mechanisms of his own language through descriptive analysis. By elementary student I mean principally the pass or general degree student at a university, but I hope the work will also have some use for the sixth-former, the training-college student, and even the honours student of English who is not a linguistic specialist.

I do not believe there is such a thing as finality in the description of a language—certainly not of a living language. A textbook presentation of the subject is *a fortiori* provisional. But more than this inevitable evanescence attaches to any work on English grammar published in anticipation of Professor Randolph Quirk's projected *Survey of Educated Spoken English*. For that, however, we have to wait a decade, and it will be longer before derivative textbooks can appear. In the near future, very great theoretical advances in methods of linguistic description are expected, but this has been the position throughout my life so far and (I would almost say 'I trust') will stay so for the remainder of it. Meanwhile, the necessity of putting something into the hands of teachers and students is desperate, and this is the sole justification of the present work. It hopes to be no more than an interim measure. I am appalled by the frequency with which I have to say that the facts about a given usage are simply not known (analytically known, that is). But there are many reaches of English structure concerning which a clear statement of ignorance would be a step forward.

Most chapters are provided with exercises, though many teachers will prefer to devise their own. It is unfortunate that though the substance of the book emphasises spoken English, the material of the exercises has to be drawn not from real speech, but from literary sources, and I would like to make two suggestions in this connection. First, I should be sorry if anyone conducted a course on *Modern English Structure* without considering the tape-recorder as essential a piece of equipment as the textbook. Second, the book is conducted as if it were a class in which all participate; the *we's* throughout it are emphatically not editorial. If a group of people work through the book as a team, and keep the tape-recorder on during their discussions, they will be providing themselves with material for analysis far more rewarding than anything I can offer.

References are given throughout by author and year of publication; full details of the publications referred to are given in the bibliography.

I hope that my indebtedness to general linguists, phoneticians, and recent writers on the structure of English will be clear from the references in my text; what may not emerge so boldly is a more indirect, but very great, debt to the work of the great observers of the detail of English usage, from Henry Sweet through Otto Jespersen, G. O. Curme, H. Poutsma, H. E. Palmer, E. Kruisinga and P. A. Erades, to R. W. Zandvoort. The Linguistics Association has provided a forum for discussion from which I have benefited in many ways; amongst its members I am aware of a special obligation to Professor Randolph Quirk, Dr. M. A. K. Halliday, and Messrs. J. C. Catford, John Sinclair and W. Haas, some of whom have allowed me to refer to their unpublished work. The Council of King's College, Newcastle upon Tyne, allowed me study leave during the Michaelmas Term, 1961, and this enabled me to complete the book much more quickly, and much less incoherently, than I could otherwise have done. Professor Peter Ure and my colleagues in the Department of English, especially Dr. Angus Macdonald, were so accommodating as to make possible the rearrangement of my teaching so that I could take up the grant of study leave. Though I fear they did not suspect it at the time, several generations of undergraduates have been teaching me what little I know about how to put across linguistic material to people whose central interests lie elsewhere. The staff of the University Library, King's College, have been unfailingly helpful. My sister-in-law Jean Strang and Miss K. O'Rawe have provided skilled secretarial help. Mrs. Jean Bone has spent much time checking the typescript. My colleague, Mr. James

Maxwell, has had the outstanding kindness to go through the entire typescript and has made many acute comments and corrections; he, like others too numerous to mention, has provided references for interesting usages and illuminating discussion of matters I wished to treat. My most overwhelming debt is to my husband, Colin Strang; I could not begin to formulate or acknowledge it in its totality, but I should like to record that it includes both a corrective element, directing attention to obscurities of expression and inconsistencies of thought, and a creative one—the seeking out of examples and the formulating of neat analyses of complex data. A meticulous examination of the whole typescript is only the final round of his contribution to the book.

Newcastle,
March, 1962

Note to the Second Edition

It was foolish of me to suggest in my original introduction that a textbook could be useful to elementary students without offending against the standards of professional linguists. Linguists, as a profession, do not have an agreed body of doctrine, and cannot properly be spoken of in the lump. I doubt if anything could be written about the English language that did not offend against the principles of some linguists. Even if it could, the aim would be unduly limited and negative. One can more appropriately think in terms of providing a text which some scholars think worth putting into the hands of students beginning the analytical study of the English language.

The successive reprintings of the book, with minor changes, indicate that it has not wholly failed in respect of an aim so formulated; though revision is now necessary if it is to continue to serve any purpose. I should like to use the occasion to specify more clearly than before not only my aim but also my intended audience.

In addressing the book to beginners, especially those with English as their native language, I was thinking especially of English English students, that is, of people whose linguistic preconceptions have been shaped by such studies as fall under the title of English in the educational system of this country. In 1961–1962 I had less understanding than now of how sharply the assumptions (and consequently the needs) of such people differed from those of students reared in other parts of the English-speaking world. Even those from Scottish or American schools need a rather different presentation. If I had to single out a tendency in these studies which has particularly directed my selection and arrangement of material, I would choose the pervasive tendency of so-called English Language teaching to induce students to turn a blind eye to the facts of usage. In such a situation the beginning of higher study must provide a corrective; it seems to me natural that this corrective should take the form of encouraging a habit of attention—attention which can only, in the first instance, be to the facts of surface structure. No-one can afford to stop at the level of surface structure, but some need a good deal of help to get even that far.

My own reading during the past five years would in any case have led to extensive revision, but I am happy to acknowledge that I have learnt a great deal from reviewers of the first edition, and from those, both colleagues and students, who have offered comments more privately. They form a large and distinguished body, and almost without exception their observations, even when critical, have been positive and helpful. I single out for mention two people, Randolph Quirk and Colin Strang, for the extent of their help, and for the blend of learning, insight and gentleness that makes their comments so welcome; but to all who trace, however blurred, the lineaments of their advice, I offer my warmest thanks.

In addition to changes and expansions of a regular kind I have made one alteration in the mode of presentation. The Bibliography continues to serve two purposes—it lists the main works cited in the text, and provides a guide to further reading. But it now seems advisable to set out plans for directed reading at the conclusion of each chapter or group of chapters. At first sight it may seem odd that a few items in the new sections on *Further Reading* (especially those at the end of Chapter II) are not included in the general Bibliography, but I believe this decision can be defended. The Bibliography, in so far as it is a guide to further reading, sets out to indicate what can most usefully enter the sights of any student in a one-year course, who is giving at least some proportion of his time to English Language. Its value is nullified if it is over-ambitious. Yet some particular student may wish to follow up one or another point in a chapter, and be glad to know where to do so. I am delighted to be able to include so much new material in the suggested reading; but the deletions from the old Bibliography do not mean a lessening of respect for earlier work—only that I have had to take a sadly constricted stand about priorities for my envisaged audience.

Acknowledgements

The author and Publisher wish to thank the Bell Telephone Laboratories, Murray Hill, New Jersey for permission to use the photographic material on the plates which appear in the book, and the following for permission to use copyright material: the authors and Longmans Green & Co. Ltd. for the extracts from *Problems and Principles* by David Abercrombie (previously appearing in an article in *English Language Teaching*), 'Lexis as a Linguistic Level' by M. A. K. Halliday in *In Memory of J. R. Firth* edited by C. E. Bazell, *Patterns of Language* by A. McIntosh and M. A. K. Halliday, and 'Syllable Quantity and Enclitics in English' by David Abercrombie in *In Honour of Daniel Jones* edited by David Abercrombie; Victor Gollancz Ltd. for the extract from *Take a Girl Like You* by Kingsley Amis; David Higham Associates Ltd. for the extract from *The Day of the Sardine* by Sid Chaplin; the Syndics of the Cambridge University Press for the extract from *Studies in Words* by C. S. Lewis; Mrs Anne Wyndham Lewis for the extract from *Paleface* by Wyndham Lewis; Methuen & Co. Ltd. for the extract from *King Solomon's Ring* by Konrad Lorenz; Curtis Brown Ltd. and the Trustees of the Rose Macaulay estate for the extract from *Staying with Relations*; MacGibbon and Kee Ltd. for the extract from *Absolute Beginners* by Colin MacInnes; William Heinemann Ltd. for the extract from *The Acceptance World* by Anthony Powell; Martin Secker and Warburg Ltd. for the extract from *Colloquial English and Communication* by Randolph Quirk; the University of California Press for the extract from *Selected Writings* and *Abnormal Types of Speech in Nootka* by Edward Sapir; the author and Macmillan & Co. Ltd. for the extract from *The Masters* by C. P. Snow; Basil Blackwell Ltd. for the extract from *Philosophical Investigations* by Ludwig Wittgenstein; the author and the Linguistic Society of America for the extracts from 'Descriptive Statement and Serial Relationships' by Randolph Quirk in *Language* 41; George Allen and Unwin Ltd. for the extract from *Language* by Leonard Bloomfield; the authors and Mouton et cie, The Hague, for the extracts from 'A Phonetician's View of Verse Structure' by David Abercrombie in *Linguistics* 6, and *Investigating Linguistic Acceptability* by Randolph Quirk and Jan Svartvik; Dennis Dobson Ltd. for the extract from *The Unpleasant Profession of Jonathan Hoag* by Robert A. Heinlein; the author and The Observer Ltd. for 'The American Language' by John Crosby; The Times Publishing Co. Ltd. for the extracts from *The Times;* the author and Otto Harassowitz Verlag for an extract from *The Categories and Types of Present-day English Word-Formation* by Hans Marchand; and G. L. Trager and Henry Lee Smith Jnr. for an extract from their book *An Outline of English Structure.*

Contents

Chapter

CHAPTER I

The Nature of Language

§1. Language is so much taken for granted as a component of normal human experience that we characterise as infancy ('being without speech') the only stage in our lives when experience is not saturated with language. Many people do not reflect on the part language plays in their lives, but most people pay tribute to it by taking some interest in questions about its origins, development and correct use. They are as ready to ask how the armadillo got his name as how the elephant got his trunk, and equally ready to listen to stories in answer to both questions. This book is about the most general aspects of how English works, but much that is true of English is true of it simply because it is a language and because it is language. For that reason we may start by considering some questions about language in general.

§2. One of the questions people do not very readily ask about language is what it is. By and large, for practical purposes, they know—that is, they know in general how to recognise an example of it when they meet one. Even at this level there are difficulties. For instance, we talk about *the language of mathematics* or *music* or *the dance,* but if a foreigner who did not talk English asked us to point out examples by which he could learn the meaning of the word *language* we would not show him a sum or a samba. If he asked about, say, *the language of music,* we could refer him in general terms to the practice of extending meanings figuratively, and we could show that the extension is secondary because if he knows what is meant by *language* he will understand its use in *the language of music,* but the converse is not true. A more serious difficulty arises when we have to face expressions like *the language of bees.* This might, like our first difficulty, be resolvable by reference to some notion of figurative meaning, but the question is precisely whether the expression is figurative or not—that is, whether it can be used because of some significant but partial similarity between what we ordinarily call language and bee-communication, or whether they are so alike as to fall under the same definition. There are two problems: we have first to think out what we regard as essential to language and then to ask whether this is found in the signalling system of bees.

Now there have already been countless definitions of *language*; the truth is that the semantic spread of the word in ordinary usage is so great that any manageable definition will leave out or distort something. I do not believe that what we need in this book is yet another definition, but rather a working account or description that will bring out those characteristics most important to our understanding of how language functions.

Note

For interest, I append three definitions of language that have something like classic standing. I do not discuss them, but their value should be pondered in the light of what follows in this chapter:

(1) From the *Oxford English Dictionary* (henceforward referred to as *OED.*) the relevant sense is 2, 'Words and the methods of combining them for the expression of thought.'

(2) Jespersen (1933) §1.2, 'Language is nothing but a set of human habits, the purpose of which is to give expression to thoughts and feelings, and especially to impart them to others.'

(3) Sweet (1891) §16, 'Language is the expression of ideas by means of **speech-sounds** combined into **words**. Words are combined into **sentences**, this combination answering to that of ideas into thoughts.'

§3. To many it will seem alarmingly unscientific to struggle on without a definition of our most basic term, and as questions of definition are persistently troublesome in all linguistic studies it is worth saying a word about the use of definitions. The chief difficulty arises when we have to limit a word in current use to some more rigorously defined sense, and this is well illustrated by the term *language* itself. In *Philosophical Investigations* Ludwig Wittgenstein wrote:

'Instead of producing something common to all that we call language, I am saying that these phenomena have no one thing in common which makes us use the same word for all,—but that they are *related* to one another in many different ways. And it is because of this relationship, or these relationships, that we call them all "language". I will try to explain this.

'Consider for example the proceedings that we call "games". I mean board-games, card-games, ball-games, Olympic games, and so on. What is common to them all?—Don't say: "There must be something common, or they would not be called 'games'"—but *look and see* whether there is anything common to all.—For if you look at them you will not see something that is common to *all*, but similarities, relationships, and a whole series of them at that. To repeat: don't think, but look!—Look for example at board-games, with their multifarious relationships. Now pass to card-games; here you find many correspondences with the first group, but many common features drop out, and others appear. When we pass next to ball-games, much that is common is retained, but much is lost. Are they all "amusing"? Compare chess with noughts and crosses. Or is there always winning and losing, or competition between players? Think of patience. In ball-games there is winning and losing; but when a child throws his ball at the wall and catches it again, this feature has disappeared. Look at the parts played by skill and luck; and at the difference between skill in chess and skill in tennis. Think now of games like ring-a-ring-a-roses; here is the element of amusement, but how many other characteristic features have disappeared! And the result of this examination is: we see a complicated network of similarities overlapping and criss-crossing: sometimes overall similarities, sometimes similarities of detail.

'I can think of no better expression to characterize these similarities than "family resemblances"; for the various resemblances between members of a family: build, features, colour of eyes, gait, temperament, etc. etc. overlap and criss-cross in the same way.—And I shall say "games form a family"' (from §§65–67).

If we are inventing a technical term as an analytical instrument, we can give it whatever meaning we like. If we want to take over a term in common use, we must reckon with this principle of family resemblances operative in the semantic spread of words in ordinary use. Of course we can still arbitrarily adopt a rigorous use if we explain what we are doing, but we do so at a price. First, there is always danger of confusion because our minds are so accustomed to the more flexible general use. Second, the next writer on our subject is liable to adopt quite a different arbitrary definition, so that readers who try to pursue the subject have to learn a new set of definitions with each book they tackle. There are, for instance, well over two hundred different definitions of the term *sentence* for language-students to cope with. But above all, we shall have fragmented a subject which we all, partly because of our linguistic habits and experience, feel hangs together. For these reasons I shall try to give definitions only of technical terms; for words in common use I shall give descriptions or working accounts designed to throw light on, rather than to depart from, ordinary usage. In the case of the word *language* I want to approach the description from three directions: considering the type of structure it is, the type of function it has, and how it can be delimited in relation to neighbouring phenomena.

Note

A survey of definitions of *sentence* up to the date of his writing is given by Fries (1952), Chapter 2.

§4. Structurally, language is an articulated system of signs, primarily realised in the medium of speech. We shall spend the next few paragraphs considering what this means. It is a **system,** not a mere collection of parts, because in any given language the functioning parts hang together and condition each other.   We can see this most clearly if we go outside our own language and compare its conventions with those of other languages.   In vocabulary, for instance, the semantic spread or functional range of Modern English *sheep* is limited by the co-presence of *mutton* in the language, as contrasted with that of, say, *mouton* in French; the semantic spread of Swedish *farmor* (paternal grandmother) is limited by the presence of *mormor* (maternal grandmother) in the same vocabulary, as contrasted with that of English *grandmother*.   Each unit is delimited by its neighbours, and therefore all are ultimately interdependent—like the English parochial system in which the borders are all mutually determined and no interstices are left over.   The same features can be observed in the organisation of grammar: for instance, in Modern English, which has no pronoun dual, the plural is used with reference to, or in connection with, more than one, but in Old English, which had, the plural was used in connection with more than two.   A comparable type of mutual conditioning can be observed in the elements of the sound system; and again in the relationships between the various component systems of a language—the question of just what is expressed by means of vocabulary and what by means of grammar in a given language, for instance (consider how you would render *Cosi fan tutte* into English).   By taking examples outside English I have tried to bring out aspects of English structure that might otherwise be overlooked; I do not mean to suggest that all languages somehow or other cover the same ground semantically, for this is not the case.   The total semantic coverage of a language depends on the total experience of the speech-community using that language, and experience differs from community to community.   When we compare languages, therefore, there are always some similar and some distinctive ranges of meaning expressed.

Notes

1. The conception of language as an articulated system of signs is fundamental in F. de Saussure (1916), and is expounded there most fully in Part I.   An English version is available in Saussure (1961) and the complex history of the original text can now be traced in Saussure (1967).
2. It would strictly be more correct to say that language is systematic than that it is a system, for the various systems that make up any given language are not integrated with each other to the same extent or in the same way as are the internal parts of a single system.   J. R. Firth (1948), p. 151, uses the term **polysystemic** for this characteristic of language.   This refinement of thinking is very proper, but to give prominence to it at the present stage may obscure the much more fundamental contrast between a system and an aggregation, which is one of the first things to grasp when looking at language-structure.

§5. The kind of system language is, is an articulated system. The word **articulated** is ultimately derived from Latin *articulus*, diminutive of *artus* 'joint', and it is here used to refer to the property in languages of being able to build up units of one order into units of another order, that is, not merely something bigger, but something functioning in quite a different way from its component parts (compare the difference between single vertebrae and the backbone they compose). In English, for example, the two words *but* and *bit* are each made up of three sounds in a given order; the difference between them is made by the middle sound. Now the difference of sound between *u* and *i* does not have any significance in itself (see how differently it functions in other paired sequences like *hut, hit; fun, fin; sun, sin*), but these sounds are the means of making a distinction between two units of a different order from themselves (namely, words). You will notice that at this level the articulations are almost wholly governed by convention; we acquire whole words when we learn our mother tongue, and if we want to be understood we do not form too many new ones for ourselves. But words themselves can be articulated into units of another, more complex order, usually called sentences, and this is where an element of personal creativeness enters into our utterances. If we know a language we can always articulate from its words (if it has words) sentences we have never heard before, and we can count on their being understood by speakers to whom, likewise, they are new.

Along with this difference between words and sentences goes another. Though words, unlike speech-sounds, have meanings, sentences have meanings of a much more particular and complete kind. Negatively, we can say that *but* is not the same as *bit*, but positively we can only give for each a considerable range of possible meanings. Once they are put into sentences each is relatively precisely located within that range: '*Try a bit harder*', '*Please give me a bit of that*', '*There was no bit in the carpenter's shop*', '*In communication theory the unit of information is the bit*', '*He bit a piece out of the apple*'. In some cases the particularising may proceed further, as when a sentence spoken by an actor in a play is interpreted by the hearers in the light of the knowledge that it is part of a play. Some years ago a good deal of panic was caused when a news announcement about the invasion of earth from another planet was included in a broadcast play, for listeners who had just tuned in did not realise that it was a play. So the progressive articulatory structure of language can be seen as a way of making increasingly precise the meaning of the component parts. The relevance of context to the significance of individual units must never be overlooked. It may even have to serve as the sole means of distinguishing two like-sounding utterances, such as *The sun's rays meet* and *The sons raise meat* (example from C. F. Hockett, 1958, §2.1).

But context, as we have already suggested, must not be thought of as nothing more than environment in the utterance. It includes the immediate social setting of the utterance, the function of the total relevant linguistic structure in its social setting, and even the entire cultural matrix in which the language functions. As a simple example, consider how you would explain the meaning or function of such linguistic structures as '*Good morning*' or '*Your worship*' without reference to social and cultural institutions. Such forms of expression are also a particularly clear pointer to the interpretation of talk about linguistic forms 'having meaning'. By this and similar expressions throughout the book, I do not suggest that the meanings forms have are anything like distinct objects, 'ghosts in the machine'; *meaning* in the relevant sense can be analysed as equivalent to *use* (cf. Wittgenstein, 1953, §43, 'For a *large* class of cases . . . the meaning of a word is its use in the language'). There are, I think, compelling reasons to keep the word *meaning* for the kind of uses linguistic forms have, as long as we do not let it lead us into the error of dualism.

Notes

1. The use of the term *articulated* expounded in this paragraph must not be confused with that current in phonetic studies, cf. §§26 ff.
2. The importance of context in the widest sense in the study of language is stressed in the work of Malinowski, Firth, Sapir and Pike. The dangers of 'ghost in the machine' theories are examined not only by Wittgenstein, but also by Ryle (1949), who is not concerned with meaning in language, but with other matters in which the temptation of dualism is strong.
3. In this paragraph I have introduced the term **context** in a dual sense, building on common usage and on the practice of earlier linguists and anthropologists. It is now usual to distinguish the senses by use of separate terms—**co-text** for linguistic environment, and **context** for cultural setting. This useful distinction is introduced by McIntosh in Bazell etc. (1966, 303, Note 2, where the term *co-text* is attributed to J. C. Catford).

§6. What language is a system of, is **signs**. The word *sign*, like the word *language*, has many different meanings, but the one chiefly relevant here is 'a mark or device having some special meaning or import attached to it' (*OED.*, sb. 2). Note that the mark or device is not chosen necessarily as being inherently representative, or expressive, or symbolic, of its import; the association of the one with the other is arbitrary, conventional—in the words of the *OED*. the meaning or import is attached, and it is people who do the attaching. With most linguistic forms this is obvious enough; what is not always realised is that even the relatively few and peripheral elements in language that are to some extent imitative or onomatopoeic differ from language to language and from time to time according to the conventions of usage—

the Anglo-Saxons expressed sympathy by saying '*He! He!*' and as is well known, English bells go *ding-dong* and German ones *bim-bam.* Such forms are also subject to phonetic changes whereby their originally imitative character is completely obscured, as happened in the development of Latin *pipio* to French *pigeon,* itself borrowed into English to become the modern form *pigeon.* But even this limited measure of imitativeness is unusual, and characteristically linguistic forms are conventional in the sense that we use them as we do because that is what we have learnt as the practice of the speech-community we belong to; and they are arbitrary in the sense that we can give no other reason for our predecessors' use of them than that they too inherited them from yet earlier generations.

Scholars have distinguished in various ways between *signs* and *symbols,* but it is probably most convenient in linguistic work to reserve *symbol* for those things selected to stand for others by reason of some inherent aptness or appropriateness, and *sign* for those selected independently of any such considerations. Thus, though all language may be used symbolically, and some linguistic forms do have expressive or imitative value, the reasons for using a particular form in a particular function in a given language are independent of its symbolic value. Accordingly, linguistic forms can best be described as signs.

Notes

1. The case for this distinction between signs and symbols is argued by Saussure (1916), p. 101. Unfortunately, the importance of the symbolic use of linguistic forms has caused many scholars to write of them as being symbols. What is involved here is not necessarily a difference of opinion, but often only a difference of emphasis, between those who concentrate on the factors determining the forms, and those who concentrate on the way the forms are used. Students must be prepared to meet divergent terminology in this and other matters, cf. the usage of Edward Sapir, for instance in the passage quoted in §11 below.

2. What is said in this paragraph about a sign and its import must be interpreted with that caution against dualism already recommended in §5. Cf. again Wittgenstein (1958), p. 5, 'The mistake we are liable to make could be expressed thus: We are looking for the use of a sign, but we look for it as though it were an object *co-existing* with the sign .. The sign .. gets its significance from the system of signs, from the language to which it belongs.'

§7. Though we have used the term *sign* in talking about the structure of language, it is in fact a functional term—that is, there is no particular kind of thing that is or is not, can or cannot be, a sign. Anything is capable of being one; it is a question of how it is used, that is, of whether a meaning or import is attached to it. In this sense, regardless of the form chosen as their exponent, signs are necessarily mental products. They are also necessarily two-sided—there must always be, on one hand, the thing that is a sign of something, and on the other, the thing it is a sign of. The exponent may well be something existing in its own right, but it does not function as, that is, become, a sign until it signifies something. There are, then, three things we may think of, the exponent, its import, and their union, the sign. The French language copes with this situation more neatly and lucidly than English, having the words *signifiant* for 'that which signifies', *signifié* for 'that which is signified', and *signe* for what results from *signifiant* and *signifié* in mutual dependence on one another, namely, the sign. We shall keep to the English terms **exponent**, **signification** and **sign**, but our special use of them may be easier to remember if you bear in mind the French forms. The mutual dependence of exponent and signification must always be remembered; though we distinguish them in analytical work so as to be able to focus attention on each separately, they have in reality no separate existence, since each is only an aspect of the sign.

§8. There are two further things to notice about signs. First, since they are mental products, the distinctions between them reflect, not external reality (whatever that may be), but the mind's way of classifying its experience. The distinctions between signs, like the association of exponent and signification, are to some extent arbitrary within the speech-community. This again may best be seen by looking outside the familiar distinctions of our own language. Whorf (1956), pp. 208–216, gives many vivid examples, of which we may quote two. Where English has one word, *snow*, Eskimo has distinct words for falling snow, slushy lying snow and hard-packed snow, but no generic word for snow; we think of snow as a distinct kind of thing, for which, if we have experienced it, we naturally have a word, but we do not generally realise that this is not a view emanating from our experience of the world so much as from our experience of the English language. The second goes deeper. Where English has the sentence '*I clean it (gun) with the ramrod*', Shawnee has '*Nipēkwālakha*', in which *Ni-* corresponds to 'I' and *-a* to 'it', but the remaining components are *pēkw* ('dry space'), *ālak* ('interior of hole'), *h* ('by motion of tool, instrument'). Accordingly (and this is the second point), what a sign signifies is its signification (cf. §7); it does not signify an object, or, if it is a linguistic sign, anything in the external, non-linguistic world. Words are certainly not just names of things, though some of them (e.g. proper names) are used to refer to things. A sign-system is a mental system for whose validity questions about the external world are immaterial.

§9. The characteristics we have so far unravelled from the complex called language do not constitute a sufficiently exhaustive account. For example, all the features we have identified so far can be found in a traffic-light system. The units in the standard English type of traffic-light installation are mutually delimiting, (partly) arbitrarily selected, and capable of rudimentary articulation (the combination red and yellow having a signification not deducible from that of its parts). Yet it would be a departure from ordinary usage to speak of traffic-lights as forming a language, and it is ordinary usage we are now examining. What does such a system lack that it is not ordinarily called language? There is a difference of degree, in that it is immensely less complex. There is a more radical difference of kind: traffic-lights cannot be spoken, and language in its central ordinary sense is always something capable of being spoken. I would not depart so far from ordinary usage as many linguists have done in recent years and say that only speech is language, writing is not properly language. Language has two aspects; it is the mental systems we have already discussed, and it is the body of utterances framed in terms of these systems. The primary medium for that framing is speech—primary in that it came first and is still most widespread in the experience of mankind, and in the sense that for almost all human beings it is the first linguistic medium they learn to use (there are a very few exceptions like Helen Keller). Speech has so great a lead over its rivals that its use as medium should be incorporated into our working account of what language is. Those who maintain that writing is not language argue that writing is a mere reflex or transfer of speech (an imperfect one at that). In a society so highly sophisticated and literate as our own the relationship is certainly not so simple, and its nature probably varies from person to person; the problem is one for psychologists, and it will not do for linguists to assume they know the answer without investigation. It is best, therefore, to accord speech primacy among various possible linguistic media to the extent of mentioning it in our working description, and to the extent of excluding from language what could not be realised in speech, but not to the extent of identifying language exclusively with speech.

Note

Definitions of language which identify it exclusively with speech are fairly common among American linguists; examples are C. F. Hockett (1958), §1.2, and J. B. McMillan in *Applied English Linguistics* (Allen, 1958), p. 9. A different view is taken by M. Joos (1948), §5.02, who defines language as 'a set of neural patterns in the speech center', one of the six aspects of speech as he analyses it. An interesting example of the interaction of speech and writing in English is found in 'The Gnu Song' (Flanders and Swann, 'At the Drop of a Hat').

On the relationship between spoken and written English see Bradley (1913), McIntosh and Halliday (1966) Paper Six, Abercrombie (1967) Chapter I. On written language generally, see Gelb (1953); on spoken language generally Strevens (1956).

§10. The reference to language as two-sided, system and realisation, must be expanded, particularly as I differ from some recent linguists in taking the two sides to be essential, though system is primary. Once again, French is useful here. Saussure distinguished between *langage* (the total complex), *langue* (language as system), and *parole* (language as realisation); unhappily, in the published form of his work (for which he was not responsible) the distinction is not absolutely clear and consistent, and the attempts to anglicise his terms have not been altogether success- ful. In any case, this facet of language can perhaps best be understood if we apply to it the philosophical distinction between **types** and **tokens** first elaborated by C. S. Peirce in relation to a linguistic example. There is one word *the* in the English language, but instances of it occur very frequently—perhaps thirty times on a page this size. The instances, or tokens, exist in the sense of being phenomena, having a definite location and time of occurrence; the types, e.g., the word *the*, exist in the sense that they are rules determining the shape and function of the tokens. That not only single words, but all linguistic forms, constitute a **type- token complex** has been increasingly realised in the last few years. Accordingly, no account of language which excludes from it the type- system can be valid, since that is what both causes and enables the tokens to function; language, or a language, cannot be defined as the total of utterances of speech-communities or a given speech-community. On the other hand there is something alien from ordinary usage, I would almost say perverse, about taking the language to be only a type-system, and distinguishing between language (as the type-system only) and medium (e.g., speech, writing). Using the term *language* for the whole complex, system and realisation, enables us both to retain and to il- luminate ordinary usage.

Note

Linguistic applications of Peirce's type-token distinction can be found in Yule (1944), Strang (1958) and Herdan (1960). For the notion of a language as consisting only of its (speech) tokens, cf. Z. S. Harris (1951), §2.4, 'For the purpose of descriptive linguistic investigations a single LANGUAGE or dialect is considered over a brief period of time. This com- prises the talk which takes place in a language-community.' On the distinction between *language* and *medium* see Abercrombie (1967), Chapter I.

§11. It is usual to identify language not only in structural, but also in functional terms, and here the notions of language as a means of expres- sion and as a means of communication are central. They do not, however, provide an exhaustive or sufficiently exclusive account of the functions of language. Expression and communication are carried on by means other than language, and language has other functions besides these. A stimulating account of the functions of language has been given by Edward Sapir (1949), pp. 10–12, 15–16:

'In the first place, language is felt to be a perfect symbolic system, in a perfectly homogeneous medium, for the handling of all references and meanings that a given culture is capable of. The content of every culture is expressible in its language.... It is highly important to realize that once the form of a language is established it can discover meanings for its speakers which are not simply traceable to the given quality of experience itself but must be explained to a large extent as the projection of potential meanings into the raw material of experience. If a man who has never seen more than a single elephant in the course of his life, nevertheless speaks without the slightest hesitation of ten elephants or a million elephants or a herd of elephants or of elephants walking two by two or three by three or of generations of elephants, it is obvious that language has the power to analyze experience into theoretically dissociable elements and to create that world of the potential intergrading with the actual which enables human beings to transcend the immediately given in their individual experiences and to join in a larger common understanding. This common understanding constitutes culture.... [The forms of language] predetermine for us certain modes of observation and interpretation.... No matter how sophisticated our modes of interpretation become, we never really get beyond the projection and continuous transfer of relations suggested by the forms of our speech.... Language is at one and the same time helping and retarding us in our exploration of experience....

'A further psychological characteristic of language is the fact that while it may be looked upon as a symbolic system which reports or refers to or otherwise substitutes for direct experience, it does not as a matter of actual behavior stand apart from or run parallel to direct experience, but completely interpenetrates with it.... It is generally difficult to make a complete divorce between objective reality and our linguistic symbols of reference to it; and things, qualities, and events are on the whole felt to be what they are called. For the normal person every experience, real or potential, is saturated with verbalism. This explains why so many lovers of nature, for instance, do not feel that they are truly in touch with it until they have mastered the names of a great many flowers and trees, as though the primary world of reality were a verbal one.... It is this constant interplay between language and experience which removes language from the cold status of such purely and simply symbolic systems as mathematical symbolism or flag signaling.... It is important to realize that language may not only refer to experience or even mold, interpret, and discover experience, but that it also substitutes for it in the sense that in those sequences of interpersonal behavior which form the greater part of our daily lives speech and action supplement each other and do each

other's work in a web of unbroken pattern. If one says to me
"Lend me a dollar" I may hand over the money without a word or I
may give it with an accompanying "Here it is" or I may say "I
haven't got it" or "I'll give it to you tomorrow". Each of these responses is structurally equivalent, if one thinks of the larger behavior
pattern.'

Sapir proceeds from this account of the role of language in the experience
of individual and community, to a discussion of its expressive function,
which, as he says, is in no danger of being overlooked. Later he con-
siders the communicative function and others that may be regarded as
coming roughly within its orbit. Answering those who would define
language as a communication-system, he says:

'To say that thought, which is hardly possible in any sustained sense
without the symbolic organisation brought by language, is that form
of communication in which the speaker and the person addressed are
identified in one person is not far from begging the question. The
autistic speech of children seems to show that the purely communicative aspect of language has been exaggerated. It is best to admit that
language is primarily a vocal actualization of the tendency to see
realities symbolically, that it is precisely this quality which renders
it a fit instrument for communication.... Language is a great force of
socialization, probably the greatest that exists. By this is meant not
merely the obvious fact that significant social intercourse is hardly
possible without language, but that the mere fact of a common speech
serves as a peculiarly potent symbol of the social solidarity of those
who speak the language. The psychological significance of this goes
far beyond the association of particular languages with nationalities,
political entities, or smaller local groups.... The extraordinary importance of minute linguistic differences for the symbolization of
psychologically real as contrasted with politically or sociologically
official groups is intuitively felt by most people. "He talks like us"
is equivalent to saying "He is one of us".

'There is another important sense in which language is a socializer
beyond its literal use as a means of communication. This is in the
establishment of rapport between the members of a physical group,
such as a house party. It is not what is said that matters so much as
that something is said. Particularly where cultural understandings of
an intimate sort are somewhat lacking among the members of a
physical group it is felt to be important that the lack be made good by
a constant supply of small talk. This caressing or reassuring quality
of speech in general, even where no one has anything of moment to
communicate, reminds us how much more language is than a mere
technique of communication.'

Sapir concludes with a brief account of the role of language as 'the most potent single known factor for the growth of individuality' (p. 17). The manifold insights conveyed by Sapir are summed up by the terse account of language by Bloomfield as a means of bridging the discontinuity between nervous systems by means of sound-waves (1935, Ch. II, especially p. 27). Both Sapir and Bloomfield think of language as being essentially speech, though Sapir does expressly include thinking in language in his account.

Notes

1. For a full-length study of language as one kind of behaviour-pattern amongst others see Pike (1967). On the multiplicity of the roles of language cf. also Wittgenstein (1953), p. 23. Language is identified in terms of five defining characteristics by Hill (1958), pp. 3–9.
2. Sapir, in the passage quoted in this paragraph, uses the word *autistic* in relation to a kind of speech-use common in early childhood—a use of language which is its own satisfaction, and is not directed towards other people. The now familiar medical use of the term *autistic* developed after the date at which Sapir was writing and should not be read into his account. He is not referring to a pathological condition.

§12. The third line of approach to our working description of language was to be through delimitation, that is, by trying to see what is distinctively characteristic of human language in comparison with other communication-systems of a partially similar kind. The relevant known systems are those of certain other kinds of animal, and it is in this connection that post-war scientific studies have led to most radical re-thinking by linguists. The subject has recently been surveyed by C. F. Hockett (1958, Ch. 64), who concluded that the animal systems must be examined in respect of seven criteria, features which are not found together, or in pronounced degree, in anything but human language. On this view human language is not altogether different in kind from animal systems of communication, but can be placed higher on a scale on which they too can be graded. The criteria are:

1. **duality** (i.e., having the equivalent of both a sound-system and a grammatical system; being, in our terms, articulated): possibly present in bee-dancing;

2. **productivity** (i.e., having a capacity for 'speakers' to frame new 'utterances' which will be understood by other users of the system, cf. §5 above): found in bee-dancing;

3. **arbitrariness** (cf. §6 above): slightly present in bee-dancing and gibbon calls;

4. **interchangeability** (i.e., having the property that all potential transmitters of messages are also potential receivers, and vice versa

[this constitutes a further ground for the exclusion of traffic-lights as in §9 above]): found in bee-dancing and gibbon calls;

5. **specialisation** (i.e., degree of remoteness of the communicative stimulus from the response it triggers; cf. §§4, 9 and 10 above): present in bee-dancing and gibbon calls, to some extent in stickleback courtship, and possibly in the care of their offspring by herring gulls, but found in immensely higher measure in human language;

6. **displacement** (i.e., capacity for producing messages removed in time and place of transmission from the key features in their antecedents and consequences): found in bee-dancing;

7. **cultural transmission** (i.e., property of being learnt by new users, not transmitted genetically): possibly present in gibbon calls.

During the last decade, however, interest has centred on the second of these criteria ('productivity'). There has been widespread return to the belief that the nature (not merely the extent) of the creative or productive element in human language (in its everyday, not only in its poetic, uses) is distinct from anything in animal communication systems. The subject is reviewed in a number of works, among which a beginning might well be made with Chomsky (1966), Lenneberg (1964) (especially the editor's own paper), and Fodor and Katz (1964) (paper by Lenneberg).

Note

In linguistic study we often meet structures which can best be differentiated, not on the model of a set of pigeon-holes, each occupied clearly and distinctly by something quite separate from what is in the other pigeon-holes, but rather as fitting at different points on a continuous graded scale, with overlap, and borderline cases, and no clear dividing lines. For such a continuum M. A. K. Halliday has introduced into linguistics the term **cline**.

§13. The problem of delimitation has also been considered from a zoologist's point of view, by Konrad Lorenz (1952), Ch. 8, especially pp. 90–91, and he makes the following distinctions:

1. Since the 'language' of animals is (normally) genetically fixed and not culturally transmitted (cf. §12.7 above), it is [generally] the same in a given species wherever in the world that species occurs. We may add that (except for the special case of mutations) this holds not only 'wherever' but also 'whenever', whereas human language not only varies from person to person and community to community (cf. §14 below), but also from generation to generation (cf. §15 below).

2. An animal in using its 'language' does so without conscious intention of influencing others of its species: 'even geese or jackdaws reared and kept singly make all these signals as soon as the correspond-

ing mood overtakes them'. What in animal behaviour is functionally nearest to human language is structurally quite different, e.g., the intelligible acts of a dog trying to persuade his master to let him out. 3. The power of parrots and large corvines to imitate human speech is structurally similar to, but functionally different from human language. Such speech is learnt, but normally the sounds 'have no "meaning" and bear no relation whatsoever to the inborn "vocabulary" of the species'. There have, however, been cases where the sounds uttered seemed to be associated with a definite thought, and Dr. Lorenz is able to quote one indubitable instance of a raven truly learning to use a human word: 'My raven Roah ... was not only shy of strange people, but also had a strong aversion to places where he had once been frightened or had had any other unpleasant experience. Not only did he hesitate to come down from the air to join me in such places, but he could not bear to see me linger in what he considered to be a dangerous spot. And just as my old jackdaws tried to make their truant children leave the ground and fly after them, so Roah bore down upon me from behind, and, flying close over my head, he wobbled with his tail and then swept upwards again, at the same time looking backwards over his shoulder to see if I was following. In accompaniment to this sequence of movements—which ... is entirely innate—Roah, instead of uttering the above described call-note [sc. krackrackrack], said his own name, with human intonation. The most peculiar thing about this was that Roah used the human word for me only. When addressing one of his own species, he employed the normal innate call-note.... The old raven must, then, have possessed a sort of insight that "Roah" was my call-note. Solomon was not the only man who could speak to animals, but Roah is, so far as I know, the only animal that has ever spoken a human word to a man, in its right context.'

These two important discussions remind us that we must not think of human language as separated by a chasm from other activities, but as shading off in various directions by gradual transitions towards other kinds of structure. Whether we accept the view that human language forms a cline with some animal communication systems or not, there is clearly an instance of serial relationship between them. This term was introduced by Quirk (1965) and is discussed in the present work at §176.

Note

I have not discussed systems in machines which might be regarded as having kinship with human language. What kind of distinction can be made in this case should be clear from §11.

EXERCISES

1. Discuss the definitions of *language* quoted in the Note to §2.
2. Comparing the vocabulary of English and any other language(s) you know, what evidence do you find that the system of the language imposes its own classification on the speaker's experience?
3. Write down any words or other special forms that in your own usage are the mark of your belonging to a particular group within the English-speaking community. What would be the effect of their use outside the group?

FURTHER READING

In studying each chapter readers should look up the references and the passages quoted. Items from the Bibliography particularly relevant to the issues raised in this Chapter are noted below, though naturally many of these items also bear upon issues that will be treated later in the book. I give first a list of studies written, by and large, in such a way as to avoid demanding specialised knowledge from the reader: Brown (1958); Carroll (1953); Firth (1964), especially *Tongues of Men*, Chapters 1–7; Gleason (1961); Gleason (1965), especially Chapters 1–4; Jespersen (1922); Malinowski (1923 and 1935); Miller (1963); Quirk (1968); Robins (1964), especially Chapters 1 and 9; Sapir (1963); Schlauch (1943); Sledd (1959); Strang (1965); Whorf (1956). Slightly more demanding than these, though not more demanding than works cited in the text are: Hjelmslev (1953), Martinet (1962), especially Chapter I, McIntosh and Halliday (1966), Papers One, Two, Five.

It should hardly need saying that readers will not find complete agreement, in views or terminology, among all these scholars, nor, *a fortiori*, between their work and mine.

CHAPTER II

The English Language

§14. We have been concerned so far with what language is. The properties which characterise it are exemplified in English, but naturally do not suffice to tell us what English is. There is no more one simple answer to this question than to the question what language is, but we shall follow the same principle in considering it, that is, we shall ask what the ordinary usage is and what it implies. As before, it will seem odd to some people that there is a question to be asked: they know what English is in the sense that they can recognise an example of it. If I were now to switch to writing in German, they would be able to say: 'Up to such and such a point, the paragraph is written in English, and afterwards in German. English is the language the first part of the paragraph is written in.' But as before, recognising central examples is not the only skill involved in knowing what English is: we must also have an idea where it is appropriate to draw the boundary-line. Some people think of American English and British English as two languages, others as one, appealing respectively to the principles that any substantial divergence of usage results in the existence of two languages, or that a high degree of mutual intelligibility is a sufficient condition of sameness of language. A more difficult case is posed by, for instance, Melanesian Pidgin, which is clearly related to English in a way that, say, Turkish is not, but which has a relatively low degree of mutual intelligibility with it. Just how much intelligibility ought we to insist on? There does not seem to be compelling ground for any one answer.

§15. It is if anything even harder to draw the line in the historical dimension, for there all the transitions are gradual to the point of imperceptibility. Our language is only minimally different from that of our parents or even our grandparents, and so on through the generations until eventually we come to forms yet more incomprehensible to the modern Englishman than those of Melanesian Pidgin:

'Hwæt we gardena in geardagum
Theodcyninga thrym gefrunon
Hu tha æthelingas ellen fremedon'
('Listen: we have heard about the glory of the national kings of the

Spear-Danes in former days, how those princes performed valorous deeds.' Symbols no longer used in English spelling are transliterated in the quotation.)

Of course, if we go back far enough we find that most of the languages of Europe, together with a number of Asiatic ones, derive from the same original language. It would be absurd to say that therefore they are all one language now, yet at any one period in time the change and divergence from generation to generation would be slight or imperceptible. We must draw a boundary, but no one place seems more suited than any other to be its site.

§16. This problem is baffling, but it is of a familiar kind. For instance, in the colours of the spectrum there is a continuous gradual change from red to violet. But people who are not colour-blind can tell red from yellow, and in most cases blue from purple. It is a mistake to think that the indeterminacy of boundaries makes our central notions less clear or valid. For ordinary purposes this is all that matters, but the purposes of study are rather more special. Linguists do sometimes need to say, 'I shall take so much and no more to constitute language x'; but the boundaries so established are determined arbitrarily for a given purpose and have no value apart from that purpose. It is perfectly reasonable to say that one and the same text may be counted as in English for some purposes and not for others. For most purposes it would be merely perverse to say that the language Shakespeare wrote is not English; but if I am asked what is the English inflection for the third person singular present indicative of verbs, I shall have to say that it is -(e)s: I cannot give -(e)th as an alternative. The fact that Shakespeare does have it as an alternative will not affect my answer. For some purposes, then, the language Shakespeare writes is not English (we would ordinarily say, is not the same as present-day English). Now it is clear that if we are going to describe the structure of modern English we cannot talk about all its varieties at once. We have to select one variety as central for our purposes, though we may need to refer to others. However, an important feature of English, indeed, one dimension of its structure, is the range of its varieties, and the subject deserves our attention.

Notes

1. I have said that all varieties of English cannot be analysed at once, but actually a brilliant, highly technical analysis of the principal kinds of current English has been made by Trager and Smith (1951). The following chapters will show that while acknowledging the importance of this work, I disagree with it at many points.
2. In these preliminary chapters any necessary grammatical terms are

traditional ones whose use is assumed to be familiar. A more careful terminology is adopted and explained in later chapters; the index should be consulted in cases of uncertainty.

§17. Generally, linguists do not make an absolute distinction between a **language** and a **dialect**; but if the two terms are used together in a single discussion, *language* is the more general: a language can include a wider range of varieties than a dialect, and, as we shall see, different kinds of varieties. A dialect of a language is the form of it used by a geographical or social sub-section of its speakers (the **speech-community**). The form of language used by each individual speaker is called an **idiolect**. But the scale idiolect–dialect–language is not the only one on which the variants co-existing in a speech-community can be placed. Intersecting it are three others. The first is of **medium**. We use different forms of English for writing and for speech. How written English 'utterances' are constructed we all (if we are literate enough to be reading this book) know well from a long period of overt training in reading and writing. But generally we have not been trained in the conscious analysis of spoken English, and most people are surprised, even incredulous, when the evidence of the tape-recorder compels them to attend for the first time to how ordinary spoken English utterances are constructed. This is a subject about which far too little is known, but Randolph Quirk has published transcriptions of conversation by educated speakers which indicate the gulf in grammatical construction between spoken and written English (1955, p. 182; –, – –, – – –, indicate pauses of increasing length and no pauses occur except those so marked; further transcriptions and discussion can be found in Smith and Quirk, 1954):

'he – seemed of course he had that kind of n er I I'm er I I er I I er er are you northern by any chance I was going to say that kind of northern – – er – scepticism or at least questioning mind – – which er – but of course he would mislead you with that he er he gave you the impression that he only er you know he gave you the impression that he was – sceptical and at times sceptical and nothing else – – – but I think he er – – I think he appreciated the course there you know – from one or two things he said when I bumped into him.'

Secondly, within each of the media, there are different types of English for different social roles—in writing, for the letters we send as clients, daughters, friends, employers, etc. and in speech, for our utterances as lovers, shoppers, lecturers, etc. These are not just differences of style in the ordinary sense—that is, of the way we exploit commonly available resources; but truly of language—that is, of what resources are available. Differences of this kind cut across those of class or local

2+

dialect: any of us may draw on variable kinds of English for these various roles whatever sort of dialect we speak. Equally they cut across differences of medium—the conversation of two intimately friendly dialect-speakers may be represented in writing a novel or, with a further return to speech, the script of a broadcast play. In view of the possible confusion we have just referred to it is unfortunate that this kind of difference has come to be called a difference of style. To minimise the risk of confusion I shall use the word in its technical sense with single inverted commas, thus, 'style'. It is easy to underestimate the institutionalised status of this kind of variation in English; we are more ready to acknowledge its importance in an exotic language. In *Abnormal Types of Speech in Nootka*, Sapir wrote:

> 'An interesting cultural and linguistic problem is the use in speech of various devices implying something in regard to the status, sex, age, or other characteristics of the speaker, person addressed, or person spoken of, without any direct statement as to such characteristics. When we say "big dog make bow-wow" instead of "the dog barks" it is a fair inference that we are talking to a baby, not to a serious-minded man of experience. Further, when we hear one use "thee" where most would say "you" we suspect that we are listening to an orthodox Quaker. . . . Such implications are common in all languages and are most often effected by means of the use of special words or specific locutions. . . . A more specialised type of these person implications is comprised by all cases in which the reference is brought about . . . by morphologic or phonetic means. . . . [in Nootka] the physical classes indicated by these methods are children, unusually fat or heavy people, unusually short adults, those suffering from some defect of the eye, hunchbacks, those that are lame, left-handed persons, and circumcised males.' (Reprinted in 1949, pp. 179–181.)

Knowledge of this high degree of differentiation in an American Indian language may stimulate us to reflect on what kinds of differentiation persist in our own language (consider the use of swear-words as markers of nouns and verbs etc. in some circles as a signal that a man is talking to men). When, after reading Chapters III and IV, you practise transcription, you will find it necessary to decide on the appropriate 'style' in order to settle how you would speak a given sequence: even in phonology English has an equivalent to the Nootka system, though the terms of the system differ. Identification of linguistically varying 'style' in English is difficult for two reasons. It involves adaptations of which we normally have little consciousness, and it is not (unlike the choice between -(e)th and -(e)s) mandatory. How a speaker selects his 'style' depends partly on how he, as an individual, adjusts to the groups he belongs to. That we, as members of the English-speaking community, have a sense of appropriate 'style' independent of the practice of individuals is plain from such familiar comments as 'He speaks like a book!'

§18. The kinds of variation considered so far depend on the user of the language—on his social and geographical affiliations (which may be life-long), his choice of role and mode of adjustment to it, and his selection of medium (all of which normally vary from occasion to occasion). The last dimension of variation depends not on the user but on the use; it is called **register**. Naturally it can be exemplified from positive characteristics of utterances used for various purposes, but isolated positive examples often seem trivial, or accidental, or capable of alternative explanation. For instance, the presence of such a lexical form as *drop goal* will indicate that English is being used for the purpose of talking about football; but not everyone is convinced that this kind of feature is enough for the identification of a dimension of linguistic variation (the common, though mistaken, belief, is that English must be used for talking about something, and it is self-defeating to identify a separate register for everything that can be talked about). Phonology gives some more immediately convincing examples —consider the phonology of parade-ground English or of TV (monologue) advertisements; again it may not seem to provide a very comprehensive analysis, but only to mark off a few phonologically peculiar uses from the great mass of 'normal' ones. Positive examples from grammar perhaps offer more convincing examples—not in terms of what is absolutely permitted or not permitted, but in terms of relative frequency. Consider the high rate of passives in the English of scientific exposition, or of imperatives in the English of advertising. Perhaps most telling are negative instances—instances of what can or must be omitted in certain registers. Notice the regular absence of an object in certain kinds of written instructions:
Mix well and turn into a greased pie-dish (a written form that could never be used by a cookery demonstrator speaking her instructions);
Please tear off (written instruction on the lining flap of a match box);
Ease off with penny (written instruction on the lid of a cream jar);
in the last two cases it is worth thinking how you would phrase the instruction in speaking to a blind man.

This kind of omission (which we shall call **deletion**) is not simply (as is often thought) merely a matter of space saving. The kind of deletion characteristic of written instructions (object-deletion) is quite different from that occurring in diaries (subject deletion when the subject is first person) and in classified ads. (article deletion). In lay usage, telegraphic English is space-saving, rather than special-register English, but amongst journalists a distinct register has developed (cf. Evelyn Waugh's *Nurse unupblown*; and note that the distinguishing character- istics of many varieties are most clearly delineated in the simplified, exaggerated forms bestowed on them by parodists).

Note

I have not attempted to show what is meant by social or geographical dialects, because the terms and their uses are well known; the reading suggested at the end of this Chapter indicates sources for study of dialectal varieties of English. 'Style' and register are, however, terms that need introducing with more care. For a further treatment see Joos (1962) and Strevens (1964).

§19. What we have so far distinguished among the possible varieties of a language might be found anywhere. English is, however, one of a re- latively small group of languages which have developed a variety not locally restricted, which is called a **standard language.** The expres- sion **Standard English** is used in many different ways both popularly and by linguists, but a most lucid account has been given by David Abercrombie (1953):

'Another kind of English exists, however, which is better not classified as a dialect. It stands in striking contrast to all other varieties. Not only is it different from the dialects linguistically, that is to say in the same ways that they are different from each other, but— and this is the important point—it differs from them socially and politically also. Unlike the dialects, it is not tied to any particular region or country, but is a *universal* form of English; it is the kind used everywhere by educated people. It is, moreover, the *official* form of English, the only kind which is used for public information and administration. It thus has a quite different standing in the English-speaking world from the dialects, and this non-dialectal kind of English is best called Standard English. . . .

'Standard English is easy enough to identify—you are reading it now, for example. In its written form it appears in all public docu- ments put out in countries whose official language is English; and in its spoken form, it is heard in announcements from all radio stations which broadcast in English. . . . Although it is called "English" it no longer has any necessary connection with England. . . . It would be misleading, of course, to claim that Standard English is *exactly* the same wherever in the world it may be spoken or written. There are undoubtedly differences . . . but they are really trivial and insignificant beside the astonishing homogeneity of Standard English the world over' (pp. 114–5).

For linguistic purposes there are no class-distinctions between languages or their varieties. But from the point of view of standing in the world, such distinctions obviously exist. From this point of view it is the present-day, internationally current, Standard English that is the most important variety, and that will, accordingly, be taken as basis for analysis in this book.

§20. Even this limitation does not provide us with an altogether uniform variety of English. As far as words and usage are concerned, I shall work with the Standard English of Great Britain, which is most familiar to me and is probably known to my readers. But it is not there so much as in matters of pronunciation that divergences within Standard are most noticeable. If English is one of a small group of languages having a standard form, it is quite exceptional in having the kind of pronunciation that I shall take as basis. This is an accent which can be heard from speakers originating in any part of England, but still local in the sense that it is confined virtually to English people and those educated at English public schools. Frequently people refer to it as Standard English, but this practice is not to be recommended, both because that term should be used for a kind of English, not merely a kind of accent, and also because the description *standard* can better be applied to what is accepted throughout the English-speaking world than to what is virtually confined to the English of England. This kind of accent can best be called by the name assigned to it by A. J. Ellis **Received Pronunciation (RP.).** Of this, too, David Abercrombie has wise things to say:

'RP, as a matter of fact, is an accent which is more than unusual: it is, I believe, of a kind which cannot be found anywhere else. In all other countries, whether English-speaking or not, all educated people have command of the standard form of the language, but when they talk it they have an accent which shows the part of the country from which they come. One of the accents of the country, perhaps, is popularly regarded as the "best" accent, but this is always an accent which belongs to one locality or another.... In England, RP is looked on as the "best" accent, but it is not the accent of the capital or of any other part of the country. Every town, and almost every village, contains speakers of RP whose families have lived there for generations. It is significant that the question "where is the best English spoken?" is never debated by the English. Those who speak RP are set apart from other educated people by the fact that when they talk, one cannot tell where they come from' (p. 117).

§21. It is abundantly clear that English is not a simple entity, but one of extreme complication. It is made up, not of just one uniform linguistic system, but of countless hosts of systems. Although linguists have not been able to agree upon a general definition of a language, they have developed terms for dealing with this aspect of the question. All the idiolects which are mutually intelligible with one another are said to form an **L-simplex**. Any two or more idiolects which are mutually intelligible with one another are said to be linked in a **chain**, and all idiolects which are so linked form an **L-complex**. Thus, among the eight idiolects taken as points of reference in Figure 1, we find a single L-complex, but a series of L-simplexes, viz., A–B–C–D–E, F–D–B, D–G–E, C–H–E.

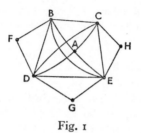

Fig. 1

Of course, in a real L-complex the points of reference are likely to run into millions, but the principle is the same. But although the notions of L-simplex and L-complex enable linguists to deal more accurately with the question 'What is a language?' than do ideas and words in common use, they are not perfect instruments, because the notion of mutual intelligibility is itself only relative, though attempts are being made to quantify it. In the historical dimension, of course, any language could be regarded as forming an L-complex, and it cannot be determined how much forms an L-simplex. The varieties of English co-existing to-day probably also form one L-complex (perhaps with the exception of Pidgin); it is not known how many L-simplexes they constitute.

Note

Hockett (1958, Ch. 38) gives an account of L-simplex and complex, and surveys work on the quantification of degrees of intelligibility.

§22. What emerges from our consideration of the varieties of English is the difficulty of drawing precise boundaries. Such a difficulty arises too from a completely different source, namely that English, even of a single variety, is a pretty amorphous entity. Concerning its vocabulary the Editors of the great *Oxford English Dictionary* write:

'The Vocabulary of a widely-diffused and highly-cultivated living language is not a fixed quantity circumscribed by definite limits.

That vast aggregate of words and phrases which constitutes the Vocabulary of English-speaking men presents, to the mind that endeavours to grasp it as a definite whole, the aspect of one of those nebulous masses familiar to the astronomer, in which a clear and un-mistakable nucleus shades off on all sides, through zones of decreasing brightness, to a dim marginal film that seems to end nowhere, but to lose itself imperceptibly in the surrounding darkness. In its constitution it may be compared to one of those natural groups of the zoologist or botanist, wherein typical species forming the characteristic nucleus of the order, are linked on every side to other species, in which the typical character is less and less distinctly apparent, till it fades away in an outer fringe of aberrant forms, which merge imperceptibly in various surrounding orders, and whose own position is ambiguous and uncertain. For the convenience of classification, the naturalist may draw the line, which bounds a class or order, outside or inside of a particular form, but Nature has drawn it nowhere. So the English Vocabulary contains a nucleus or central mass of many thousand words whose "Anglicity" is unquestioned; some of them are only literary, some of them only colloquial, the great majority at once literary and colloquial—they are the *Common Words* of the language. But they are linked on every side with other words which are less and less entitled to this appellation, and which pertain ever more and more distinctly to the domain of local dialect, of the slang and cant of "sets" and classes, of the peculiar technicalities of trades and processes, of the scientific terminology common to all civilized nations, of the actual languages of other lands and peoples. And there is absolutely no dividing line in any direction: the circle of the English language has a well-defined centre but no discernible circumference. Yet practical utility has some bounds, and a Dictionary has definite limits: the lexicographer must, like the naturalist, "draw the line somewhere", in each diverging direction.' (General Explanations, Volume I, p. xxvii.)

What is said here of vocabulary is true of all levels of English structure: the centre is unmistakable, but the circumference can only be drawn on the arbitrary decision of the analyst. There is, therefore, no such thing as *the* right decision about it—though naturally there are some wrong ones!

§23. The expression **levels of structure**, used in §22, requires some explanation. The traditional primary classification of linguistic studies is threefold: the study of sounds (**phonology**), of patterns (**grammar**), and of vocabulary [lexis] (**lexicology**). Here again, it has become clear that the divisions are imposed by the analysts, and do not emerge from the linguistic material. We do not, therefore, want to keep them unless they justify themselves by being useful in practice. And, practically speaking, since the facts of any language are too complex to be handled without some arrangement into classes, it is convenient to classify them in terms of relative generality. The rules of greatest generality are handled by phonology; those of medium generality by grammar; and those of least generality by lexicology. But these three types of study should not be thought of as occupying separate compartments so much as ranges on a cline (cf. §12, Note); which material is assigned to each in the analysis of a given language depends partly on the language, but also partly on the inclinations and purpose of the analyst of it. Consequently, one range or level of structure cannot well be treated in isolation from the others, particularly the middle one, grammar, which shades off into both its neighbours. It is largely because of the artificiality of grammar conceived in isolation that the term itself has gone out of favour with linguists, and the term *structure*, which suggests the affinities between all levels of linguistic organisation, is preferred. Likewise the term *level* is used as a reminder that the ranges are ordered on a cline, not separated in pigeon-holes.

The purpose of this book is to give an account of the observable rules of English at the middle range of generality, but to set this work into its essential context of phonology and lexical study.

Note

The idea of identifying the subject-matter of grammar in terms of rules of a middle range of generality is found in R. H. Robins (1951), p. 93. The notion of levels of linguistic structure is general in the work of J. R. Firth (and his colleagues), cf. especially 1957_2, pp. 192 ff.

§24. We have now introduced another word that needs comment. I spoke of linguistic rules, but I must make clear that in language a **rule** is a practice to which users of the language conform; it is nothing else. That is why I spoke of 'observable rules'. If the rules set down in grammars and other linguistic studies have any validity, it is solely because they are accurate descriptions of the practice of the users of the language. A language (as system) has no existence outside the minds of its speakers, and there could not possibly be any evidence for it but the utterances they frame in the light of their knowledge of the system. If we consult grammars, dictionaries and handbooks of usage on particular linguistic questions, this is only as a short-cut to usage itself, the only repository of authority. It has unhappily been the practice of many grammarians, especially in the last two centuries, to write of rules as if they had a source outside usage—in logic, in the nature of things in general, in authority—authority of other languages, past forms of the same language, the judgement and practice of eminent individuals, or God Himself. This indefensible practice has brought the term *rule* itself into disrepute among linguistic scholars. In the sense we have given it, it remains useful: only we must be on our guard against assigning any prescriptive force to rules as we formulate them. They must be products of observation, not directives for behaviour. 'Doctors do not *make* the rules of health or of cell structure; they try to determine what these rules are and to come to terms with them.' (Quirk, 1966_2.) The English linguistic scholar is in an analogous position.

It must be added that a cheerful directive to observe and describe, not prescribe, is by no means the end of our problem. Though there is nowadays a widespread tendency amongst linguists to assume that a speaker will recognise an acceptable sentence in his language when he meets one, and will clearly distinguish it from a deviant one, recent work has shown the assumption to be inadequately founded. If a linguist cannot obtain reliable judgements by simply asking speakers to class usages as acceptable or deviant, it is also clearly impractical for him to observe by just waiting to see which sentences are produced (in any case, that method would never allow him to pronounce any sequence deviant, since it always *might* turn up). Consequently, much more sophisticated techniques of enquiry have had to be devised; these methods, with some findings for English, are recorded in Quirk (1966_1), Quirk and Svartvik (1966). It is abundantly plain from this work that, though there are clear-cut cases, there is also a considerable area in which acceptability is not a matter of yes-no, but one of more-less. No simplistic account can be given of the rules of even one relatively homogeneous variety of English. Many generalisations that follow in this book should be read in the light of this caveat.

EXERCISES

Here are some specimens of different kinds of English. What can you deduce from the variety of English used about the context of situation, about the character, sex, age, class and social role of the speaker (if there is one) and the person(s) (if any) addressed?

(a) 'Soon as it's dark the place is alive with characters that fancy the odd door or a dozen or two window panes—ideal for greenhouses. Enough to give you the Willies: saws, hammers, and axes going, torches flashing, and chaps carrying the stuff, some like coffin-bearers, all like bodysnatchers hugging the shadows. That's for our parish. You pass through it to the park: a bloody flat wilderness of ashes with the odd swing or two. You skid down the south end of this under the viaduct and the road bridge and that's where the burn flows out into daylight again—out from under sixteen million tons of filth. You're in No Man's Land here. There's a house or two occupied by tinkers, hawkers and scrap men and what-not, and two gas lamps. Nobody can see what's happening at night on those big slopes.' (Sid Chaplin, *The Day of the Sardine*, 1961, p. 17.)

(b) "'I'm sure I should be speaking for the college in saying that it would be foolish—it would be worse than that, it would be presumptuous —only to accept money for general purposes. But you see, Sir Horace, we have suffered quite an amount from benefactions which are tied down so much that we can't really use them. We've got the income on £20,000 for scholarships for the sons of Protestant clergymen in Galway. And that's really rather tantalizing, you know."

"'I see that. But let me put a point of view some people might take. Some people—and I think I include myself among them—might fancy that institutions like this are always tempted to put too much capital into bricks and mortar, do you know what I mean? We might feel that you didn't need to put up a new building, for instance."' (C. P. Snow, *The Masters*, first published 1951, quotation from Penguin edition, p. 116.)

(c) 'The family, if you can call it that, consists of three besides myself, plus numerous additions. The three are my poor old Dad, who isn't really all that old, only forty-eight, but who was wrecked and ruined by the 1930's, so he never fails to tell me, and then my Mum, who's much older than she lets on or, I will say this for her, looks, certainly three or four years older than my Dad, and finally my half-brother Vern, who Mum had by a mystery man seven years before she tied up with my poppa, and who's the number-one weirdie, layabout and monster of the Westminster city area. As for the numerous additions, these are Mum's lodgers, because she keeps a boarding-house, and some of them, as you'd expect if you knew Ma, are lodged in very firmly, though there's nothing my Dad can do about it, apparently, as his spirits are squashed by a combination of my Mum and the 1930's, and that's one of the several reasons for which I left the dear old ancestral home.' (Colin MacInnes, *Absolute Beginners*, 1959, p. 29.)

(d) 'Dear All,
So glad to hear every one is thriving. Do not worry about me, I am very fit and happy and you know your strong girl. Of course I am wrapping up warm, but here in the South we do not get it as cold as you, I think. There is one of those big stoves in the kitchen come sitting room and I can tell it will be all snug in the winter. I have made such a nice friend at school, she is called Mrs. Carter. Of course, I know what you are saying Dad, "All Southerners are sly and deceitful," but really I must say I have found them very . . .' (Kingsley Amis, *Take a Girl Like You*, 1960, p. 157.)

(e) 'You shall be taken to the place from whence you came, and thence to a place of lawful execution, and there you shall be hanged by the neck until you be dead, and afterwards your body shall be buried in a common grave within the precincts of the prison wherein you were last confined before your execution; and may the Lord have mercy on your soul.'

(f) 'In regard to formulation, the established pattern of creating an increasingly complex compound by grafting on to the pure root synthetic a number of builders, designed to accentuate and correct the characteristics of the pure detergent, plus others which serve specific duties, will probably continue in an attempt to produce a balanced domestic product.' (J. R. P. Monkman in *Penguin Science News* 53, Autumn 1959, p. 23.)

Can you say anything about the linguistic evidence which leads you to form the conclusions you have drawn? You should consider this question again when you have worked through the book.

Remember that the specimens quoted above were formulated in written English; what conclusions can you draw about the speaker and the situation from the passage transcribed from actual speech in §17?

FURTHER READING

For an introduction to the history of English, from writers who look at history in relation to structure, see: A. C. Baugh, *A History of the English Language*, London, Routledge and Kegan Paul, second edition, 1959; W. F. Bolton, *A Short History of Literary English*, London, Arnold, 1967; Margaret Bryant, *Modern English and its Heritage*, Macmillan, New York, second edition, 1962; A. H. Marckwardt, *An Introduction to the English Language*, Oxford University Press, New York, 1943 (or any reprint), especially Chapters III–VI; Margaret Schlauch, *The English Language in Modern Times*, Warsaw, 1959; H. C. Wyld, *The Historical Study of the Mother Tongue*, London, John Murray, 1906; H. C. Wyld, *A History of Modern Colloquial English*, London, Fisher Unwin 1920. On history and variation in language generally, see Martinet (1962), especially IV, V, and W. P. Lehman, *Historical Linguistics*, Holt, Rinehart, and Winston, New York 1964.

Descriptions are now available of an enormous range of varieties of English. The tradition of recording English rural dialects (that is recording them as dialects, not just writing in them), goes back to the seventeenth century (John Ray, *A Collection of English Words not generally used*, London 1674; with additions, 1691), and produced enormous monuments of nineteenth-century scholarship (A. J. Ellis, *Early English Pronunciation*, Parts 1–5, London, Early English Text Society, 1869–1889 and Joseph Wright, *English Dialect Dictionary*, London 1898–1905, six volumes, the last including Wright's *English Dialect Grammar*). In the middle of the present century a new survey was undertaken, and its results are partly in print (Harold Orton, *A Survey of English Dialects*, Leeds, 1962). The Linguistic Survey of Scotland is investigating both urban and rural varieties (Angus McIntosh, *An Introduction to the Linguistic Survey of Scotland*, Edinburgh 1952).

Plainly the American standard varieties of English have been minutely recorded, and they have the advantage of a major dictionary with a fairly recent thorough recension (Webster's *Third New International Dictionary*, 1961). American dialects too, come under review, in *The Lingusitic Atlas of the United States and Canada*, H. Kurath and others, 1954. For a brief but authoritative survey of the work see Raven McDavid's contribution to Hockett (1958). In the U.S.A., too, the study of the special problems of urban dialects is further advanced than in England, see W. Labov, *The Social Stratification of English in New York City*, Centre for Applied Linguistics, Washington D.C., 1966. The Englishes of many other parts of the world are now described; for some recent examples see F. G. Cassidy, *Jamaica Talk*, London, Macmillan, 1961; F. G. Cassidy and R. B. Le Page, *Dictionary of Jamaican English*, Cambridge University

Press, 1967; George Turner, *The English Language in Australia and New Zealand*, Longman's, London, 1966; A. S. C. Ross, *Pitcairnese*, London, Deutsch, 1964. An account is being prepared of the English of Tristan da Cunha as its occupants spoke when they arrived in England.

CHAPTER III

The Sounds of English

(A) Phonetics

§25. A sequence of spoken language constitutes a continuum of sound, constantly varying from inception to pause. But we commonly think of it not as a continuum, but as a succession of segments. In the two English sentences 'I'm going to play' and 'I'm going to pray' we are aware of a difference of meaning and a difference of form each dependent on the other. Speakers think of the difference of form as located in a particular bit of sequence, and the role of segmentation in the production and reception of speech justifies our use of it in description. Thus we may say that in speech, the primary medium of language, the basic units for the differentiation of one utterance from another are **speech-sounds**, and in order to understand the structure of utterances in a given language we must first have studied its **sound-system.** The work is twofold: we must know which sounds are used and how they are organised into a system. It is the structural organisation that is central to the functioning of language, and study of it is called **phonemics**, or better, **phonology.** But we cannot make sense of that until we have studied the material organised, the sounds themselves, and this study is called **phonetics.** The two kinds of approach must be distinguished in all types of linguistic (and other behavioural) studies. From the adjectives **phonetic, phonemic,** K. L. Pike (1967, Ch. 2) abstracted the new terms **etic, emic,** both of which can enter indefinitely into new formations. In an etic approach all data of a given kind (e.g., all possible vocal sounds) are studied; in an emic approach what is studied is the structuring of data in a given language or culture (e.g., how the unmeasured diversity of sounds ever spoken in English utterances is grouped into a relatively small number of sounds, each set serving to distinguish one utterance from another).

The purpose of the present chapter is to equip students to talk about the sounds of English, and some warnings are in place. First, it is never really satisfactory to teach, especially to begin the teaching of, phonetics, through the written medium alone. Next, no phonetic description can be complete: how much detail is included depends on the purpose of

31

the presentation. In this study phonetics has a purely ancillary role, and the presentation is accordingly both meagre and slanted towards English; naturally, this does not mean that English is inherently more important or more 'normal' than other languages—only that it is our subject. Lastly, we can best avoid repetition by describing the character of common English sounds when we describe their organisation in Chapter IV. At the moment we aim no higher than mastering a set of notions and a vocabulary for talking about vocal sounds in general. Those who find in this chapter too many terms and too little illustration may prefer to turn first to Chapter IV and to refer back to this chapter (with the help of the Index) for explanation of the terms there used. Sooner or later, however, the difficulties must be faced.

Note

More extended treatment of the two main branches of general phonetics, authoritative and very clearly written, are now available in Ladefoged (1962) and Abercrombie (1967).

§26. The sounds of speech are produced by a tract of the body whose primary (biological) functions are not linguistic. There are **speech-organs** only in the sense that some organs are secondarily used for speech. As sounds must be made before they can be studied, the study of their production, **articulatory** (also called **genetic**) **phonetics**, is the primary, and was the senior, branch of the subject. Once sounds are made, they exist as waves (usually) in the air: the measurement and analysis of these waves is called **acoustic phonetics**. The sound waves do not fulfil their central linguistic function until they impinge upon a human ear and are in some sense transmitted to a human brain: there is accordingly scope for a third branch of analytical study, **auditory** or **perceptual phonetics**, but that, compared with the others, is relatively little developed. Most recently, a fourth branch of study, complementary to the other three, has arisen through the use of **speech-synthesisers.**

Note

The following sections on articulatory phonetics draw heavily on K. L. Pike (1943), to which I refer all who wish to pursue the subject further.

§27. Sounds can be defined as 'vibrations with characteristics of frequency, intensity, and duration which produce certain sensations of audibility when impinging upon the ear' (Pike, 1943, p. 45). Speech-sounds are those sounds produced by the vocal apparatus which are used in speech. A sketch sagittal section of the vocal apparatus is given in Figure 2; students can save a great deal of time later on if they memorise now the labels for the parts of the vocal apparatus.

§28. In the vocal apparatus are five principal **cavities** which can contribute to the sounds of speech: the **lungs, œsophagus, pharynx, nose** and **mouth**; any one or combination of these when shut off by a **closure** forms an **air chamber.** Vocal sound results when a stream of air in one or more chambers is set into movement by an **initiator,** i.e., some mobile part of the walls of an air chamber which by moving makes the chamber larger or smaller. The usual initiator for English sounds is the lungs, and the usual movement is towards the centre of the air chamber, i.e., **compressive.** Sounds made by movement of the initiator away from its centre are not a regular part of the sound-system of English (so in describing *English* sounds there is no need to specify that they are compressives; it can be taken for granted). An initiator with its air chambers is called an **air stream mechanism.**

In the normal air stream mechanism of English sounds the outgoing lung air may escape through the nose and mouth, in which case the

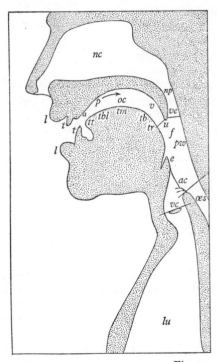

Abbreviations

l, l = lips
t, t = teeth
a = alveolar ridge
p = palate
v = velum
u = uvula
tt = tongue tip
tbl = tongue blade
tm = tongue middle
tb = tongue back
tr = tongue root
ve = velic
f = faucal pillars
np = nasopharynx
e = epiglottis
pw = pharyngeal wall
$œs$ = œsophagus
vc = vocal cords (glottis)
ac = aretynoid cartilage
lu = lungs
oc = oral cavity
nc = nasal cavity
Slant lines mark off the entrance of cavities.

Fig. 2

sound produced is described as a **nasal**; or (with velic articulation, cf. Fig. 2 and §29), through the mouth alone, in which case the sound produced is described, if necessary, as an **oral**—where nothing is specified the sound is assumed to be oral. Within the class of oral sounds a distinction must be made between those in which the air escapes over the centre of the tongue (**centrals**), and those in which it escapes over or round the side(s) of the tongue (**laterals**); where nothing is specified, the sound is assumed to be central.

§29. We have already implied that the production of differentiated vocal sounds is not dependent simply on the use of static resonating air chambers. All moveable parts of the vocal apparatus can cause **stricture**, i.e., 'the partial or complete closure of an air passage' (Pike, 1943, p. 120), and in so doing act as **articulators**; the place undergoing contact or near approach is called a **point** or **region of articulation**. There is an indefinite number of **positions of articulation** (described in terms of articulator(s) and/or point of articulation), but those commonly distinguished are:

> **bilabial** (between both lips);
> **labio-dental** (lower lip and upper teeth);
> **dental** (tongue tip between teeth);
> **post-dental** (tongue to back of upper teeth);
> **alveolar** (tongue tip to alveolar ridge);
> **palato-alveolar** (tongue blade to palatal edge of alveolar ridge);
> **alveolo-palatal** (immediately behind the position last described);
> **palatal** (tongue middle to hard palate);
> domal (tongue tip to dome of palate);
> **velar** (back of tongue and velum);
> uvular (uvula and back of tongue);
> **velic** (velic and wall of nasopharynx);
> pharyngeal (root of tongue and pharyngeal wall);
> faucal (between the faucal pillars);
> epiglottal (epiglottis and pharyngeal wall);
> **glottal** (between the vocal cords);
> œsophageal (sphincter closure of the orifice of the œsophagus).

Those not given in bold face are not used as **primary strictures** (cf. §33) in normal RP. English (though some may be heard in dialects, e.g., a uvular *r* in Tyneside); the velic and glottal have different functions from the rest (cf. §§ 28, 32, 47). It is on the remainder that beginners should concentrate, therefore.

Where articulation involves complete closure the sound produced is described as a **stop**; where it involves near-closure with audible friction, the sound produced is described as a **fricative**. A stop consists of two parts, the formation and release of the closure, but in a third class of sounds, called **affricates**, the formation of closure is followed by local friction in roughly the same region of articulation.

Even when there is no impediment of these three kinds to the escape of the air-stream, the character of the sound produced can be varied over a considerable range by changing the shape of the resonating chambers, and this kind of modification is chiefly due to movements of the tongue and lips. Sounds so produced are called **resonants**.

§30. Articulated sounds may further be differentiated by the variable shape of the articulators and strictures involved in their production. From side to side an articulator may be flat, grooved, rounded, etc., and from back to front straight, cupped, humped, protruded, retracted, etc. A set of distinctions more frequently used in the elementary description of English concerns degree and shape of stricture. In size the stricture may be relatively **extensive** or **restricted**; from side to side relatively **narrow** or **wide**; from top to bottom relatively **close** or **open** (with intervening stages). In shape it may be wide and shallow (or close), i.e., **slit**, or narrow and deep (or open), i.e., **rill**. It will be apparent that most of these terms are used most often of the tongue, and for that another set of terms is also useful, **front**, **central** and **back**, indicating the region of the mouth towards which the tongue, if raised, is raised.

§31. There are also several types of articulation. One is so common that it is called **normal articulation** (when necessary: usually nothing is specified and the articulation is assumed to be normal). In this, an articulator approaches a point or region of articulation, causing stricture, and after a period of time (variable, **long** or **short**) releases. Two other types of articulation have some use in English. In **flap articulation** 'the articulator gives one rapid tap against its articulating region, and then immediately releases; approach and release together are formed by a single ballistic movement' (Pike, 1943, pp. 125–126); it follows that prolongation is impossible. This type is common only between the tongue tip and the alveolar ridge, as in a common RP. pronunciation of *r* in *berry*. **Iterative articulation** 'is formed by the repeated, rapid, and automatic approach and release of some stricture' (ib., p. 125); various forms are possible, of which **trills** are heard in some varieties of normal English speech—of tongue tip against alveolar ridge in Scottish *r* and of uvula against back of tongue in Tyneside *r*. In RP. a trilled *r* is heard only outside normal speech, for instance in singing or declamation.

§32. There is, however, one iterative articulation of trill type that is used in all varieties of English, that of the vocal cords or glottis, which by rapid opening and closing produce a characteristic vibration known as **voice** (its absence being **voicelessness** or **breath**). The distinction between **voiced** and **voiceless** is one of the basic dichotomies in the classification of sounds, and beginners should develop their kinaesthetic sense of the presence of voice by laying the fingers of one hand lightly against the front of the throat and familiarising themselves with the vibrations felt during production of voiced sounds such as *b, d, g, m, n, l, v, z,* and all ordinary English vowels, but not felt during production of voiceless sounds such as *p, t, k, f, s.*

Although voice is, etically, an iterative articulation, it is rarely thought of as articulation. This is because it functions differently from other articulations. In English (and many other languages) the air column, after passing through the vibrating vocal cords, is always modified by movements of other articulators, so that functionally the iterative articulation of the vocal cords is less like an articulation than a **modifier** of the air stream which is, in its modified or unmodified state, itself the carrier for other articulations, which accordingly we think of as having a different rank. Although we are trying to reserve functional considerations for the next chapter, it is necessary to introduce the notion of functional ranking among articulators even in a presentation of phonetic material, because this ranking appears to be largely independent of the structure of particular languages.

Note

The notion of the glottis as modifier rather than articulator refers only to its use in iterative articulation. By closure and release in normal articulation it can also produce a stop, which is used in RP., though it too functions differently from other stops in this particular language, cf. §47, conclusion.

§33. From the discussion in §32 it is clear that laymen and linguists alike intuitively rank articulations, taking some to be more important, or at least functionally different, in the production of a given sound. Though the ranking is related to function, its basis is physical, lying in the articulatory processes involved. The two chief criteria are:

(1) A stricture in the oral cavity ranks higher than one in the nasal cavity, which in turn outranks one in the pharyngeal cavity.

(2) Within a cavity, a stricture causing complete closure outranks one causing localised friction, which in turn outranks one causing little or no friction in that same cavity.

(Cf. Pike, 1955, 8.623, where more detailed criteria are given. The theory of ranking was developed by K. L. Pike and E. V. Pike in publications listed in that work; one importance of the theory for beginners is that when a simplified description is made of any articulation, ranking is usually the basis for selecting features to mention.)

§34. A second, independent, basic dichotomy in the classification of sounds is that between sounds which have air escaping from the mouth over the centre of the tongue, but with no strong local friction in the mouth; and the rest. The former, **central resonant orals**, roughly correspond to what are commonly known as **vowels**, the others to **consonants**. But it is important to be very careful in the use of these words. First we must put right out of our heads the notion that they refer to letters rather than sounds (along with any notion that the letters systematically correspond to sounds). Secondly, we must distinguish between two further senses of each word. In ordinary use the word *consonant* (if it is used at all of sounds rather than letters) is used either to refer to an articulatory class of sounds (those produced with audible impediment to the air-stream, as opposed to vowels, which are not), or to sounds having a particular role in syllable structure (occurring with other sounds, 'con-sonant', as opposed to vowels, which may stand alone in syllable structure). The first of these notions is etic, the second emic; membership of the two kinds of class is generally similar, but does not usually, or in English, coincide entirely. The measure of similarity is such that we do not always need to make a distinction, and for the emic use, or where no distinction is needed, I shall use the familiar terms **vowel** and **consonant**. Where it is necessary to refer to the sounds explicitly as members of articulatory classes I shall use Pike's terms **vocoid** and **non-vocoid** (or **contoid**) (1947, p. 5).

Summing up, to describe the articulation of vocoids the essentials (for our purpose) are to give an account of the state of the tongue (in terms of closeness, front to back positioning, and muscular tone, **tense or slack**) and of the lips, which may be **spread, neutral** or **rounded**. As in ordinary English speech all vocoids are normally voiced, this feature need not be specified; for the same reason it is not necessary to specify that vocoids are orals using egressive lung air.

For non-vocoids we should specify whether the sound is oral or nasal; where and of what kind are the primary strictures involved; and whether voice is present. Other specifications are only needed when they are a departure from the (English) norm. It must be added that the requirement of audible impediment to the air stream in non-vocoids leaves the boundary rather indeterminate. Certain sounds without local friction and with open approximation of the articulators (such as the initial sounds of English *yet* and *wet*), are usually regarded as consonantal. We shall call them **approximants** (following Abercrombie, 1967, p. 50).

We have already pointed out that some sounds are subject to variation of length and others are not. Generally the terms **long, half long** and **short** will describe this feature where necessary, but in languages emic length is much more important than etic length, and the subject will be treated further in the next chapter.

FIG. 3

Front	Central	Back
i		u
ɪ		ʊ
e	3	o
ɛ	ə	ʌ ɔ
æ		ɒ
a		ɑ

	Bilabial	Labio-Dental	Dental	Alveolar	Palato-Alveolar	Alveolo-Palatal	Palatal	Velar	Uvular	Glottal
Stop	p b			t d				k g		ʔ
Fricative		f v	θ ð	s z	ʃ ʒ	ɹ	ç			h ɦ
Affricate				tʃ dʒ						
Nasal	m			n				ŋ		
Lateral				l						
Trill or Flap				r or r					R	
Approximant	ʍ w						j			

Diacritics.   ʻ=slight aspiration (puff of air, as after *t* in English *tip*); ₒ=voice-lessness; ‿=voice; ꓕ=dental articulation (*t* in English *eighth* as opposed to *eight*); ₁=syllabic consonant (as *-en* in English *kitten*); ə, ɪ, ʊ etc.=vocoidal colour of *l*; ~=nasal quality; •=tense; ˌ=slack;)=lips more rounded; (=lips more spread; ⁔=non-syllabic vocoid; ꞉=long; ˑ=half-long (of vowels; consonant length is shown by repetition of the symbol for the consonant); ʼ=stress; ₁=half stress; ʺ=emphatic stress; pitch can in general be marked by a brief horizontal line high or low, sloping up or down, but for English pitch cf. the marking suggested in §76.

§35. We are now equipped with the first instrument needed in phonetic work, the rudiments of a vocabulary for talking about sounds. This is indispensable for some purposes, but for others it is too cumbersome, and must be replaced by a one-to-one equivalent system for denoting sounds. In a strict sense this is impossible, for no complex muscular movement can be exactly repeated, and speech-sounds (each produced by a complex muscular movement) are as distinct as finger-prints. But we can make a reasonable approach to exhaustiveness by having a symbol for each sound that can be heard as distinct by a trained phonetician. This can most effectively be done by having a nucleus of primary symbols for common sounds, with additional diacritics to represent common types of variation. In principle any system would do, but those systems based on the principles of the International Phonetics Association are now widely used, and such a transcription is adopted here. There are, however, modifications: first, not everything need be included if we are only to transcribe English; second, the order is changed to fit our method of exposition; third, the descriptive labelling is conformed to the practice of this book. The material falls into three parts—first, the transcription of vocoids, showing the front-to-back dimension horizontally, and the close-to-open dimension vertically; other features can be shown by diacritics. Two are particularly important. Lip position varies from fully spread to fully rounded; in the English approximations to the points identified (and English here conforms to a rather general tendency among languages), there is an association between spread lip position and high front tongue position, rounding and high back position, with less marked lip-position features (roughly speaking) as the tongue position lowers. The second variable is muscular tension (as in [i, e, u]) as against laxness (in the remaining positions as realised in most varieties of English). Next, non-vocoids, with positions of articulation shown horizontally, voiceless sounds before voiced in each section; remaining features, as required, on the vertical axis (it is important to remember that different kinds of variables are shown here). The last section contains diacritics for the elaboration of the primary symbols.

Note

In addition to the precise technical terms introduced so far, it is convenient to have the general term *sibilant* for hissing sounds [s, z, ʃ, ʒ, tʃ, dʒ]; there is very little difference of position between the first two pairs, but the shape of the articulator is different—*slit* for the first pair, *rill* for the second pair, cf. §30. Another rather general term which is often useful is *liquid*, for a class including lateral, flap and trill sounds. Tongue position may be specified as *high/low* rather than *close/open*.

§36. We have said that neither descriptions nor transcriptions of speech-sounds can be more than approximations, and we have now to consider yet another sense in which this is true. In articulation parts of the vocal apparatus generally move slowly and continuously; they do not assume one set of positions and then make a clean break into another set. This is reflected in the sounds they produce: 'Speech . . . consists of continuous streams of sounds within breath groups' (Pike, 1943, p. 42). But this is not what speech strikes a listener as being; rather, he hears it as a chain of successive segments. Actually, the movement of initiators produces, within the continuous streams of sound, **crests** and **troughs** of stricture, which seem to split up the stream into a sequence of **segments**, and since we have defined sound partly in terms of its effect upon the ear (§27), we may use this auditory impression as a basis for phonetic analysis (cf. also §37.4 on the acoustic basis of segmentation). Accordingly, the phonetician, like the ordinary listener, may say that the English words *but* and *bit* each consist of three segments, and may describe or transcribe their production in terms of three successive articulations. Two segments which are produced in the same way are said to be (tokens of) the same **phone** (type).

§37. Acoustic phonetics has thrown much light on the matters raised in §36. The most important advances have resulted from use of the Acoustic Spectrograph, which produces a visible record of speech (a **spectrogram**) showing, not more detail than earlier instruments, but precisely what the ear can hear, and in very much the way that the ear hears (Joos, 1948, 3.10). On a spectrogram the three dimensions of speech-sounds (cf. §27) are shown as follows:

time (duration) on the horizontal axis (in centiseconds);
frequency on the vertical axis (in cycles per second [cps.]);
intensity by the relative blackness of the markings.

Several kinds of information or hypotheses first derived from spectrogram analysis are important for our purposes:

(1) Vocoid and non-vocoid sounds show up as different in kind. Vocoids have energy present in several bands of frequency and therefore show up as groups of dark bands on the horizontal axis. The component bands are called **formants**, and are numbered from the bottom upwards (from the lowest to the highest frequency range). Perceptual experiments with speech synthesisers have shown that it is the first two formants (F_1, F_2), and chiefly the second, that contribute most to the distinctive character of vocoids; F_3 has slight value in enabling hearers to distinguish vocoids, and the higher formants contribute to the naturalness of vocoids rather than their recognisability. From an articulatory point of view, F_1 is correlated with tongue height (and so with the shape of the pharyngeal cavity); F_2 with front-to-back tongue placing (and so with the shape of the oral cavity).

Non-vocoids produce several quite different kinds of marking. Voiceless stops have two successive parts: a blank (for the closure)

SPECTROGRAMS OF (AMERICAN) ENGLISH SOUNDS

A. SOUNDS IN ISOLATION

GROUPS 1 & 2—VOICELESS & VOICED STOP SOUNDS

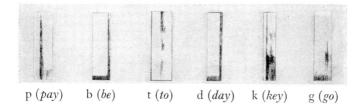

p (*pay*)   b (*be*)   t (*to*)   d (*day*)   k (*key*)   g (*go*)

GROUPS 3 & 4—VOICELESS & VOICED FRICATIVE SOUNDS

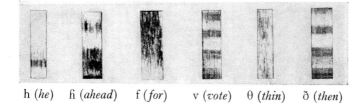

h (*he*)   ɦ (*ahead*)   f (*for*)   v (*vote*)   θ (*thin*)   ð (*then*)

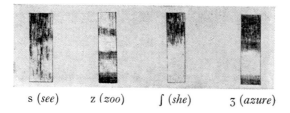

s (*see*)   z (*zoo*)   ʃ (*she*)   ʒ (*azure*)

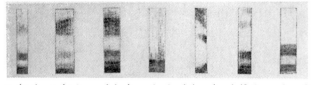

m (*me*) n (*no*) ŋ (*sing*) w (*we*) j (*you*) l (*let*) r (*read*)

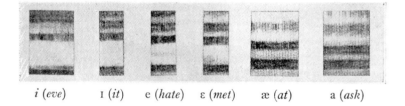

i (*eve*) ɪ (*it*) e (*hate*) ɛ (*met*) æ (*at*) a (*ask*)

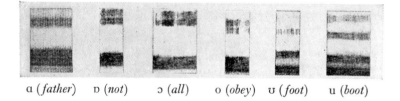

ɑ (*father*) ɒ (*not*) ɔ (*all*) o (*obey*) ʊ (*foot*) u (*boot*)

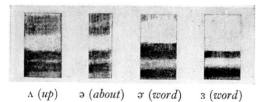

ʌ (*up*) ə (*about*) ɚ (*word*) ɜ (*word*)

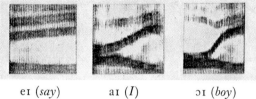

eɪ (*say*)   aɪ (*I*)   ɔɪ (*boy*)

aʊ (*out*)   əʊ (*go*)   ju (*new*)

ʍ (*when*)   tʃ (*church*) dʒ (*judge*)

B. CONTINUOUS SPEECH

Did you thank him?

Do you need anything?

Buy him something new.

Can he sing this song?

Nothing is being done now?

and a thin high spike representing the release; voiced stops are similar except that the first part has a low-frequency horizontal component (representing vocal cord vibration, and called a **voice bar**); voiceless fricatives have irregular vertical striations, with no voice bar, and voiced ones similar patterns with a voice bar, and so on. Examples can be picked out from the plate. Acoustically it is evident that speech-sounds divide into a relatively homogeneous class of vocoids and a mixed bag of remainders, the non-vocoids.

(2) The first group of illustrations in the plate shows traces from sounds spoken in isolation; the second group shows how patterns mutually influence each other in continuous speech. Now another kind of distinction shows up between vocoids and non-vocoids, for the vocoid patterns, though very variable, are always clear, but the non-vocoid patterns are often very faint or negligible—so weak that sounded in isolation they would be inaudible or at least indistinguishable. In other words, most of the information (i.e., clues to identification) in speech is carried by the vocoids.

(3) In the second group of illustrations in the plate it appears not only that successive segments are not clearly separated, but that the linking between them is something more than the presence of glide sounds that could be explained as mechanically caused by the movement of parts of the vocal apparatus from one position to another. Rather, the continuum is formed of successive overlapping waves of activity in such a way that at any one point of time two or more waves are contributing to the total spectrum of the sound. This characteristic leads to the hypothesis that in speech the brain sends out successive instructions to the vocal apparatus (**innervation waves**) which wax and wane smoothly and may be diagrammed roughly as follows:

Fig. 4

(Each wave symbolises the activity in respect of one phoneme, cf. §45.)

Moreover, each innervation wave is itself complex in structure, and its components are not always perfectly synchronised. For instance, in passing from [t] to [ɛ] in *hotel*, the release of closure for the [t] may precede the onset of voice for the vocoid, and even that onset may be too gradual to be located exactly (cf. Joos, 1948, 5.55).

(4) It follows that the impression listeners have of speech as a succession of segments is to some extent 'read into' the acoustic material, this 'reading in' being a part of the perception of speech. Such

re-cutting apparently takes place at points in the continuum where the rate of acoustic change becomes disproportionate to the rate of articulatory change (Joos, 1948, 5.5., especially 5.53); accordingly, it cannot be very exactly located, and the centres of segments are more easily identifiable than their boundaries. This agrees with Pike's finding from articulatory phonetics, that crests and troughs of stricture divide the continuum into a countable sequence of segments, though the borders of the segments cannot be precisely delimited (cf. my §36).

(5) The listener who has re-cut the speech-continuum into segments must then be able to recognise the segments, and putting together the information from (1) and (2) above we can see that recognition of non-vocoids is heavily dependent on recognition of neighbouring vocoids. This has been experimentally confirmed: the same tracing of a non-vocoid, 'pronounced' by a speech-synthesiser, is heard differently by listeners according to the quality of the following vocoid (cf. the demonstration reported by Hockett, 1958, 13.4).

(6) Some differences of vocoid quality are too small to be perceived, and the perceptual threshold for such distinctions is known. Spectrograms of what is heard as the same sound in the same context by different speakers of the same dialect may, however, show variations up to four times as large as would sound different in the speech of the same speaker; such sounds have been called phonetically identical but acoustically distinct. Presumably the reason why differences between them are not noticed is that speakers of the language have been socially trained to ignore them. The listener's identification must be based on something other than the wave structure of the acoustic impression he receives for a given segment: rather, he recognises the sounds of someone else's speech by placing them on a scale relative to each other. The process is akin to the reading of handwriting that varies from person to person. This deduction, likewise, has been confirmed by experiment with speech-synthesisers. Six versions of the sentence *Please say what this word is* were synthesised in such a way that they sounded like the same sentence pronounced by people who had the same accent but differed in their personal vocal characteristics. Then four different test words of the form *b-vocoid-t* were synthesised and played at the conclusion of the sentence (one per repetition). Identification of the test word was found to depend on the personal characteristics of the voice in the sentence leading up to the test word (cf. Ladefoged and Broadbent, 1957).

Note

For a detailed account of the use of spectrograms in linguistic study, treating of the full range of types of spectrogram and their characteristic roles in linguistics, see Pulgram (1959).

§38. In many respects the classification of speech-sounds we have outlined presents itself as a group of binary choices, some independent, some ordered in dependence. Thus, if we start off by asking of a given sound: '*Is it vocoid or not?*' then, depending on the answer '*Yes*', we are faced with the question *Tense or lax?*; thereafter the choices, as we have presented them so far, appear to be multiple ones relating to lip and tongue position. But with the initial answer *No* we can ask *Voiced or not? Stop or not?* and we face a multiple choice only later in the sequence. On reflection, it is apparent that this is a consequence not of the nature of the evidence, but of the way it has so far suited us to present the evidence. Most people are familiar with the idea that most discursive descriptions and identifications can be re-cast as a series of binary choices, and that if the series is at least partially ordered it does not have to be very long to yield a unique identification. The most popular example of this re-casting occurs in the game of *Twenty Questions*; almost as familiar nowadays is the reduction of complex material to a series of binary decisions in the programming of computers. There is thus no cheating involved in seeking to impose a series of binary oppositions on the range of sound-differences used in speech; indeed, there is substantial evidence that this is how speech (like other discriminatory activities) was acquired in the first place. In the development of the child, discrimination between the terms of a pair appears to precede identification of the single object, and *a fortiori*, discrimination of the terms of a series. Certainly, re-casting of the account of sound-variables into binary terms is a great economy in descriptive linguistic study, and throws new light on both comparative and historical problems.

Each opposition involves the presence (signalised +) or absence (signalised −) of a distinctive feature (DF), defined phonetically (i.e. in acoustic and motor [genetic or articulatory] terms). Finality in the listing of DFs depends on knowledge of all languages of the world, but the present picture is not likely to be substantially modified, and it is a surprisingly simple one. From around a dozen oppositions all known languages build up their individual sound systems, amongst which many individual systems have over two-score terms.

Note

Essentially the DF approach is the work of the eminent linguist Roman Jakobson. The account given here is derived from the exposition in Jakobson and Halle (1956). Much has been written on the method, and its application to English, in the last ten years; but it is important to distinguish the originator's account from modifications made by other scholars, and not necessarily in conformity with his views.

§39. How the distinctive features are organised into bundles to form the sounds which in a given language differentiate one utterance from another will become clear in the next Chapter. For the moment it is appropriate simply to list them, using Jakobson's 1956 inventory and description. Characteristics can be checked against spectrograms and against articulatory analyses. They are of two kinds. **Sonority features** depend on 'the amount and concentration of energy in the spectrum and in time'. There are nine of them:

I. *Vocalic/non-vocalic* (acoustically: presence versus absence of a sharply defined formant structure; genetically: primary or sole excitation at the glottis without obstruction elsewhere in the vocal tract; cf. [u] versus [k]).

II. *Consonantal/non-consonantal* (acoustically: low versus high total energy; genetically: presence versus absence of obstruction in the vocal tract; cf. [k] versus [l]. Note that vocoids are vocalic and non-consonantal; contoids are consonantal and non-vocalic; liquids are vocalic and consonantal (having both free passage and obstruction in the vocal tract); glides are non-vocalic and non-consonantal [having neither]).

III. *Compact/diffuse* (acoustically: having a higher [versus lower] concentration of energy in a relatively narrow, central region of the spectrum, accompanied by an increase [versus decrease] in the total amount of energy; genetically: forward-flanged [i.e. having resonance chamber in front of the narrowest stricture large in proportion to that behind it, as in low and back vocoids, or palatal and velar contoids] as against backward-flanged [i.e. having the front resonance chamber small in proportion to that behind the narrowest stricture, as in high front vocoids or labial contoids]).

IV. *Tense/lax* (acoustically: higher versus lower total amount of energy in conjunction with a greater versus smaller spread of the energy in the spectrum and in time; genetically: greater versus smaller deformation of the vocal tract out of its position of rest).

V. *Voiced/voiceless* (acoustically: presence versus absence of periodic low-frequency excitation; genetically: periodic vibrations of the vocal cords versus absence of such vibrations, as in [b] versus [p]).

VI. *Nasalised/non-nasalised* (acoustically: spreading the available energy over wider [versus narrower] frequency regions by a reduction in the intensity of some formants and the addition of others; genetically: mouth resonance chamber supplemented by the nasal one versus exclusion of the nasal resonance chamber, as in [m] versus [p]).

VII. *Discontinuous/continuant* (acoustically: silence [at least in the frequency range above vocal cord vibration] followed and/or preceded by a spread of energy over a wide frequency region, versus absence of such abrupt transition; genetically: rapid turning on or off of source either by closure-release or by one or more taps, versus absence of such on-off mechanism; as in trilled [r] versus [l]).

VIII. *Strident/mellow* (acoustically: higher intensity noise versus lower intensity noise; genetically, rough-edged [i.e., having supplementary obstruction versus the simpler impediment that produces smooth-edged sounds]).

IX. *Checked/unchecked* (acoustically: having a high rate of discharge of energy within a reduced interval of time, versus a lower rate of discharge over a longer interval; genetically: glottalised versus non-glottalised).

Plainly, although all criteria involve binary decisions, the decisions are of two kinds, some yes-no, some more-less; this distinction will also be observed in the remaining three features, the **tonality features**, which involve the ends of the frequency-spectrum.

X. *Grave/acute* (acoustically: having concentration of energy in the lower versus the upper frequencies of the spectrum; genetically: peripheral [i.e. having an ample resonator] versus medial [having a less ample, more compartmented resonator). Examples are velar and labial as against palatal and dental sounds.

XI. *Flat/plain* (acoustically: having a downward shift or weakening of some upper frequency components; genetically: narrowed slit sounds produced with a decreased back or front orifice of the mouth resonator with velarisation expanding the mouth resonator, as against wider slit sounds).

XII. *Sharp/plain* (acoustically: sharp sounds are characterised by an upward shift of some upper frequency components; genetically: they are widened slit sounds with a dilated pharyngeal pass, i.e. widening of the back orifice of the mouth resonator, accompanied by palatalisation constricting the mouth cavity).

Bundles of features on the two intersecting axes of sonority and tonality are used for the identification and description of the distinctive sounds of particular languages. The clear phonetic basis of the classification requires, however, that the method of analysis should be outlined here.

Note

For the classification of sounds arising from DF analysis, and for the developmental sequence of binary splitting in the child's acquisition of language see Jakobson (1956), especially III, IV; Jakobson, Fant and Halle (1952). Two papers by Halle in Fodor and Katz (1964) apply this mode of analysis to English sounds. Jakobson's *glide* is our *approximant*.

§40. A sequence of segments divides auditorily into **syllables**. Each **phonetic syllable** is produced by a single movement of an initiator (in normal English speech, by a single **chest pulse**), and often is made audible by a vocoid. The segment during which the speed of the initiator is greatest is the **syllabic**, the crest of the syllable; all other segments are **non-syllabics** (syllabics are commonly vocoids, but not always, and we sometimes need to speak of **syllabic consonants**). A syllable is **open** when it ends in a vowel; otherwise it is **closed**.

In many languages, including English, a sequence of syllables divides into **stress groups**, in each of which one, the **stressed syllable**, has stronger initiator pressure than the rest. Likewise, syllables can vary in length, and sequences of them in pace. These variables are used emically in English and will be discussed in the next chapter.

§41. We have been nearing, and now reach, the limit of usefulness of the distinction of phonetic and phonemic. The variable we have so far left out of account is that of **pitch**, which depends on the speed of vibration of the vocal cords. In ordinary speech, every voiced segment has a frequency-pattern, but that and the pitch are independent variables. How the pitch variable is used differs from language to language and will be described later.

EXERCISES

The essential exercise for the work of this chapter is to go over it, especially the early paragraphs, in conditions that do not inhibit you from practising the articulations described; a mirror is often helpful. And after that, to work at the phonetic alphabet until the symbols are so familiar that you can read or write them at something approaching your normal speeds for reading and writing. After all, any words or other sequences of vocal sound will provide material for an exercise. Just to check up that you have reached this stage, read off the following transcriptions:

['pɒtəfʌz'jobaɪdʒ] [ˀɛlˀ] ['wʌhɪm'pæŋdɔːk] [ʃɜː 'viːsnuːθ] ['ɑːrðetʃ]

FURTHER READING

The most important works are those by Abercrombie and Ladefoged referred to in the course of this Chapter. Amongst earlier works in the Bibliography, those by Jones (1951, 1952); Joos (1948); Pike (1943); Potter, Kopp and Green (1947); Stetson (1951; and Ward (1948) should be studied at this stage. Gimson (1962), which is indispensable for Chapter IV, also has much material relevant to this Chapter.

CHAPTER IV

The Sounds of English

(B) Phonology

(I) SEGMENTAL

§42. Anyone who is asked the difference between the English words *but* and *bit* can say that there is a difference of meaning which is conveyed by a difference of sound. The linguist (though he might also prefer a different formulation) can be more precise about both terms of the explanation. We are concerned in this chapter with his technique for analysing and recording significant differences between sounds—not only in this small instance, but between all contrasted utterances in a given language, namely English. In other words, we are going to apply our knowledge of phonetics to the analysis of sounds as they function in English. First we need a code of symbols to represent the distinctive sounds of our language one by one, since it is clear that ordinary English spelling fails to do this. Our list of symbols looks very like the English-slanted selection of phonetic symbols given in Fig. 3, but even apart from the fact that we are now linking them to examples in English words, it will become clear that there is good reason for the apparent repetition.

Note

The material of this chapter perhaps requires even more co-operation from the reader than that of Chapter III. Students must be prepared to work through it alone, trying out sounds and sequences as they are described, until the correlating of sound with symbol becomes second nature to them; and they should go back over Chapter III to make sure that they are as ready in description as transcription. The exercises at the end of the chapter will confirm that these skills have been achieved; they cannot substitute for the right sort of co-operation in working through the chapter.

§43. (1) VOWELS.
i: as in *see*
ɪ as in *sit*
ɛ as in *set*
æ as in *sat*

47

ɜ: as in *earth*
ə as in *about* (first syllable)
ʌ as in *cub*
u: as in *soon*
ʊ as in *put*
ɔ: as in *bought*
ɒ as in *not*
ɑ: as in *calm*

These are (relatively speaking) pure vowels, and can be described in terms of a single articulatory position each. The long and short vowels are never in English distinguished solely by length, about the phonemic role of which in English vowels there is, anyway, some doubt; so length is sometimes taken for granted and not marked in a phonemic transcription. An alternative economy is to mark length and omit the contrast of quality between the pairs of vowels concerned. But for beginners a mnemonic transcription—one which helps them remember the phonetic facts underlying their phonemic analysis—is usually most helpful. The practice of marking both length and quality is therefore recommended at this stage. From a phonemic point of view there is no need to mark the frontness of the low short vowel for which I have given the symbol /æ/. It does not contrast with a corresponding back vowel, and use of the symbol /a/ enables one to represent at one go the sound used by older RP. speakers, standard non-RP. speakers and some younger RP. speakers. Yet the difference between the two is something of which speakers are very much aware, and beginners often look for symbols to differentiate them. In this, too, it seems advisable to start with symbols which put beginners at ease, even if they do carry phonetic information which is extraneous to the needs of phonemic analysis.

A sequence of two vocoids in the same syllable is called a **diphthong**, and must be described in terms of two articulatory positions. Of course, only one of such a sequence can be syllabic, and diphthongs are called **falling** if it is the first, **rising** if it is the second. English diphthongs are all falling. Diphthongs may also be classified as **centering**, if the tongue moves towards a central position for the second element; **decentering** if it moves to a less central position. The English diphthongs are:

Centering
- ɪə as in *here*
- ɛə as in *there*
- ɔə as in *more* (in those speakers who use here a different sound from ɔ:)
- ʊə as in *poor*

Decentering $\begin{cases} \text{eɪ as in } \textit{play} \\ \text{aɪ as in } \textit{my} \\ \text{ɔɪ as in } \textit{boy} \\ \text{əʊ as in } \textit{go} \\ \text{aʊ as in } \textit{now} \end{cases}$

Many speakers, especially in certain 'styles' of speech, have two triphthongs, both falling, and with a decentering-centering movement:

aɪə as in *fire*
aʊə as in *our*.

Increasingly, however, RP. speakers tend to have either /aː/ or a new diphthong /aə/ in places where these triphthongs formerly occurred, thus reducing the number of contrastive sounds by one or two.

In continuous speech, the distinction between the simple vowels and the complex ones (diphthongs, triphthongs) is obscured because the articulatory positions are not held steady even for the simple ones; but spectrograms show that in isolated enunciations the distinction is real, and that is the situation reflected by our choice of symbols and terms. Further, in accordance with the principle that symbols for phonemic transcription should be as phonetically representative as possible (cf. §45), both elements of diphthongs are transcribed with vocoid symbols, though one is syllabic and the other is not. The student keen enough to read further in the subject must be warned that he may meet different practices in both these matters, though our usage conforms to most British and European practice.

Notice that complex vowels are not simply built out of normal English simple segments, but involve, too, the use of two segments not found alone in RP., [e] and [a]. Also the total number of complex vowels is produced with a relatively restricted system of first elements and a very restricted (three-term) system of final elements.

Note

In claiming that English diphthongs are falling I am excluding from the class of diphthongs such sequences as /juː/ in *music*, which are sometimes analysed as diphthongs. The case for treating them as consonant-plus-vowel sequences is argued by Gimson (1962), p. 89.

§44. (2) CONSONANTS.

w as in *witch*
ʍ as in *which* (distinct from the preceding only in some speakers and
                some 'styles' of RP.)
j as in *yet*
r as in *berry*
m as in *merry*

n as in *nor*
ŋ as in *sing*
l as in *like*

p as in *put*
b as in *but*
t as in *tent*
d as in *dent*
k as in *kill*
g as in *gone*
f as in *full*
v as in *very*
θ as in *think*
ð as in *then*
s as in *so*
z as in *zoo*
ʃ as in *ship*
ʒ as in *pleasure*
tʃ as in *church*
dʒ as in *judge*

h as in *hope*

§45. Each of the units listed in the last two paragraphs is distinctive in English, that is, can serve to differentiate two utterances. But as soon as we try to describe them in phonetic terms it becomes apparent that they are not themselves for the most part phonetically simple or homogeneous; rather, they are groups or families of different sounds, such that none of the differences internal to a given family serves in English for the differentiation of utterances. Such groups or families of sounds are called **phonemes**, and the transcription code we have just given is for the phonemic transcription of English. Each kind of sound, or variant, which can in given circumstances realise a phoneme, is called an **allophone**; sometimes one allophone is of much wider currency than others in a phoneme, to the extent that we can say it will occur unless something happens to prevent it. In such a case this dominant allophone is called the **norm** for the phoneme. In other cases, the phoneme does not have a norm. For examples of phonemes with and without a norm consider the accounts of /t/ and /h/ respectively below. In a phonemic transcription one symbol represents each phoneme, and although any set of distinctive symbols would do, it is usual to select symbols that are phonetically suggestive (though of course they cannot be phonetically exhaustive), and actually representative of the norm, if there is one. Nevertheless, since each symbol represents a group of sounds distinctive in a given language, the value of phonemic symbols is different from that of phonetic symbols. To indicate this difference, phonetic transcriptions are placed between square brackets, thus [ðʌs]; phonemic ones between slant lines, thus /ðʌs/. To read a phonetic transcription, you need only phonetic knowledge, knowledge of the value of each symbol; to read a phonemic transcription you need in addition knowledge of the sound-system of the language transcribed, or you do not know which variant of a phoneme belongs in a given context.

Before we go on to consider some of the phonetic variants of English phonemes, one general point must be made. Phonemes are different in every language, for they are a matter not just of sounds as 'raw material', but of how the sounds are organised in a particular system. Since most of the readers of this book will probably be native speakers of English, it may well seem to them that phonemic distinctions are big and obvious ones, while differences within the phoneme are small and trivial. It is important to realise that this impression derives, not from the facts of the case, but from one's own linguistic experience. Distinctions which are sub-phonemic in English are trivial in the sense that they have a minor linguistic function for English speakers; they are not inherently, phonetically smaller, or potentially less important. Let us take an example. To an English speaker it is perfectly evident that *r* and *l* are different sounds; but he may have to stop and think before he realises that the *l* of *like* is different from the *l* of *well*, and when he has realised it he may shrug the difference off as insignificant. But there are languages (e.g. Japanese) in which *r* and *l* belong to the same phoneme, and others (e.g. Russian) in which the difference between our two kinds of *l* is phonemic. To speakers of these languages respectively it seems that the difference between *r* and *l* is minute and trivial, and that that between our two kinds of *l* is evident and unmistakable. We are all powerfully (though not irredeemably) conditioned to perceive differences which are significant (phonemic) in our own language, and to ignore others. The first step in understanding the structure of our language is to recognise how far our experience of sounds has been conditioned by that structure. Such organisation of the etic material of experience is effected by linguistic structure at every level—lexical and grammatical as well as phonemic—and that is one reason why analytical grasp of that structure is an essential equipment of a humane mind.

Note
There are circumstances in which the distinction between phonemic and phonetic in transcription is superfluous. In such cases I use phonemic transcription.

§46. Accordingly, the two following paragraphs are an attempt to remove the veil of phonemic structuring from the reader's perception of speech-sounds, not by an exhaustive account of all possible sub-phonemic distinctions, but by pointing out some of the most perceptible in order to sharpen the reader's attention to the phonetic nature of what he hears in the future.

(i) VOWELS

These are subject to particularly wide variation from speaker to speaker, and to great changes related to their position in the stress or rhythm group (§§54–56), but the variations according to immediate phonetic context are not so striking or of so many kinds as in consonants (§47). Two points may be noted. Audible glides are liable to develop between vowels and neighbouring sounds of widely different articulation. For instance, a nasal glide can often be heard at the end of the vowel in /kɑːnt/, since the velum may be lowered in preparation for the following sound before the alveolar articulation has been made; for an example of a vowel with voiceless onset, cf. §37.3. An ə-glide is unavoidable in /mɪlk/ between the fairly close front vowel and the following ə-quality *l*. And secondly, there are notable differences in the length of vowels, depending on syllable position and following sound. It is particularly noticeable that in a stressed syllable a vowel is longest when in final position, and grows progressively shorter as it is followed by a voiced consonant other than a stop, a voiced stop, a voiceless fricative, and a voiceless stop; compare:

/biː/, /biːz/, /biːd/, /biːf/, /biːt/

(following affricates and clusters have much the same effect as their first component standing alone). The same grading of length may be observed among short vowels, and in unstressed positions, but the differences are smaller and less easy to hear. In fact, members of long vowel phonemes may be shorter than members of short vowel phonemes in a different environment. In the recognition of phonemic length, etic, physical, measurable length is less important than contrast with what else could occur in the same environment.

§47. (ii) CONSONANTS

The greatest range of variation is in the stops. If we pronounce, say, /t/ or /p/ in isolation, they consist of two processes, formation and release of closure. But in the speech continuum they may be followed by another stop, and have no release, cf. /æpt/ in conversational 'style'; or by a nasal or lateral that modifies the release, cf. /bʌtn/, /kʌpl/; or they may be preceded by another stop and have no separate closure, but only release in a freshly articulated position, as in /æpt/, /ækt/; in a sequence of three stops the middle one may be represented only by a phoneme-long silence, as in /ækt tuː/, conversational 'style'. /t/ and /k/ may vary in position as well as method of articulation; /t/ is normally alveolar, but before a dental it becomes dental, contrast /eɪt/ with /eɪtθ/; /k/ is pronounced progressively further back in /kiːp/, /kɑːnt/, /kuːl/, and once you have noticed this difference you are better attuned to spot that /t/ differs according to the following vowel in /tiː/, /tuː/. Before consonants there are yet other variants, cf. /kriːm/, /kliːn/; and after consonants others again. The capped air stream of a stop may be simply released or expelled with a puff (when the sound is said to be **aspirated**). English /p/ has considerable aspiration in /pɪn/, but less or none in /spɪn/ or /nɪp/. And stops are often unreleased in final position. Differences within the voiced stops are less striking, but of the same kinds. The fricatives markedly tend to be one-member phonemes.

/r/ is an instance of a phoneme lacking a norm. It has two principal forms—voiced alveolar fricative initially (as in /ræp/) and flapped alveolar or frictionless continuant between vowels (as in /bærən/). There is also a voiceless fricative form used after voiceless stops, as in /triː/, /kriːm/. A peculiarity in the distribution of the phoneme as a whole is that its occurrence is not governed solely by word-structure, but also by word sequence, and in such cases it cannot be assigned to one word or another, but constitutes an inter-word link. Thus, in a word sequence such as /ʌðə/ and /æpl/ potential r will be realised to break the sequence of two vowels at the word-junction (and consequently, as a flapped consonant). This realisation conforms to a tendency in English to avoid sequences of vowels in separate syllables if the first of the sequence is central or back in articulation, and weak (i.e. not the nucleus of a stressed syllable): thus we often hear /ðɪː aɪdɪərəv ɪt/, with a linking sound between /aɪdɪə/ and /əv/ but none between /ðɪː/ and /aɪdɪə/. Since neither the history nor the written form of the language suggests r as the linking-sound in that sequence, some speakers break it instead with a glottal stop, thus, /ðɪ aɪdɪəʔəv ɪt/; and some extrapolate from this to sequences like /ʌðə/ and /æpl/, linking its parts too with a glottal stop. Non-RP. speakers tend to use linking-r in situations ruled out by the definition just given, e.g., in /drɔːrɪŋ/, RP. /drɔːɪŋ/.

Like /r/, RP. /l/ lacks a norm and varies rather according to position than to phonetic context. A lateral consonant can take on the resonance of any vowel, and two resonances are used in RP. Before a vowel and between vowels /l/ has the resonance of /ɪ/ ('clear *l*'); after a vowel it has /ə/-resonance ('dark *l*'). Compare /liːv/, /iːl/, /lɪlɪ/. Also like /r/, /l/, which is commonly voiced, becomes voiceless after voiceless stops, cf. /kliːn/. Lastly, it can be a syllabic, as in /kɛtl/; cf. also the /n/ of /kɪtn/, and /m/ in some speakers' pronunciation of /rɪðm/, /prɪzm/, though /rɪðəm/ and /prɪzəm/ are also common. Syllabic /m/, which can lose its syllabic value, has recently lost ground to the full syllable /əm/, which cannot; in poetry written before 1900 words like *solemn* may require a monosyllabic pronunciation rather than the present disyllabic one.   Other (perhaps all) non-vocoids can take on syllabic value in certain circumstances (especially in conversational 'style'), e.g., /ŋ/ in /ŋkjʊ/ and /s/ in /s ə lɒŋ weɪ/.

/h/, which in English occurs only in initial position, is not really a non-vocoid by our definition (§34), but in English its function is always non-syllabic, and accordingly in a phonemic account it belongs under the consonants.   It varies in character according to the resonance of the following vowel, cf. /hæt/, /hɑːt/, /hiːt/, /hɪt/, /hʌt/, /hɒt/, /huːt/, heɪt/.   It is usually thought of as voiceless, because that is how we pronounce it in isolation, but spectrograms show that in continuous speech voiced /h/ is commoner.   /h/ has a true non-vocoid variant [ç] in a common RP. pronunciation of the sequence /hj/, as in /hjuːdʒ/, with an initial voiceless front palatal fricative.

In addition to these specific modifications, tokens of phonemes generally vary according to variable conditions of stress and position in the rhythm group (§§54–56): consider the length of the first /m/ and the quality of the second vowel in two pronunciations of /hʌmdrʌm/— first alone, and secondly in the sequence /hʌmdrʌm bət hɔʊlsəm/.

Lastly, one consonant commonly heard in English, including RP., is never distinctive in RP., and so is not included in our inventory of phonemes.   It is the glottal stop.   We have mentioned its correspondence in certain instances with linking-*r* in different RP. speakers, but it has wider functions, especially in introducing a stressed syllable beginning with a vowel, initially in a word or medially, as in /ʔɪndiːd/, /krɪʔeɪʃn/; also before the syllabic consonant of /ʔŋkjʊ/. In other forms of English the glottal stop is an allophone of the /t/-phoneme, and sometimes has this status in RP., functioning before /n/, e.g., in / tɒʔnəm/.

§48.   It is time to direct attention to the composition of our inventory of phonemes.   The reason for including some items will be immediately clear.   If someone asks, 'What did you say?' the answer might be '/pɪn/', '/bɪn/', '/tɪn/', '/dɪn/', '/kɪn/', '/fɪn/', '/θɪn/', '/sɪn/', '/ʃɪn/', '/wɪn/', etc., and each would be a different answer, differentiated by the first segment, so we could say that /p/, /b/, /t/, /d/, /f/, /θ/, /s/, /ʃ/, /w/, are different phonemes.   This procedure of substituting one component for another in a given position of the same 'frame' is called a **substitution test.**   Applying the method to other frames, we could establish yet other phonemes.   But there are some problem cases; indeed, on some matters there is no scholarly agreement.   Consideration of these cases forces us to sharpen our notion of what a phoneme is; where there are differences of interpretation we can point to the underlying differences of view about what phonemes are.

(a) /h/ and /ŋ/ are included though there is no pair of utterances distinguished simply by them. Such a minimal contrast would be impossible, since /h/ occurs only in initial position, and /ŋ/ only in medial and final position.[1] We can justify keeping them apart on twofold grounds of common sense—first, they are 'obviously' different to phonetically naive native speakers of English, and this is not normally true of intra-phonemic distinctions; and secondly, they are phonetically remote from one another genetically and acoustically. These grounds of common sense are important, but they are not easy to work into our description of the phoneme (§45)—indeed, no satisfactory definition incorporating them has ever been framed. They are principles we must not lose sight of, but exactly how we can use them is not yet clear.

In this case, however, we can draw on another argument. For English use of /h/ and /ŋ/ shows that our substitution test has not been adequately framed as a way of determining phonemic contrast. If two sounds are used in a language, to prove that the difference between them is phonemic, we need not show that substituting one for another can produce a different utterance; it is enough to show that it produces nonsense. This proviso refers strictly to sounds, not to silence as member of a phoneme (cf. §47). Thus, in answer to the question, 'What did you say?' the answer might be '/bɪə/', '/pɪə/', '/dɪə/', '/tɪə/', '/gɪə/', '/sɪə/', '/ʃɪə/', '/mɪə/', '/nɪə/', '/lɪə/', '/fɪə/', '/vɪə/', '/rɪə/', '/wɪə/', or '/hɪə/', and the conversation could proceed normally; the analyst would deduce that /h/ was phonemically distinct from all the other initial sounds in the answers. But if the answer were *'[ŋɪə]' (where * denotes a hypothetical form not recorded), nonsense would have been uttered, and the conversation could not proceed normally (some linguists prefer to say that the form *[ŋɪə] never occurs in English). The fact that *[ŋɪə] is nonsense, or never occurs, does not prove [ŋ] is a phoneme of English; it does prove it is not an allophone of /h/ or anything else. Therefore if it does occur (as in /lɒŋ/, /læŋk/, etc.) it must constitute a distinct phoneme. A parallel argument applies, *mutatis mutandis*, to /h/, and to certain other phonemes of restricted positional occurrence: /ʒ/, not occurring initially (except perhaps in such a name as *Jeanne*), and /j/, /w/ and /ʍ/, which on my analysis do not occur finally. A good contrast is provided by the intra-phonemic distinction of clear and dark /l/: phonetically naive English speakers often do not realise they are different; objectively, they are phonetically similar; and if substituted for one another out of their normal contexts

---

[1] Except in the unique, limited 'style' form /ŋkjʊ/, where in any case it is syllabic, and so cannot interchange with /h/, which never is.

they produce, not nonsense, but alien-sounding pronunciations (try saying [lˀɪlˀɪ] for [lᶦɪlᶦɪ] and [mɪlᶦk] for [mɪlˀk]).

(b) The remaining controversial items are those that clearly belong somewhere, but not everybody agrees that they should be entered as units, or as the units I have taken them to be. Their phonemic nature and status is still controversial. My analysis depends on the great importance I attach to the native speaker's reactions to the forms of his language (cf. Pike, 1947, p. 62, and Jones, 1957, especially §§1–5). The items /tʃ/ and /dʒ/ are exceptions to the common pattern of one-to-one correspondence between segment division and phoneme division; such exceptions are not rare. The substitution test can give no clear answer as to whether each is one phoneme or two, but native speakers of English commonly feel them to be one (in a way that they do not feel phonetically parallel /tr/, /dr/ to be unities). It makes little practical difference whether they are taken to be single units or (with e.g., A. Cohen, 1952, pp. 25, 43–45) sequences of two units.

(c) A similar problem is raised by the diphthongs and triphthongs, and we give a similar answer. In some cases, e.g., /əʊ/, some native speakers have difficulty in distinguishing two segments. For 'phonetic suggestiveness' I represent the diphthongs as bipartite, but I count them as single phonemes. Some scholars who treat diphthongs as sequences of two phonemes also maintain that phonetically and phonemically the so-called 'long' vowels are diphthongs, and so sequences of two phonemes (cf. e.g., Trager and Smith, 1951, 1.21, 1.23). The evidence of spectrograms does not support this view as a phonetic analysis (cf. Potter, Kopp and Green, 1947, pp. 55–56), and native reaction does not support it as a phonemic one. It is mentioned because enterprising students are likely to meet it.

Note

The theoretical difficulties of defining the phoneme have been very great, though in recent years they have attracted a declining amount of attention. In all probability the issue was a pseudo-problem. There is no difficulty in thinking of phonemes as those sounds differences between which result in differences of meaning; the difficulty arises if we add the condition that everything in the sound-continuum must be accounted for phonemically, must be assigned, in a definite and clear-cut way, as all, or part of, and no more than one phoneme. Some stretches along the continuum, as we have seen, are partly like one segment, partly like two; a decision seems arbitrary, and if we are forced to make one, it may be made *ad hoc* for one purpose and changed for another. The phoneme concept is an excellent servant, a tyrannical master.

§49. It is difficult to deduce from our inventory of phonemes anything very precise about the type of phoneme system English has. We cannot give an indisputable figure for the total number of phonemes involved—both because even within RP. individual speakers vary somewhat (in respect of /ɔː/:/ɔə/, /w/:/ʍ/, /aɪə//aʊə/:/ɑː//ɑə/) and because estimates vary substantially according to the sense of *phoneme* adopted. On our interpretation the maximum a speaker has is 48 segmental phonemes; on most other interpretations it is less, sometimes considerably less. On any reckoning the number in English is at about the mid point among known systems, which range from about 13 to about 75 (cf. Hockett, 1958, 11.2; but of course these figures cannot be any more final than those for English). A large number of phonemes does not mean that a language is unnecessarily complicated. On the contrary, it means (i) that the meaningful units of the language can be relatively short, because there are so many possibilities of diversification in small compass; (ii) that the language need only draw on a small fraction of the theoretically possible sequences of phonemes, and this greatly increases ease of communication. Just as in written English, if we see a *q* we know a *u* is to follow, so in speech, after each phoneme only limited possibilities are open for the next one, and so cumulatively throughout an utterance, until we can be fairly sure how it is to continue. This progressive limitation of the speaker's field of choice makes possible a less demanding style of utterance for him, a less intense concentration for the listener, and generally, communication in the presence of disturbance or other adverse conditions. An important form of this progressive limitation is discussed in §51.

In estimating the kind of phoneme system a language has, we take account not only of the total, but also of the balance between consonants and vowels; on any analysis English is not an extreme language either way.

§50. So far we have considered segmentally distinctive sounds, but it is obvious that other kinds of sound-contrast, such as those of stress and intonation, operate over longer stretches. Before we consider these cases, however, it should be said that it is not necessarily best to treat segmentally everything that can conceivably be treated in that way. Already, some oddities we have met in the segmental evidence have directed attention beyond the segment. For instance, when we describe /r/ in segmental terms we cannot really account for linking *r*; it is cheating to say that it occurs between words, because we have given no indication that words are relevant to segments (indeed, we have discussed segments as elements contributing to the identification of words). When we ponder this case, we see that linking *r* does not stand alone as a joining-phenomenon in English; compare the linking *n* in *an aim* (as distinct from *a name*). We do not usually speak of linking *n*, because the realisation is not so phonologically consistent as that of linking *r*, and possibly even more because our spelling tradition has come to suppress the *n* where it is not realised phonologically, but it has not suppressed the *r*.   But the example with *n* illustrates another point.   When, before a vocalic word-onset, *n* is present, two sequences which are identical in phonemic transcription (/əneim/) are in fact quite different in sound (*an aim, a name*).   Something marks the boundary between what, for the moment, we may call words.   Once we are aware of this, we can find it extensively—compare *ice cream, I scream* (stressing the two in the same way); *that's come* and *that scum*; *nitrate* and *night-rate*. Again, the abnormal distribution of /h/ and /ŋ/ indicates a restraint operating from a unit larger than the segment; so does the odd status of the glottal stop in many varieties of English.

Even in cases where we are not driven into difficulties by the attempt to describe segments in purely segmental terms we may find it possible to effect an economy by arranging the information in a different way, for instance, the difference between /kiːn/ and /kuːn/ may be described segmentally in terms of a vocalic element high, long and tense, but respectively front and back in quality.   The front element is preceded and followed by front-quality consonants, and the back one by back-quality consonants.   An alternative solution would be to cream off the element of frontness/backness, and describe it as an element 'overlaying' the whole syllable.   This would be an economy in the particular case; though not necessarily for the language as a whole (consider the difference of statement that would be required for *keel/cool*). What this example shows is that there is no case for dogmatism.   Techniques for the analysis and description of distinctive sounds are various; we need to be flexible, open-minded and self-interested, i.e. quick to see what suits us best for a particular bit of enquiry.

Sound distinctions which are best described in terms of units larger than the segment—in terms of sequence, arrangement, syllable or word-position, word juncture or delimitation, etc. are called **prosodies**.   It is certainly necessary to describe some aspects of English sound-organisation prosodically; just how much should depend on the analyst's judgement, not on theoretical parti-pris.

Note

1. The strategy of replacing the single technique of phonemics by the two-pronged attack in terms of sounds and prosodies is due to Firth; see his paper *Sounds and Prosodies*, originally published in 1948, and reprinted in Firth (1957).   Other sources are Robins (1957) and (1964) 4, especially 4.4; and T. Hill, *The Technique of Prosodic Analysis* in Bazell, etc. (1966).   For an interpretation of boundary-phenomena in terms of phoneme-theory (as *juncture-phonemes*), see Trager and Smith (1951), 1.62 and 1.72, and §57 below.
2. In speaking of differences between, say, *an aim* and *a name*, I have appealed to what are sometimes called *canonical forms*.   In rapid

speech, where context or co-text plainly disambiguate the two, we often use forms that could not be distinguished. Yet if we pronounce in isolation, even without wishing to draw attention to the difference by exaggeration, the distinction is present. It is important to realise that speech (and indeed writing) does, in many circumstances, neutralise distinctions it can make. Compare the pains we take in writing the sum of money on a cheque, using two codes (words and figures), both carefully, with the scrawl that often serves for our signature. Nevertheless, in describing a system of writing we indicate the distinctions in an ideal way rather than by analysis of scrawled signatures. Similarly in the description of speech. There is sometimes an unwarranted suspicion that we are not quite entitled to refer to canonical forms in our description. If we paid sufficient attention we should see that the gap between canonical forms and everyday realisations occurs everywhere in the organisation of speech. Description of a system has to begin from canonical forms.

(II) SUPRASEGMENTAL

§51. In §40 we defined a phonetic syllable; the phonemic syllable of English is closely related, but with minor exceptions: for instance the first /s/ of /strɛs/ has a separate chest-pulse from the remainder of the word, which accordingly has two phonetic syllables; but English people hear it as having one syllable, and that is what is critical for determining the number of phonemic syllables. Such minor skewing of phonemic syllables by comparison with phonetic ones is very usual.

In general, languages permit or favour certain types of syllables; English has wide tolerance in this matter. Symbolising consonants as C (consonant cluster as C^c), and vowel (simple or complex) as V, we can, on our phonemic analysis, classify the possible types in English as: C (relatively rare); V; CV; C^cV; VC; VC^c; CVC; C^cVC; C^cVC^c; CVC^c. Within these general types of structure, however, there are complex rules as to what can occur in a given position. Some have already been mentioned in §48; a far greater number concern the limitation of consonant clusters—so many that it is easier to make a list of what is permitted than of what is not.

Initially (again on our phonemic analysis), the following clusters of two are permitted:

/pl/, /pr/, /pj/, /tr/, /tw/, /tj/, /kl/, /kr/, /kw/, /kj/, /fl/, /fr/, /fj/, /ʃr/, /mj/, /nj/, /sp/, /st/, /sk/, /sf/, /sm/, /sl, /sw/, /sj/, /θj/, /θr/, /θw/, /bl/, /br/, /bj/, /dr/, /dj/, /dw/, /gl/, /gr/, /gj/, /gw/, /hj/, /vj/, /tʃj/.

The list cannot be quite complete or definitive because of the indeterminacy of English vocabulary (should we include /sθ/ in *sthenic*?) and because of divergences of pronunciation even within RP. (/ps/ can be heard initially in *pseudo*, etc.).

3*

The list of initial three-member clusters is much smaller, and includes only clusters beginning with /s/:

/spl/, /spr/, /spj, /str/, /stj/, /skr/, /skj/, /skw/.

English is much freer in its tolerance of final clusters, and our inventory can be more definitive:

/mf/, /mp/, /lp/, /sp/, /pt/, /pθ/, /ps/, /kt/, /ft/, /ʃt/, /nt/, /lt/, /st/, /θt/, /ts/, /tθ/, /lk/, /sk/, /ŋk/, /ks/, /mf/, /lf/, /fs/, /fθ/, /n(t)ʃ/, /(t)ʃ/, /lm/, /mθ/, /ns/, /nθ/, /nd/, /nz/, /ndʒ/, /ls/, /lθ/, /lb/, /ld/, /lv/, /θs/, /dθ/, /tθ/, /θt/, /bd/, /bz/, /vd/, /zd/, /ʒd/, /dʒd/, /ðd/, /gd/, /ŋd/, /dz/, /mz/, /md/, /ŋz/, /lz/, /gz/, /gd/, /vz/, /ðz/, /tʃt/,

are permitted two-member clusters; /m(p)t/ vacillates between two and three members;

/ndθ/, /ŋkθ/, /nst/, /ŋkt/, /ŋks/, /lpt/, /lkt/, /lks/, /lst/, /lfθ/, /kst/, /ksθ/, /dst/,

are permitted three-member clusters, together with others formed when inflectional endings (/s/, /z/, /t/, /d/) are added to items on the two-member list. The permitted four-member clusters all involve inflectional endings, e.g.,

/mpts/ (/prompts/), /lfθs/ (/twɛlfθs/), /ksθs/ (/sɪksθs/), /ndθs/ (/θaʊz-əndθs/).

All clusters occurring medially in a word can be analysed into sequences permitted initially or finally in syllables, or a combination of such sequences.

English phonemes, therefore, fall into a complex set of classes according to their capacity for occurring in given situations, and the limitations on their occurrence are of communicative importance. Moreover, in the flow of speech, important clues to word-boundaries are given by consonant clusters, since there is little overlap of membership between the initial and final lists.

§52. The syllable is the vehicle of the next three forms of supra-segmental distinctive patterning—patterning in the variation of pitch, variation of intensity, and variation in pace. These three types of patterning, **intonation**, **stress** and **rhythm**, are very closely linked in English; although they are not wholly interdependent, none can be explained without reference to the others. Evidence about them is much more complex than for the segmental phonemes. It is difficult for a speaker to identify his own usage in respect of them—partly because they represent habits learnt in early infancy (pitch patterns, for instance, are usually learnt by babies before they have any lexical repertoire; accordingly, before the speech-sounds they use can constitute phonemes), and so seem to the adult to be part of the natural order of things, rather than acquired habits; and partly because the kinds of meaning they express in English are so generalised that we cannot readily isolate them for analysis. To a much greater extent than segmental phonemes they function relatively and contrastively, and therefore experimental phonetics is only negatively helpful about them.

§53. Language systems can make use of intonation in two principal ways—lexically, by associating a given level or pattern with a given sequence of segmental phonemes in the formation of words; and syntactically, by keeping it distinct from lexical meaning, and using it to contribute a certain kind of phrase or sentence meaning. English uses it in the second way: what a word means does not depend on its pitch level or pattern; what a sentence means does (sentences may consist of a single word, but then they have intonation-meaning as sentences, not words). For this reason, analysis of English intonation must be postponed till we have looked a little at English grammar.

§54. Stress is usually defined as intensity of utterance; it is a characteristic derived from the relative force of the chest-pulse underlying syllables, and its presence is manifested by modification of the total acoustic wave of resonant sounds, not by any one isolable feature of the wave. It is often interpreted as variation in loudness, but measurements do not support this view. Daniel Jones wrote:

'Stresses are essentially subjective activities of the speaker. A strongly stressed syllable, for instance, is one which he consciously utters with greater effort than other neighbouring syllables in the word or sentence.... To the hearer, degrees of stress are often perceived as degrees of loudness.... In actual language it is often difficult, and may be impossible, for the hearer to judge where the strong stresses are' (1950, pp. 134–135).

A further difficulty about stress is that, like those of intonation, its manifestations can be placed on a continuous graded scale, and do not divide neatly into physically distinct types.

While it is difficult to identify stresses by paying attention to them as stresses, plainly we do pick them out and respond to them when we listen to speech in the primary way—as hearers, not analysts. This curious fact is connected with the mode of their production and reception. To understand this we must go back to fundamentals, and we can best do so by using the words of David Abercrombie:

'Speech, as is well known, depends on breathing; the sounds of speech are produced by an air-stream from the lungs. This air-stream does not issue from the lungs in a continuous flow, as might

be thought at first.   The flow is "pulse-like": there is a continuous
and rapid fluctuation in the air-pressure, which results from alternate
contractions and relaxations of the breathing muscles.   Each muscular contraction, and consequent rise in air pressure, is a chest-pulse
(so called because it is the intercostal muscles in the chest that are
responsible); and each chest-pulse constitutes a syllable.   This syllable-producing process, the system of chest-pulses, is the basis of
human speech.

'This, however, is not the whole story of the production of the
air-stream which we use for talking; there is in addition a second
system of pulse-like muscular movements on which in part it depends.
This system consists of a series of less frequent, more powerful contractions of the breathing muscles which every now and then coincide with, and reinforce, a chest-pulse, and cause a more considerable
and more sudden rise in air-pressure.   These reinforcing movements
constitute the system of stress-pulses, and this system is combined
in speech with the system of chest-pulses.'

(1964, pp. 5–6; now reprinted in Abercrombie 1965).

Note, too, the wise comment:

'Our perception of speech depends to a considerable extent on the
hearer identifying himself with the speaker.   As we listen to the
sounds of speech, we perceive them not simply as sounds, but as
clues to movements.   It is an intuitive reaction of the hearer to be
aware of the movements of the various organs of speech which the
speaker is making.   We perceive speech in muscular terms.' (*ib.*
p. 7).

For this mode of perception, involving the listener's self-identification
with the speaker, Abercrombie uses the term *phonetic empathy* (*ib.* p. 8).

What English speakers apparently do single out are not so much
degrees as contrasts of stress, identifying pulses as strong or weak relative to neighbouring syllables.   There are therefore only two significantly distinct grades, though physically more varieties can be dis-
criminated.   The two-grade system is the basis of differentiation in
verse and prose alike.   Notice, however, that a pair of disyllabic words
we think of as segmentally alike, but prosodically differentiated by
stress, such as ¹*import*/*im*¹*port*, also, and perhaps more importantly, differ
in the length and intonational characteristics of their respective syllables.   So far, in discussing the stress system, we have conflated two
things, which must now be distinguished.   The sequence of strong and
weak pulses is a syllable-producing sequence.   But not every pulse
carries an articulated syllable—not even every strong pulse.   The

point was elucidated by Abercrombie, and can best be put in his words:

'I must next make an important point: that a stress pulse can occur without sound accompanying it. There is one famous and often quoted example of this; attention was drawn to it first, I think, by Daniel Jones. The phrase "thank you", when spoken in a per-functory way, is often pronounced in England in a way that can be represented in phonetic transcription as ['k̩kju]. As far as the ear is concerned, the first syllable has disappeared; as most people say the phrase, however, it is still present in the speaker's movements—and present, moreover, as a stressed syllable.

'In this instance, although there is silence in the place of the initial stressed syllable, the speaker makes a movement of the articulators as well as of the breathing muscles: he actually says a long [k] at the beginning of the word. But a stress-pulse may also occur in English at a point during an utterance where there is a gap in the sequence of words, and there is no articulatory movement. This is what happens when I say something like the following: "A funny thing happened to me, on my way here this evening". Between "me" and "on", as I said the sentence then, there is what may be called a "silent stress-pulse", as distinct from an actual "stressed syllable" (which would be a stress-pulse with some articulatory movements superimposed on it). We can say, therefore, that that utterance contained six stress-pulses, one of which was silent and the other five were stressed syllables (*fun*ny, *hap*pened, *me*, *way*, *ev*ening).

'Such silent stresses are not a matter of chance nor of the speaker's whim, and they merit more linguistic investigation than they have received so far. When one starts listening for them they turn out to be surprisingly frequent in conversation, and even more frequent in prose read aloud. Moreover, as we shall see, they are an integral part of the structure of English verse.

'From now on, therefore, I shall use the word "stress", by itself, to mean simply the rhythmical recurrence of the reinforced chest pulse; it may coincide with an articulated syllable, which will then be a stressed syllable; or it may be a silent stress.

'One must not suppose that because a silent stress is silent, it therefore does not exist for the hearer. There is a stress, even if not a stressed syllable; and this stress is felt by the speaker and (because he would do the same if he were speaking) "empathised" by the hearer.'

Words of more than one syllable have at least one **inherent stress**, that is, one syllable that in continuous speech will be stressed if there is nothing to cause suppression of the stress. The sort of thing that will cause its suppression is occurrence in parenthesis or the presence of a focus of attention elsewhere in the sentence. Monosyllables may or may not have inherent stress. If a word has two inherent stresses, one is usually **optional**, i.e., more liable to suppression than the other. The first stress may be optional, as in *intonation*, or the second, as in *humdrum*. Which stress is optional may depend on the function of the word—usually, in the numerals from *thirteen* to *nineteen* the first stress is optional except in counting, when the second stress is. Inherent stress is positionally fixed in the sense that it normally has a definite place in each word it occurs on, but variable in that words do not all have stressed syllables in the same, or a simply definable range, of places.

In addition to the inherent stresses, whose positioning is determined lexically (though their realisation sometimes depends on syntactical features), there are **special stresses**, serving to focus contrastive attention at a required point in the sentence (i.e., wholly syntactically determined). Compare:

'*I didn't*

with

*I '*didn't*.

Special stresses may occur on any syllable in a sentence. The distinction between inherent and special is not a question of degree, but of what determines the presence of one and the same phoneme of stress.

There is, however, more to be said about the systematic use of degrees of stress in English. First, among syllables lacking full stress there is regular (phonologically conditioned) patterning of a stronger and a weaker type, with a tendency for the weaker to be juxtaposed to a stressed syllable, and then the two to follow each other alternately within the boundaries of the word; an unrealised optional stress usually takes the stronger form. Consider the stress patterns of some words from this paragraph—*systematic*, *phonologically*, *paragraph*.

Lastly, there is extra strong or **emphatic stress**, which like ordinary stress correlates with the beginning of intonation contours. It has significance at the level of indicating how a sentence it is used in is being used, but it does not serve, like ordinary stress, to make lexical distinctions. It is partly like, partly unlike, a separate stress phoneme, but if we think of stress not as an absolute property, but in terms of contrast, we need never distinguish more than two phonological terms, stress and unstress.

Note

For a fuller treatment of stress see Chomsky, Halle and Lukoff in *For Roman Jakobson*, Halle, etc. (1956). On accent and juncture in English see Abercrombie (1965) and (1967, chapters 3 and 6); Arnold (1967); Fry (1955); Gimson (1962, chapter 10).

§55. The second variable carried by the syllable is that involving duration and pace—the variable whose patterns are responsible for *rhythm* in language. Rhythm can arise from the patterning in time of either chest-pulses or stress-pulses. In the first case the language will display regularity (not necessarily sameness) in the duration of syllables; such a language is said to be *syllable-timed*. In the second case the regularity will be in the recurrence of stresses, and the language is said to be *stress-timed*. English is a stress-timed language. The basic unit of rhythm in English is the *foot*, which runs from the beginning of one stress to immediately before the onset of the next. It should hardly need saying that this is an inescapable unit of patterning in English as such; it is not a special characteristic of verse.

Since the recurrence of the stresses is patterned in time, and since the number of syllables (if any) intervening between stresses is not fixed, it follows that syllables are not of fixed duration. Consider the three sequences:

> *The man's here*
> *The manor's here*
> *The manager's here*

All three consist of two feet. They start with a preliminary unstressed element, followed by stresses on /mæn/ and /hɪə/. In the first, nothing intervenes between the two stressed syllables (i.e. the feet are monosyllabic); in the second one syllable intervenes (i.e., the first foot is disyllabic, the second monosyllabic); in the third, two syllables intervene (i.e. the first foot is trisyllabic, the second monosyllabic). Yet the rhythm is constant; if we beat the stresses they come at equal intervals in the three sequences and within each of the sequences. Plainly, then, the duration of syllables is not inherently fully fixed, i.e. there is no one length that a given syllable must have in any circumstances. The environment in the foot accounts, in our example, for some 'stretching' (in the monosyllabic feet), and some 'squashing' (in the trisyllabic foot; the terms are in quotes because they imply the existence of a norm, for which we have no evidence).

It does not follow from this element of environmentally-conditioned 'give' in the length of syllables that English syllables entirely lack patterned duration as an inherent property. We may compare the co-existence of inherent and special systems in stress. How the inherent and the environmentally-conditioned fit together has only recently been described in detail. The exposition that follows depends on Abercrombie's account in *Syllable Quantity and Enclitics in English* (in Abercrombie, 1964, and reprinted in Abercrombie, 1965). Having defined the foot, and taken it as the basic unit of analysis, he says:

'The quantity of any syllable is a proportion of the total length of the foot within which the syllable occurs, and it is relative to the quantity of any other syllable in the foot. We cannot therefore say anything about the quantity of a syllable until we know its place in the foot.

'Perhaps at this point a reminder should be issued, to prevent possible misunderstandings, that (1) syllable quantity is not directly dependent on either (a) vowel quantity or (b) stress; (2) the foot is independent of word boundaries.

'It is clear that, since feet are of even length, as they must be if delimited by the isochronous stress pulse, the number of syllables in a given foot will have a direct effect on their length. In a monosyllabic foot the quantity of the syllable and the quantity of the foot coincide; here phonematic structure is totally irrelevant. In /four/large/black/dogs/ every syllable has the same quantity, though their phonematic structures are very different. In a disyllabic foot it is obvious that neither syllable can be as long as the syllable in a monosyllabic foot; and in a trisyllabic foot some at least of the syllables must of necessity be shorter than those of a disyllabic foot. The number of syllables in the foot is, however, not the only thing which must be taken into account when establishing the quantity of a syllable. The often-quoted minimal pair of sentences produced by Scott

take Grey to London
take Greater London

shows how two disyllabic feet, /Grey to/ and /Greater/, having, moreover, the same phonematic structure /greɪtə/, may be composed of clearly different syllable quantities. An examination of types of disyllabic feet will provide the simplest illustration of the principles underlying syllable quantity in English (as exemplified in my own pronunciation).

'For the purposes of analysis it is convenient to regard disyllabic feet as being in triple time; that is to say a foot is to be looked on as containing three units of time, between which the syllables are divided.'

§56. While monosyllabic feet are necessarily of one kind, disyllabic feet are of three kinds, which Abercrombie identifies thus:

'The first, which we may call type A, has a short syllable followed by a long syllable, that is to say, in musical notation, ♪ ♩, or 1 time-unit followed by 2 time-units. Examples are /shilling/, /never/, /atom/,

/cuckoo/. I shall represent the syllable quantities of this foot as ᴗ —, making use of the symbols of traditional metrical notation, in spite of their misuse these days, and intending that they should be taken literally. A convenient name for it is a "short-long" foot (it is a pity we cannot call it an "iamb", which, in the original sense of that word, it is; but it would probably be too confusing).

'The second type of disyllabic foot, Type B, contains two syllables of equal length, ♩. ♩., or 1½ time-units followed by 1½ time-units. Examples are /greater/, /firmly/, /centre/, de/cisive/, /matches/. The traditional metrical notation does not provide us with a symbol for this syllable quantity, but a satisfactory one can easily be invented by turning the "short" symbol upside-down ∩. The foot can thus be represented as ∩∩. It is convenient to call this an "equal-equal" foot (we could not really call it a spondee, even if the term was not spoilt, since a spondee is essentially a foot in duple time).

'These two types of feet, therefore, give us three different syllable quantities:

short	ᴗ	♩	1 time-unit
medium	∩	♩.	1½ time-units
long	—	♩	2 time-units

It is clear, also, that a third type of foot is possible, which we can call Type C, "long-short", or ♩ ♩. Examples are /Grey to/, /tea for/two, I'll/see you a/gain to/morrow, per/haps I/did. (We had better not call this a "trochee", for the same reason that "iamb" is best avoided.)

'The three types of disyllabic foot, therefore, are:

A ᴗ —
B ᴗᴗ
C — ᴗ.'

Though English speakers have long been conscious enough of these patterns to be able to manipulate them for effect (they are amongst the most durable aspects of the sound-organisation of English) they have long eluded analytical understanding. Presumably the reason lies in the complexity of the conditions governing their incidence. Not only does environment in the foot have to be taken into account in the determination of syllable length, but also which foot occurs depends on two kinds of factors—partly the incidence of word-boundaries, partly phoneme-structure within the word.

Type C is simplest since, as the examples show, it occurs if and only if there is a word-boundary within the foot. We understand the remark that 'the foot is independent of word-boundaries' as meaning that foot boundaries need not occur at word-boundaries; the *kind* of foot that occurs is, however, related to the placing of word-boundaries.

Conversely, feet of Types A and B both normally occur where there is no word-boundary within the foot, and the end of the foot coincides with a word-boundary (i.e. the two syllables of the foot fall on a di-syllabic word with first-syllable stress, or on the last two syllables of a longer word with penultimate-syllable stress). Which of the two occurs in a particular case is determined by the second kind of factor, by phoneme-structure. The simplest way of describing this might be in terms of a prosody of shortness versus length extending over the first (i.e. stressed) syllable of the foot, or better, over the whole word. But to identify it in more familiar segmental terms we can use a symbolism in which:

(1) C stands for *consonant* (or for *consonant-cluster* if the difference is immaterial; if the difference matters, the number of consonants must be indicated by repeating C);

(2) V stands for *vowel*; but the short vowels are indicated by V^1, the long vowels and diphthongs by V^2; if the difference between V^1 and V^2 is immaterial, V alone is used;

(3) Brackets mean that an element may, but need not, occur.

We are dealing with a structure of, essentially, five places—the consonantal opening of the first syllable, its nucleus, another consonantal margin, a second nucleus and a final closure. It is the second and third places in conjunction that vary in such a way as to determine foot type. The rules may be summarised discursively, and then in a formula. The outer framework, whose variations are of no account, is as follows:

Place I: may be filled by one or more consonants, or left empty;
Place IV: must be filled by a vowel (or syllabic consonant);
Place V: may be filled by one or more consonants or left empty.

For the sequence of Places II and III there are three possibilities. The first, V^1 in Place II, C in Place III, yields Type A. The other two yield Type B; namely, either V of any kind in Place II, with two or more consonants in Place III, or V^2 in Place II, with zero or a consonant in Place III. Thus:

	Place I	Place II	Place III	Place IV	Place V	
(i)	(C)	V^1	C	V	(C)	= Type A (*meadow, records, silly*)
(ii)	(C)	V	CC(C)	V	(C)	= Type B (*limpid, fainting, youngster, helpings*)
(iii)	(C)	V^2	(C)	V	(C)	= Type B (*drawing, open, orchards*)

Of feet with more syllables Abercrombie writes:

'There is a greater variety of syllable-quantity patterns in trisyllabic feet. The syllable quantities can clearly be heard to be different in, for example, each of the following feet:

/one for the/road
/anything /more
/seven o'/clock
/after the /war
/nobody /knows

The factors which govern these quantities are of the same sort as in the case of disyllabic feet; but there is no need to discuss in detail how they apply. Here too word-division plays an important part, and it does in still longer feet also.'

It is time to take up the ominous word 'normally' used of the conditions for feet of Types A and B. Certain habitually unstressed monosyllables sometimes function rhythmically as if they were part of a preceding stressed monosyllable; we may say in such cases that there is a conflict between their grammatical status (and their written appearance) which is that of a word, and their phonological status, which is that of part of a word. Forms showing such conflict are *enclitics*. Examples are the second elements of *take it, did he?, is there?, tell him*. In structures of this kind Type B is more common, but A does occur.

Note
The further characteristics of patterning involved in metrical structure are analysed by Abercrombie in *A Phonetician's view of Verse Structure*, in Abercrombie (1964₂ and 1965).

§57. The last suprasegmental feature that need be mentioned is rather different. In careful pronunciation *that's come* and *that scum* differ from each other. Their segmental phonemes are the same, and they are alike in stress patterning. What then remains to distinguish them? Clearly, there is a difference in the way of getting from the /t/ to the /s/ and the /s/ to the /k/ in the two expressions, and perhaps also in the tokens of these phonemes. The kind of transition occurring between one stressed meaningful element and another seems to operate as an extra distinctive property, something like an extra phoneme. It is called **open juncture** and symbolised $+$. Accordingly, we would transcribe *that's come* as /ðæts+kʌm/ and *that scum* as /ðæt+skʌm/. We may summarise the incidence of this feature by saying that it occurs at the boundaries of morphemes (meaningful elements, cf. §64) between any two phonemic stresses (note that it does not occur between *that* and *s* in *that's*, where there are two morphemes but only one stress). Quite a number of pairs of English utterances are distinguished only by the presence or absence, or the variable placing, of this feature. It is an important resource of the language, especially in formal 'styles' or in conditions where disturbance or lack of context make communication difficult. The *locus classicus* for juncture in English is Trager and Smith (1951), especially 1.62 and 1.72; cf. also §50 above.

Exercises

1. Make a phonemic transcription of the following passage; include the intonation contours (which will cover the marking of phonemic stress): '"My dear, they could have got a laugh there. You agree, don't you, Mr. Starling? You see how easily one could have got a laugh? Why, if I'd been playing it, I'd have put in quite a different inflection," and Ruby imitated what Billie Carlton had just said upon the stage. "You see? If she'd said it that way, she'd have got a laugh."' (F. Tennyson Jesse, *A Pin to See the Peepshow*, Penguin edition, p. 141.)
2. Pick out ten sounds from the above passage which are allophonic variants of a phonemic norm. Describe the conditions responsible for their occurrence and indicate the main features of their articulation.
3. How many segmental phonemes have you in your own English? Does the number vary in different 'styles'?
4. Give an example of one English syllable of each of the general types listed in §51, and one illustrating each of the permitted initial and final clusters. Which clusters function as signs that a syllable is (a) beginning, (b) ending?

Further Reading

The works listed at the end of Chapter III and those referred to in the course of this Chapter are the most relevant. In particular, Gimson (1962) should be consulted for detailed descriptions of the range of realisations of phonemes in RP.

CHAPTER V

The Structure of Utterances

(A) The Rank-scale

§58. In Chapter I we considered the articulatory structure of language as proceeding from the distinctive, but non-significant speech-sound, which we now call the phoneme, through orders of significant elements of increasing particularity up to the utterance in context. We also guarded ourselves against the temptation of thinking that a house built out of bricks provides a sufficient analogy to this kind of structure. The **utterance** has been defined by Z. S. Harris (1951, 2.4) as 'any stretch of talk, by one person, before and after which there is silence on the part of that person'. This definition, obviously, embraces a very wide range of structures—from a monosyllable lasting perhaps an eighth of a second to a Kremlin speech lasting several hours. Such a wide-ranging term is needed, but its usefulness can be greatly increased if it is restricted. It is therefore usual to distinguish between **minimum** and **expanded** utterances, where a minimum utterance is the least form that could stand alone as an utterance, and any addition represents some form of expansion. But this distinction is not much use without an idea of what constitutes the same essential structure; it seems reasonable to interpret '*He came as quickly as he could*' as an expansion of '*He came*', but not to interpret '*The dish ran away with the spoon*' as an expansion of '*Away*', though it is undoubtedly longer. In grammatical study we examine how words etc. combine in a given language into larger structures of more specific significance, that is, among other things, what kinds of expanded utterance are possible. For this we need a scale of linguistic terms, names for structures, but *utterance* is really an historical term, a designation of events.

§59. Accordingly, we distinguish another complex unit on a different scale from the utterance, namely, the **sentence**. This term we shall use to describe those linguistic sequences that have internal but no external grammatical relations—which are grammatical structures, and self-contained ones. In this sense the term is not equally useful for all languages, but it is indispensable for English, in which the disjunction of what is grammatically self-contained from what is not is one of the most absolute in the language. There is a little indeterminacy, but that is inescapable in linguistic analysis.

At this date, unfortunately, it is not possible to propose using the term *sentence* without justifying the practice. How much dissatisfaction there has been is indicated by the number of attempts at definition (Fries, 1952, Chapter 2), for there is no need to redefine a term unless you are dissatisfied with your predecessors' use of it. It is for this reason that some recent writers have attempted to make *utterance* do the work of the traditional term *sentence*. But we have already seen that the two terms belong to different scales, one historical, the other linguistic. It is better to face the difficulties about *sentence*, and try not to be misled by them. Basically the trouble is that our formal education has made us more conscious of what is a sentence, i.e., is grammatically self-contained, in writing, than of what are the corresponding structures in speech. Also, of course, a written sentence is deceptively easy to identify; as Cobbett put it long ago, 'A *sentence* . . . means one of those portions of words which are divided from the rest by a single dot' (1817, Letter 1). It ought, after all, to be easy enough to say what kinds of structure we do divide off in this way. Then the danger is that we too readily assume that these structures are identical with the grammatically self-contained units of speech. Although some 'styles' of spoken English do have structures equivalent to those delimited as sentences in writing, others, very frequently used, do not. An example of one that does not—by no means an extreme or exceptional example, was given in §17. That such structures are usual in informal educated speech has been amply demonstrated in recent years by tape-recorded material; that they are effective as utterances is evident from the fact that we manage to carry on impromptu conversations. So we can deduce that they have a regular patterning that could be described—only so far it has not been systematically described. What, therefore, we shall have to describe here are those structures that are common to written English, of a direct, not highly wrought kind, and spoken English of a not too impromptu kind. This is clearly not because such kinds of English are more important than others, through numerical predominance or as an ideal, but because most is known about them. To these kinds of English our sense of *sentence* is relevant, and if necessary we can make it more precise by distinguishing the spoken and written structures as **sentence(S)** and **sentence(W)**.

Notes

1. A linguist professing to replace *sentence* by *utterance* but failing is Harris (1951), cf. especially 2.4 and 2.32; Fries (1952) follows a similar course and is described by Sledd (1955) as boxing a 'noisy but inconclusive round' with traditional notions of the sentence. The sensible view is still that of Bloomfield, adapted above: 'In any utterance, a

linguistic form appears either as a constituent of some larger form, as does *John* in the utterance *John ran away*, or else as an independent form, not included in any larger (complex) linguistic form, as, for instance, *John* in the exclamation *John!* When a linguistic form appears as part of a larger form, it is said to be in *included position*; otherwise it is said to be in *absolute position* and to constitute a *sentence . . .*

'An utterance may consist of more than one sentence. This is the case when the utterance contains several linguistic forms which are not by any meaningful, conventional grammatical arrangement (that is, by any construction) united into a larger form, e.g., *How are you? It's a fine day. Are you going to play tennis this afternoon?* Whatever practical connection there may be between these three forms, there is no grammatical arrangement uniting them into one larger form: the utterance consists of three sentences' (1935, 11.2).

I have not referred at all to some traditional kinds of sentence definition in terms of meaning (e.g., 'the sentence is a relatively complete unit of meaning' or 'expresses a single thought'). Bloomfield has stated (see above) a principle on which they can be ignored, namely that they do not say anything about linguistic forms; not only are they in this sense irrelevant, but in practice they are both unclear in application and partial in coverage.

2. Linguistic analysis can operate with units larger than the sentence (see Harris, 1952), but the connections above the sentence level are largely semantic. Sentence-linking items such as *however, nevertheless*, can, though, be regarded as forming a quasi-grammatical link between sentences.

§60. Plainly sentences are meaningful structures made of other, usually, but not necessarily, smaller, meaningful structures. The only other meaningful structure we have mentioned so far is the **word**. Of course, there are words in sentences, but it does not make sense to say that sentences are constituted, in any direct sense, of words. If you doubt this, you can try building sentences word by word. Write a word that could begin a sentence, and pass it to a friend for him to add one word that he thinks could continue the sentence; conceal the first word, and let another person add a third word; continue in this way, revealing each time only one word before the one to be added. The resulting strings will only rarely and accidentally look at all like English. If we cannot think of single words as the building-blocks of sentences, would we do better with strings of two, or three, or four, or even ten, words? Well, yes, better. We should notice a gradual improvement until at about four-word stretches there would be chunks that did approximate to acceptable English and chunks that did not. Even at ten words, the grammar would be fairly acceptable, but the topic would swing abruptly in a way abnormal for genuine sentences. Since we do not find a cut-off point at which the deviant ends and the normal begins, it looks as if we must orient our search differently, and look, not for the number of words that enables us to build acceptable sentences, but for a structure of a different kind, which can be realised in varying numbers of words, but which contributes indispensably to our formation and grasp of sentences.　We must expect to find at least one structure of this kind, and must be prepared to discover that we need to search for more than one.

Note

On word-sequence building of first- to tenth-order approximation, see Miller (1951) Chapter 4.

§**61.** If we resume our search from the sentence end, we immediately spot a kind of structure sometimes co-extensive with a sentence and sometimes forming part of one.　This seems a promising starting-point. We may take an example from written dialogue.　In the sequence:

> 'You asked me a specific question.　I've answered it.　You did not ask me what the substance was; you asked me to find out whether or not it was blood.'　(Robert A. Heinlein, *The Unpleasant Profession of Jonathan Hoag*)

there are three sentences (W); the written form enables us, as experienced readers, to translate them into three sentences (S).　The same structures could, however, be re-arranged, with a semi-colon in place of the first full stop, giving two sentences in all, or with a full stop in place of the semi-colon, giving four sentences in all.　The changes are not immaterial; they bring about real differences; and we cannot make them everywhere—if we changed the second full stop we should not be left with a sequence of whole, acceptable sentences, but should need to change the wording too.　But some changes can be made, affecting purely punctuation (and what it corresponds to in speech), which still do leave nothing but acceptable sentences in the whole sequence.　We may say that as well as sentences there are sentence-like structures, that is, structures which can constitute whole sentences, but do not invariably do so in use.　To them we shall give the name **clause**, and we shall say: a sentence consists of one or more clauses; one or more clauses constitute a sentence.　In doing so, we do not merely isolate an important constituent, but also implicitly change our metaphor for the way sentences are made.　We have already noted that various kinds of juncture between clauses can occur if there is more than one clause in a sentence, some kinds involving verbal change.　That being so, we are not dealing with building blocks or bricks, but with a more abstract **constitute–constituent** relationship; we shall continue to work with this notion as long as it proves useful.

Notice that we cannot speak of clauses as constituents of *larger* structures, since a sentence may consist of a single clause.　Sentence, clause, and the further constituents we shall identify, represent points on a **scale** that only in a limited sense moves from greater to lesser in extent; not size, but function in the next higher unit consistently differentiates the units at each point on the scale (except the last, which has no higher unit). To this scale Halliday gives the name **rank-scale**; we can speak of a structure as higher (or lower) in rank without necessarily implying that it is larger (or smaller).

Since a single clause in many cases constitutes a sentence we must take clauses as the real starting-point in our search for constituents; nothing is lost by doing so. Indeed, it is only units that function in a higher unit (unlike sentences) that can be the place of operation of systemic contrast. Therefore we must search for at least one further unit on the scale before we reach the word; the argument that words are not direct constituents of sentences holds for words in clauses.

You may have noticed that the use of the term *clause* proposed here is not yet wholly clear-cut, but already appears to be in conflict with traditional definitions (e.g., that a clause is a structure containing a finite verb). The approach here takes function (as constituent of the higher-ranking sentence) to be the primary defining characteristic of clauses; certain types of structure often go with this function, but they are not the basis of the definition, and we shall recognise verbless clauses (cf. §67). Two points of clarification should, however, be made. First, it does not follow that because we define clauses as immediate constituents of sentences, every bit of a sentence must be clearly assigned to a particular clause and not to any other. Actually, not everything in a sentence is involved in its constituent structure— intonation, for example, clearly is not. And some elements that do belong to constituent-structure may be Janus-like, contributing to two clauses at once (e.g., *what* in the sequence *You did not ask me what the substance was*). Second, though we are not defining clauses in terms of their internal structure, we shall see that certain structures are closely associated with them. When such characteristics occur in a function that is not clausal, they may be referred to as clause-like; we shall consider at §65 an aspect of grammatical organisation in which it becomes necessary to distinguish clause-like items that are non-clausal in function (and the same will hold for other units on the rank-scale).

§62. In the search for sentence-constituents we were guided by an intuitive notion of equivalence, and we cannot do better than try the same notion on clause-analysis. Consider the three structures:

This is the house;
This is the house that Jack built;
This is the cock that crowed in the morn . . . that Jack built.

The opening elements (*This is*) are the same; the whole sequences are equivalent in grammatical **rank** (i.e. are sentences consisting of one clause each, cf. §61). By simple subtraction we conclude that there is grammatical equivalence between the three remaining components, however varied in length and in internal structure. Nothing mediates between them and the clause; they are **immediate constituents** of their respective clauses. We may tentatively conclude that whatever they are is an **element of clause-structure**, and we may give that element its traditional title **complement** (abbreviated C; there is not usually any ambiguity between the grammatical and the phonological use of the abbreviation).

It cannot then escape attention that structures which are equivalent at C have also another dimension of equivalence. They all fit in the first position of the clause (there are, in fact, a few exceptions [see Chapter VII], and the converse does not hold). Thus, we can also say:

The house is this one;
The house that Jack built is this one;
The cock that crowed in the morn . . . that Jack built is this one.

Here, we have identified another element of clause-structure, having pretty well the same kinds of **realisations** as C, one to which we can give the traditional name **subject** (abbreviated S; again, there is usually no ambiguity with the medium-abbreviation S). In our present set of examples this leaves only one piece over, and that piece necessarily also constitutes an element, namely *is*, the **predicator** (P). Like S and C, it can take more complex forms, though its range of possibilities is more limited, and the tie between P and the form-class *verb* as its realisation is uniquely close (see Chapter IX). Briefly, we may add that if we find other elements they may be identified as **adjunct** (**A**) (as *on the elbow* in *the swinging door hit John on the elbow*), and that when clauses are strung together it is sometimes necessary to mark that an element serves as S in relation to one clause and as C in relation to another, or that the S/C contrast does not apply within a clause; for this the label Z may be used. It should be added that the elements of a clause can include more than one C or A, but only one S and one P, though either may be simple or compound. In *I'll give him the book at college to-morrow* the structure is SPCCAA. It is clear from this example that Cs and As may each vary in kind. The different realisations of A can, if necessary, be classified by their function, as locative (*at college*), temporal (*tomorrow*), conditional (*if possible*), purposive (*for fun*), etc.; of course, the reason for such discriminations must be formal, not functional—for example, to account for the relative order of multiple As. The two realisations of C in our example certainly need to be differentiated if we are to proceed to a finer, or more delicate, analysis. Both can be classified as **objects**, and distinguished by the traditional names **direct** and **indirect object**. The difference can be stated in terms of order: the indirect object comes first if neither contains a preposition (as in our example) but alternatively the direct is followed by a prepositional indirect object (*I'll give the book to him*). Both kinds of object can be distinguished from a further type of C, **non-object** C, as in *He became a monk*. The distinction can be seen within the clause and in comparison between clauses. Within the clause different types of verb relate S and C according to whether C is object or non-object (cf. §69). Clauses with C of object type usually (not invariably) correspond to structurally parallel clauses in the same way that *He'll be given the book* and *The book will be given to him* correspond (structurally, not in range of use) to *I'll give him the book*. But there is no **A monk was become by him* corresponding to *He became a monk*. Do not be misled into thinking that C types in English depend on case.

S and P are simple in the examples given so far, but compound in *Jack and Jill . . .*, *Stop, look and listen*. For the elements that enter directly into clause-structure we may use the term **phrase**. A clause consists of one or more **phrases**; one or more **phrases** constitute a clause.

§63. One kind of phrase, that exemplified in *at college, to him, up the hill*, has a constituent-structure which still does not necessarily take us to word rank. In *up the hill* we have a bi-partite structure; *the hill* is habitually a phrase of S or C type (*The hill is on your right, Let's climb the hill*), but in other instances it needs something before it to function as a phrase (*Jack and Jill went up the hill*). We may distinguish the *up the hill* type as a prepositional phrase, having itself a structure of constituents we may call **groups**. There is a very large number of instances in which the distinction between phrase and group need not be specified in analysis of constituent-structure, because each phrase consists of one group. The item may then be called by either term. But, as we have seen, there are occasions when the distinction is needed. Moreover, if we turn for a moment to a matter other than constituent-structure, we find an important distinction. Phrases, like clauses and sentences, usually have no single head; such structures are called **exocentric**, and contrasted with structures which have a single head and are, as a whole, of the same kind as that head. Thus, nominal groups (*every conceivable kind of flower, the finest recording I've ever heard*) have heads (*flower, recording*) and these heads, are like the groups they belong to, nominal. Structures of this second kind are **endocentric**. Unlike sentences, clauses, and phrases, groups are characteristically endocentric.

With the group, or phrase/group, we reach an element whose immediate constituents are words. Notice that *word* (which we have hitherto accepted in its common uses, without definition) is thus defined as a unit of a certain rank in the constitute-constituent scale of grammar (it also has phonological characteristics that commonly, but not necessarily, coincide with its grammatical one; enclitics are forms that are grammatical but not phonological words, and grammar, which makes meaningful distinctions, is taken to be prior to phonology, the means of making such distinctions).

As with sentences, we shall find it advisable at times to distinguish spoken and written (word[S] and word[W]). Word(W) has a clear-cut sense; it is a sequence of letters after which a space is left in writing; but the clear-cut distinction is not by any means always applied in the same way (for discussion, and further references, see Marchand (1961) Chapter I). *A fortiori*, it will not systematically coincide with a particular kind of structure in speech, which in general we take to be primary, and which must be our guide where written usage is not self-consistent. Notice, too that such a form as *I've*, which in speech and writing forms a unit, cannot be a word in our sense, since it includes two groups, S and P. It is a phonological conflation reflected in the written form.

Notes

I have indicated a primary, or central, sense of **word**, and suggested that other senses, current in popular usage, have a certain relevance in linguistic study. This kind of distinction, between central and peripheral senses (with the corollary that there are central and peripheral instances of the thing in question) will crop up rather frequently. Other criteria for the word, which are to some extent relevant in English, are given by Bloomfield: 'Forms which occur as sentences are free forms. . . . A free form which consists entirely of two or more lesser free forms . . . is a phrase. A free form which is not a phrase, is a word. A word, then, is a free form which does not consist entirely of (two or more) lesser free forms; in brief, a word is a minimum free form. . . . For the purposes of ordinary life, the word is the smallest unit of speech. . . . The fact that the spacing of words has become part of our tradition of writing, goes to show . . . that recognition of the word as a unit of speech is not unnatural to speakers' (1935, 11.5).

He also (loc. cit.) suggests that *uninterruptability* is characteristic of word-structure, the only exceptions in all known languages being so rare as to seem almost pathological. English does admit of exceptions, but the effect is somewhat bizarre, of 'BELGRAVIA. "ABSO-BLOOMING-LUTELY LUVERLY". Adam fireplace, chandeliers. "AND ALL THAT. . . ."' (advertisement in *The Times*, August, 1960). Two other subsidiary criteria are worth mention. One is *unguessability*, lack of motivation. The word is typically one of the kinds of linguistic form whose function cannot be deduced from the functions of its parts together with their grammatical arrangements; a structure whose function can be so deduced is said to be *motivated*. In this the word differs from the phrase, group, clause and sentence. This is not a very clear or decisive criterion. Guessability is of a more-less, not yes-no kind (compare *polyglot* with *cabbage*: *cabbage* is not motivated, but for some speakers *polyglot* is, though the motivation comes from outside English; and some sequences such as *greenhouse* and *ice cream* are motivated to some extent, but we cannot guess their exact functions). The last criterion is linked with unguessability. We have great freedom in composing phrases, groups, clauses and sentences; we are free because the meaning of the whole is deducible. We cannot in the same way make up new words; their meaning is not deducible, and we should not be understood. On the other hand, some inventiveness is open to us, just as much as the meaningfulness of elements permits us (see Chapter XII); and in this words are unlike phonemes, which we cannot make up at all. Note, however, that occasionally highly successful new words are deliberately created, relying on no more than a very general suggestion of meaning in their component parts, e.g. *supercalifragilistic-expialidocious*.

§64. The words in *This is the house that Jack built* have no obviously meaningful subdivisions. Since grammar is a level of organisation concerned with meaningful distinctions, the material of these sentences does not immediately require us to look any further. But much other material does. If we return to the sentences 'You asked me a question. I've answered it.', it is clear that at least two forms, *asked* and *answered*, do have meaningful subdivisions—*ask-*, *answer-*, and *-ed*. These word-constituents must therefore be brought into our scale, and they are given the name **morpheme**. A word consists of one or more morphemes; one or more morphemes constitute a word. Below this, on a scale of meaningful distinctions, we cannot go.

We have naturally begun with the analysis of clear instances. But not all examples are so clear. For instance, if *ask-ed* is more than one morpheme, then we might feel inclined to argue that *was* must be, though the two components do not follow one another in time but are, as it were, superimposed. And if *was*, why not *is*? And what of *built* as contrasted with *build*? Can we find an end of this analogical cutting into morphemes? This, like the problems of phoneme-definition, is an issue on which much ink has been spilt (see *Note* below). The grave problems arise if we worry about whether a particular item is (inherently) a morpheme in the language, and about what is to count as a recurrence of the same morpheme. What is here suggested is an approach that identifies bits of utterances as being, or not being, morphemes where they occur, applying the criterion of minimum grammatically-meaningful unit, and word-constituency; it is true that certain items are, not merely in context, but habitually, morphemes, but we are not postulating that being a morpheme in the language is an inherent property of items.

Note

The presence of a semantic requirement in the definition of the morpheme means that it cannot be used rigorously, for the range of all possible meanings has not been, and perhaps cannot be, mapped out so exactly as to show clearly in every case whether two meanings are 'the same' or not. For instance, not everyone would agree with Hockett (1958 15.1) that *large* is the same morpheme in *He's a large man*, and *by and large*, but in a case of dispute, to what principle can the disputants refer? Some linguists have tried to get over the difficulty by abandoning Bloomfield's requirement of a twofold likeness and depending on a single one, likeness of distribution. Thus, Trager and Smith (1951, p. 53) 'Inspection of the linguistic material shows immediately that similar sequences or combinations of phonemes keep recurring. . . . And from time to time recurrent gaps in distribution are noted. . . . The recurring partials, including zero-elements, are the MORPHEMES of a language' (and similarly Harris, 1951). By a judicious regulation of what shall count as the frame-work or context by which the recurrent partials are to be determined, homonyms such as *pear, pair, pare* can still be kept apart. A more serious difficulty is that it still seems useful to count as one morpheme such forms as /-s,/ /-z/, /-ɪz/ in their common function of forming regular noun plurals in English, and even to count in a single morpheme of 'pastness' in the verb such things as the change of /eɪ/ to /ʊ/ in *take*, *took*, along with forms of entirely different phonemic composition; this is justified on the grounds that such sets of forms are complementary in distribution. But unless objective grounds are given for setting up the 'grid' whereby complementarity is determined, this amounts to no more than saying that different-sounding forms count as one morpheme if they have the same function or meaning. In fact, the attempt to cut out the element of dependence on meaning from the definition of the morpheme has led full circle to a definition which, under elaborate disguise, depends entirely upon meaning. The problem has similarities to that discussed in the Note to §63.

Meanwhile, it is clear that the related definitions from Hockett and Bloomfield each have virtues. Bloomfield's, by specifying 'no partial phonetic-semantic resemblance' solves the problem of what is to count as the same morpheme: any resemblance, however slight, brings forms into the orbit of the same morpheme. This, however, proves difficult to apply, for we have lost our scale of likeness, and some forms are certainly more alike than others. Hockett, by giving first place to meaning, leaves himself, as we have seen, many doubtful cases, but his definition opens the way for the useful notion of morpheme alternants, that is, phonemically different (or even zero) forms (like /-s/, /-z/, /-ɪz/ in noun plurals) which are united by complementary distribution or identity of function. Recently Hockett, indicating the weaknesses of the terms *phoneme* and *morpheme* as variously understood, has refined upon the idea of distributionally-established morphemes by pointing out that it is not morphemes, but their alternants that are made up of phonemes (1961).

There still remains the difficulty, admitted by Harris (1951, p. 253), that the sheer size of sample required for a distributional morphemic analysis rules it out of practical consideration. (See also Strang [1964].)

§65. The total scale in English grammar, therefore, has six ranks—sentence, clause, group, phrase, word, morpheme. It is likely that all languages have scales constructed in this way, though we cannot assume that any single language will necessarily have the same number of points on the scale. The relationship of consisting-constituting that prevails throughout the scale is a **taxonomic** one (a scale is a **taxonomic hierarchy**). It is, therefore, perfectly possible to have a sentence consisting of one clause consisting of one group consisting of one phrase consisting of one word consisting of one morpheme—like the Spanish Captain's daughter's 'No!'

Note, however, that a structure that characteristically functions at one rank may be downgraded to a lower one in a given higher-ranking unit. So in 'the cock that crowed in the morn' we have a clause-like structure *that crowed in the morn* constituting a part of a group. Or, in 'the man-who-came-to-dinner's hat is still in the hall' the clause-like structure *who came to dinner* is down-graded to become a constitute of the group-like structure itself down-graded to morpheme rank as a constituent of the word *man-who-came-to-dinner's*. This down-grading is called **rank-shift**. It 'moves' a unit which habitually has one rank to function in a given structure at a rank below, perhaps considerably below, its habitual one.

Convenient symbols for use in analysis are:

///	sentence boundary
//	clause boundary
/	group boundary
¦	phrase boundary
(space)	word boundary
+	morpheme boundary
[[ ]]	boundary of rank-shifted clause
[ ]	boundary of rank-shifted group

Note

The grammatical theory from which the exposition here is adapted is that of M. A. K. Halliday; see especially Halliday (1961), Halliday McIntosh and Strevens (1964), particularly Chapter 1. A simple, clear summary appears in Leech (1966). What Halliday calls *rank-shift* was earlier called *down-grading* (Hill, 1958, p. 357). The introduction of *phrase* into the scale follows Quirk (1968), Chapter 11.

(B) System

§66. In tracing a scale of taxonomically-related units we have incidentally illustrated other notions—those of **structure**, the pattern of relationship between **units** on the **scale** (a *morpheme* enters into the *structure* of a *word*, etc.) and of **place** in structure (the *position* occupied by a *morpheme*, etc.). The units are the recurrent bits over which patterning occurs, and they fall into **classes** according to their tendency to occupy the same place. Each place is a point of choice, at which the speaker selects one from a number of items in paradigmatic relationship. At the rank of word there are four places in *This is the house*: at them we have chosen, respectively, *This* (instead of *that, here*, etc.); *is* instead of *was, indicates*, etc., *the* instead of *a, my*, etc.; and *house* instead of *book, idea*, etc. Reflecting on even these few examples we may suspect that two rather different kinds of choice are involved. In the first and third positions (the *this, the* positions) we can in good conscience put *etc.* to our list; but really very few items are left that could occur in those positions, and it would be very little trouble to list them exhaustively. In the fourth position (the *house* position) we can think of thousands of items that would fit; if we rashly ventured to claim that they were numberless we should turn out to have been more literally right than one commonly is in using that expression (see Chapter XII). The last remaining position is more complicated. The items that differ from *is* in approximately the way that *was* does are few; those that differ in the way that *indicates* does are extremely numerous. In this position it seems that both kinds of choice are exemplified at once. At any place, the items that can occur constitute a *class*; but certain classes have the additional properties of a *system*. That is, they have a fixed, relatively small, and stable number of terms amongst which choice has to be made, and all terms are mutually exclusive of each other (in the case of *is*, the system of **tense** is involved, which in English is two-term, **past** and **non-past**; we cannot avoid choosing a tense, and choosing one excludes choice of the other). It is noticeable that many systems in English grammar are two-term—so much so that we may consider this the characteristic form of a system. As in phonology, choices which appear to be multiple can sometimes be arranged as ordered binary choices and such re-arrangement, far from being arbitrary, often throws light on the resources and our use of them.

The general properties of those classes which do not constitute systems are more negative; they are classes which do not conform to the requirements for systems. But one point should be made about them. Nothing in our definition of class suggests that class-membership is a yes-no matter of pigeonholing. Items that go together in a class in one place will not necessarily share the same privilege of occurrence in all positions. Classes will prove to have multiple membership and divided membership if we look at them at a primary level—that is, in the sense given. But it is natural to try to institutionalise the idea of class: to say, for instance, that there is a class of adjectives because of the large area of membership-overlap between the class of attributive adjectives and the class of predicative adjectives. In this derivative sense, classes will have central and peripheral members. These ideas will be developed and applied in later Chapters.

§67. The analysis of systems operative in English grammar is a very large task. It is simplest to begin with the systems of the largest relevant unit, clause-in-sentence-structure. In fact, as we go down the rank-scale the picture becomes so complicated that we must reserve whole chapters for parts of topics; within the clause the three big distinctions are between S/C structures, P structures and the rest, and that threefold division will be the basis of our later treatment. Here, only clause-systems will be outlined. There are four sets of choices, with relationships between them:

(i) Two-term system of **dependence**. A clause is **independent** (symbolised α) if it has a form in which it could stand as an independent sentence; otherwise it is **dependent** (β). In *It is fine today: we will go out*, both clauses are independent; in *Because it is fine today we will go out*, the first is dependent. Notice that the index of dependence may be a special word, as in the example just given, but other indications are possible. Almost all clause-systems exploit variables involving P to differentiate their terms. The sign of a dependent clause may be neutralisation of contrast in the terms of a system operative at P. Thus, to independent *He will go*, *He would go* corresponds a single dependent form (*He said*) *he would go*.

(ii) Two-term system, **finite/non-finite**, in which the marked term is the non-finite, a clause lacking a finite verb, as in *the more the merrier*; *once a thief, always a thief*; *his hands in his pockets, he . . ..* In cases where the relational element P is lacking, S and C cannot be differentiated, and the nominal element is Z. For some purposes it is useful to make a further subdivision of the non-finite type on the basis of the presence or absence of P ($+$P, $-$P); the marked term is the $-$P type, which may be called **minor**. In fully **discursive** grammar, that is, in the kind of English that has traditionally been accepted as suitable for analysis in grammars, minor clauses are restricted to dependent uses, except in a few formulaic and proverbial examples. However, it is clear that another kind of English, allowing minor clauses in independent function, is widespread and perfectly effective, so that grammars ought to take account of it. In titles, labels, public signs, notices, posters and advertising, to take a few examples, minor clauses commonly function as independent. The grammar in which they do so has been called **disjunctive**, to distinguish it from the (academically) more familiar discursive grammar. The distinction is made, and its implications explored, in Leech (1966).

§68. We deal next with a complex of systems, all two-term but interrelated in such a way that they are best handled together. They are

4+

the choices that relate clauses to functions at the contextual level, i.e.
which indicate whether the clauses are serving to make a statement, ask
a question, or give an order. Roughly corresponding to these contextual
categories are the grammatical terms **affirmative, interrogative, imperative.** A fourth variable is the two-term **positive-negative** system, which can co-exist with or be superimposed on, any term from
any of the other systems.

To place a clause in this grid of systems we must first ask: *Is it
imperative or non-imperative?* The answer will not be given in contextual terms ('It is imperative because it gives an order') but in
formal terms. The element S, if present, is what is usually called
second person (but see §97), but it is commonly omitted; P has special
forms, partly dependent on the previous condition, but additionally
neutralising the systems of tense-mood-aspect contrast normally found at
P (for the P forms in question see §123ff.). Examples are: *You try some;
Do go home (John).* If the clause is imperative it can still, as we have said,
be *positive* or *negative* (see below) but the other choices do not apply.

If the clause is non-imperative it must be placed in relation to the
next choice, **affirmative** or **interrogative.** Again, these types have
characteristic contextual functions, but are linguistically identified by
their distinctive formal properties. In affirmative clauses, the normal
or unmarked order of elements S and P is SP: *He came (yesterday),
Mary won't play;* in interrogative ones it is PS (or at least part of P
before S): *Is he? Did he come?* The characteristic role of *do*-forms in
negative and interrogative clauses is considered at §130. Both can be
positive or negative.

Finally, if the clause is interrogative, it may be **polar** or **non-polar.**
These terms have characteristic contextual roles—a polar or yes-no
question asks for confirmation; a non-polar question is multiple (unspecified) choice, and asks for information; but, as usual, they are
identified by their grammatical characteristics. A polar interrogative
clause, in addition to the order of elements characteristic of all interrogatives, tends to have a distinctive intonation (see next Chapter); a non-
polar interrogative is introduced by a special word, generally known as
a *wh-form* (from the dominant written beginning of *who, what, which,
why, when, where, how;* notice that the speech onset of *who* is like that
of *how,* not like those of the other items in the list). The network of
choices may therefore be diagrammed:

<pre>
     ┌—imperative
     │
     │   ┌—affirmative (non-interrogative)
     └—non-imperative ⟨   │
                            └—interrogative ┌—polar
                                            │
                                            └—non-polar
</pre>

Finally, there is a choice positive-negative, which operates in a different dimension since both its terms can co-exist with any term from any of the systems just described. Functionally, it is an independent variable; formally, however, it is closely akin to these systems in the mechanisms it uses. The negative is its marked term, the marking taking the form of use of some form of *not*, accompanied by verbal forms akin to those of the interrogative in their use of *do*.

It is possible that yet another dimension should be recognised. There is selection for *emphasis* in clauses like *She ˡdoes like horses* as against *She likes horses*. This emphasis can occur in positive or negative affirmative or interrogative clauses with P, using a verb that operates the *do*-system. Its function is quite different from that of lexical emphasis or heavy stress, since it serves to heighten or underline the clause-selection from the positive-negative option.

Note

The classification of clauses presented here derives from original work by M. A. K. Halliday and his colleagues. See especially Leech (1966), Halliday (1967 1 and 2) and further references there. (Halliday [1967₂] refers to the central role of verbs: 'Other than in certain minor sentence functions ... the speaker of English structures his message around a verb' (p. 13).) *Declarative* is sometimes used instead of *Affirmative*.

§69. The last paragraph does not exhaust the kinds of selection operative at clause-rank. Work now in progress (see Halliday, 1967₁) will certainly lead to the inclusion of further variables into systems. Meanwhile, we must put into a simple list the major possibilities of variation in clause-structure related to the selection at P. Amongst verbs (i.e. words characteristically functioning at P) a basic and familiar distinction is between *transitive* and *intransitive*; but in addition to these major classes there are smaller, less clear-cut ones. The differences are not just within the verbs, but affect the total patterning of clauses. To describe these patterns we must draw upon terms not yet fully discussed; they are not unfamiliar terms, but if they give rise to difficulty the explanations in later chapters should be consulted.

(i) Typical clause-structures with an intransitive verb at P are *So you've arrived, It happened yesterday*. The sub-class of verbs (V) responsible for this kind of structure can be labelled VI, and the post-verb structure has no compulsory elements; it may include an *adverb of manner* (AM). The unmarked type of VI may be given the sub-script VI_1 to distinguish it from two other types—VI_2 in which a particle is indispensable (*stand up, lie down*, etc.), (more marginal) VI_3

in which a particle $+$ C (or prepositional phrase) is required (*stand in the corner, lie on the sofa*, etc.).

(ii) Transitive verbs (VT) require a nominal group at C, and may in addition have an adverb of manner at A, as in *I'm going to write a letter, Do it quickly*. Traditionally they are also identified by their capacity for passivisation (as in *The letter will be written by me personally*). The convention is a perfectly sound one; it is important, since it introduces an element we have not previously met with, that of potential. In classifying linguistic material we have to take account not only of likeness of occurrence and patterning, but also of whether items have similar potential—potential for change into what, in the data before us, they are not (see Chapter XI). Here, too, we need to distinguish subclasses—the simple form VT_1, already illustrated; VT_2 requiring a particle (as in *Please put away your books*); VT_3 requiring a prepositional phrase (*Send the letter to my house*); VT_4 requiring two C elements (*They elected him President*). Two further types require following structures in *to* (*We persuaded him to give a lecture*) and *-ing* (*He planned to avoid meeting her*).

(iii) A small group of verbs, usually symbolised V_b from *become*, which is one of the commonest, must be followed by noun or adjective at C (for the class consisting of noun or adjective where both are possible, the term *substantive* can be used), as, *He became a monk, She became prettier immediately*; additionally, as the second example shows, an adverb of manner may be present at A but there is no passive.

(iv) A small group symbolised V_s (from a common member *seem*) requires the following presence of an adjective, and may be followed by certain adverbials, as *He seems nicer, suddenly*; *she looks young today*.

(v) A small class symbolised V_h (for *have*) is identified, as requiring a following nominal at C, excluding adverbials of manner, and having no passive. The distinction between *have* and VT is perhaps more clear-cut in American than British English. *Cost, weigh, become* (=*suit, be fitting for*) are usually associated with *have* in this class, though on more delicate analysis they can be shown to differ among themselves.

(vi) Unique in many ways (including the number of contrasts in its conjugation) is *be*—so much so that it has sometimes been treated as a distinct one-member class, and not a verb at all. It clearly has great similarities with verbs as we have so far identified them—it operates at P, is the locus of the usual verb contrasts (of tense, etc.), and the means of making contrasts of clause-type. It is very much like V_b in clause patterning, but has additional patterns. It can occur with no post-verbal element (*God is*; but note that this pattern is highly restricted in occurrence), and it plays a special part in the structure of other verbs (as in such passives as *He's being examined*). Its peculiarities no doubt justify regarding it as a special sub-class, but to exclude it altogether from the class of verbs is to violate normal usage to an unwarranted extent.

Note

For this classification of verb-types in relation to clause-structure see Roberts (1964), who, however, does not treat *be* as a verb. V_b, V_s, are sometimes jointly called *linking verbs*.

§70. The framework for sentence-study here is the merest sketch of some topics. Certain of the points it raises will be explored further in Chapters VI to X; other questions it has not even touched upon will arise in Chapter XI. But there are two further points that must be dealt with here, since they concern types of relationship which are extremely pervasive. At various ranks, items may be related to each other as unequals or as equals. In cases of unequal relationship there is **modification**, with one item specifying, determining, modifying, the other, and the other being specified, determined, modified. The items involved in such unequal relationships may be called **modifier** (determinant is also current in a similar sense), or M, and **head** (determinatum), or H. Examples, in the characteristic English order M H, are *pretty girls, world production, rainbow*. In cases where the relationship is between equals we have **apposition**; naturally one item has to come after the other, but in this case the sequence does not imply inequality, as in *slave girl, John, Duke of Mumpshire*.

Another important type of relationship occurs between and within the elements of clauses. When such elements, or their components, are tied in such a way that selection within a given grammatical system is made only once for the tied elements, not independently for each of them, there is **concord** between them. When the concord is of such a kind that it depends on choice for one item, which in turn determines the choice for the other, or excludes certain choices for the other, we speak of **government**. We have an example of government in S-P concord in English. In many cases selection must be made at S for number—singular or plural. The language imposes choice between the two, but the speaker is free to choose which term he will use, according to what he wishes to say. But this choice once made in turn imposes a like selection at P; by and large, the speaker is not free to make a fresh choice of number at this point. I can decide to mention a horse in a field, or two horses in a field, but having made my decision I am bound to continue the one-horse sentence with an *is*-like verb form at P, and the two-horse sentence with an *are*-like verb form at P.

This asymmetrical relationship of government is unlike that within S, where *one* goes with *horse*, not *horses*, and *two* goes with *horses*, not *horse*, but we cannot say that one choice determines the other. The two items are selected together, as a pattern resulting from the speaker's decision of what to say.

Note

Like most constraints in English, those arising from concord should not be thought of as absolute. On relaxation of the S-V restraints in usage see Strang (1966). In another domain of concord—time-specification between verb and adverb—the restraint is now often relaxed in captions of the type 'X gives trouble at Newmarket yesterday'.

EXERCISES

Since the exposition in this Chapter is preliminary to that of the remaining chapters on grammar, exercises are of little relevance at this stage. Readers may, however, like to see what comments they can make at this point on the structure of the following caption to a photograph in *The Times* (11.x.67): 'A.A. Metal Products' tiny thick film microcircuit module, just one inch square, is the basis of the integrated circuit voltage regulator incorporated in the new range of Lucas, the car electrical component supplier, alternators. Such integrated circuits replace the earlier electromechanical design of voltage regulator (above).'

FURTHER READING

The references given in the Chapter should, of course, be followed up; beyond this, reading relevant to sentence-structure will be considered at the end of Chapter XI.

CHAPTER VI

Phonology in Grammar

§71. The subject of this chapter is **intonation**, an area of the sound-structure of English which makes differences of meaning primarily at the grammatical level, and which for this reason was held over from Chapter IV. Now that we have established some framework for grammatical analysis we are in a position to analyse intonation. Intonation is patterning of the pitch-variable in speech, a variable depending on the relative tension of the vibrating vocal cords in voiced speech. The term is usually confined to patterning which exploits this variable for grammatical distinctions, as in English, and not used when the variable distinguishes between lexical items, as in Chinese. Most speakers are aware that English exploits this variable. They notice that there is a grammatical difference (signalled in writing by punctuation) between *John's going? John's going!* and *John's going.* They notice too that intonation is responsible for certain implications in utterances—for a note of hesitation, perfunctoriness, impatience, etc. Perhaps they also notice that the meanings and implications differ in different varieties of English and can cause misunderstanding. Speakers of some English dialects can seem to be asking a question when they are making a statement; and what in British standard is a perfectly civil form of the question *Would you like a cup of tea?* can suggest to an American guest the implication *It doesn't matter to me if you die of thirst.* But although the existence of pitch-patterning serving such purposes is clear enough, exact identification of the patterns and their functions has been a slow and complex business, on which even today many views exist. The plan of this chapter is to present a brief (indeed, an over-simplified) description of the patterns, of the systems they enter into and the meanings they distinguish.

Note

The phonetic-phonological description given here is largely derived from the very careful analysis in Kingdon (1958₁), which should be studied in amplification of the mere summary possible in this book. Apart from its importance as an analysis, a particular virtue of Kingdon's study is the ease, for printer and reader, of his transcription. My treatment of intonation-systems and their meanings is, however, almost wholly derived from studies by Halliday (1963, 1964), and Paper Seven of McIntosh and Halliday (1966; Halliday [1967₃]) arrived too late for use. The two accounts are not in every respect congruent, but I have drawn on them as being, I believe, the best in their respective areas of concentration, and have tried to fit them together without undue distortion of either.

§72. As a preliminary, we may review the organisation of phonological units in the light of the notion of **scale**, presented in Chapter V in relation to grammatical units. So far we have identified the **foot** (consisting of one or more syllables) the **syllable** (constituent of the **foot**, and itself consisting of one or more phonemes); and the **phoneme** (constituent of the syllable, but not itself further reducible [syntagmatically, the DFs are simultaneous bundles, not syntagmatic constituents of the kind relevant to the composition of scales]). We can now recognise that we are dealing with a **phonological scale**, which like the grammatical one, constitutes a taxonomic hierarchy. We have reached the lowest point on the scale, and must see whether we have also reached the highest. In fact we have not; the difference, already referred to, between *'John's 'going* and *'John's 'going?* is a grammatical difference signalled by phonology and stretching over units of more than one foot. Plainly we need to recognise a tune-carrying unit, consisting of one or more feet. For the tune itself we may use the name **tone**, and for the unit carrying it, **tone-group** (symbolised //). There is no evidence that the description of English requires postulation of any further unit of which the tone-group is a constituent.

Note

 The phoneme, minimum unit on the phonological scale, is not relevant to English intonation-systems. The tones are carried by syllables and sequences of syllables. More precisely, the intonation-systems are closely tied to the sub-system of stressed syllables. Notice in this connection that intonation depends on the presence of voice; all English stressed syllables contain a voiced component, but some (relatively few) unstressed ones do not.

§73. The last paragraph referred to intonation-systems, in the plural. In fact, there are three. The different meaningful tunes make up the **tone-system**. Each tone is identified by a pitch-movement—rising, falling or mixed—uniquely associated with it; other levels and movements of pitch may be present too, but one is definitive. There are five tones, whose character and functions will be discussed at §§76–82. We have also seen that each succeeding tone in the sequence of speech marks the presence of a fresh tone-group; the tone-group may contain subsidiary patterns too, but it remains one and the same tone-group until the domain of the next tone is reached. The structure of the tone-group presents us with two further variables, which are the basis of the other two intonation-systems of English. Within the tone-group there must be a point—one or more syllables—at which the defining pitch-movement of the tone occurs; this point, a syllable or the first of a group of syllables, is called the **tonic.** The place of the tonic is not fixed, but varies, and varies meaningfully, thus creating an independent set of choices. For example, the sentence *I'm going,* without special marks, has the tonic on the second syllable; on the other hand, if strong stress on the first word (W) is indicated, the tonic will shift, the characteristic tune occurring on the first syllable. This is a change of **tonicity,** and it is important to notice that tonicity has varied while the tone is held constant. The second variable concerns the extent of the tone-group—how much of a grammatical sequence is co-extensive with a tone-group. For example the clause *John's going today* would ordinarily be read off with a single tone-group, but it can constitute two, in which case it might be written as *John's going—to-day*; the tone is the same, but it occurs twice in the clause, where before it occurred once. This system, affording choice in the placement of tone-group boundaries, is called **tonality.** Notice that in both cases the first example given is more ordinary or normal than the second, not necessarily because it occurs more often (though that may be so), but rather because in each case the second seems to carry an extra meaning or special implication; the conventions of our writing clearly show which is felt to be normal. We shall find a similar feature in the distribution of tones. Here and elsewhere in the analysis of intonation we may call the 'normal' case **unmarked**, and the 'special' **marked.** Halliday writes:

'The meaning of tonality and tonicity can be summarised quite shortly. First it must be said that it is *not* the case, in my opinion, that the tone group can be used to define any unit in English grammar. In a slight majority of cases, if my own samples are representative, the tone group corresponds in extent to the grammatical clause; but it is also frequently, and under fairly definable conditions, either more than one clause or less than one clause. Indeed it is this range of possibility that makes tonality meaningful: the tone group can be thought of as representing a unit of information, and the speaker is free to choose how many units of information he is conveying and where he divides them; this decision is not imposed by the grammar (that is, by the non-intonational features of the grammar) except within rather wide limits. In other words tonality is an independent grammatical choice.

'For the sake of brevity I shall consider here only those cases where one tone group is co-extensive with one clause. This can be regarded as the unmarked or neutral state of affairs, since it is easiest to describe all other possibilities as being in contrast with this one. That is to say, where you have, say, two tone groups in one clause

4*

this is most easily explained by reference to the difference between this and the "one-clause–one tone group" situation.

'Within each unit there will be one, or in compound tones two, of what we may, following Lee Hultzén, call "information points". These are represented by tonicity, the placement of the tonic. Here again we can recognise an unmarked state: this is that the tonic, or more strictly the beginning of the tonic, will fall on the last *lexical* item in the tone group. . . . By contrast, of course, the tonic can start anywhere: certainly on any word, and probably, with enough ingenuity, on any morpheme; if it falls on a lexical item that is not clause-final, or a final item that is not lexical, this can be regarded as marked tonicity, giving contrastive information—an information point has been chosen in contrast to what the structure would lead us to expect.' (1966, pp. 119–120). (For the term *lexical item*, see §184.)

This contrastive effect is just what we have seen in the singling out of *John* by tonicity upon it, and by the divided tonality of the clause *John's going—to-day*, which focuses attention on the to-dayness of his going. Where the difference between the three intonation-systems is not particularly relevant, pitch-patterning may be referred to by the general term *intonation-contour*.

§74. While punctuation helps us in the written analysis of tonality and tonicity, it gives very little assistance in the indication of tone-contrast. For this reason special means of transcription must be found; even so, much must depend on the reader's ability to apply his practical knowledge in the search for analytical understanding.

Kingdon divides the notes and tunes of English speech into two kinds, the level or Static Tones, and the moving or Kinetic Tones. It is an important distinction. Since (following Halliday) we are using **tone** for the moving patterns or tunes, we must re-name Kingdon's Static Tones; the term **notes** can be used in this sense. Our first impression in listening to many English sentences is that they, or at least the central parts of them, proceed on a series of downward-stepping notes on successive stressed syllables. Consider the tune of the following, particularly the notes of the stressed syllables:

> '*Tell me* '*what on* '*earth you* '*think you're* '*doing.*
> '*Bring the* '*book to* '*school on* '*Tuesday* '*morning.*
> '*Mary* '*told me* '*John had* '*had his* '*breakfast.*

Or, with initial unstressed syllable:

> *I* '*want you to* '*read the* '*other* '*book as* '*soon as you* '*can.*
> *The* '*garden is* '*looking* '*perfectly* '*lovely to-*'*day.*
> *A*'*bout a* '*hundred* '*thousand* '*people* '*live in the* '*city.*

The final foot comes outside the pattern of downstepping level notes; we have already seen that its stress is normally the tonic, and the sentences just given all have unmarked tonicity.   Also, what precedes the first stress is outside the series.   Otherwise, the note for each stressed syllable is level, but each is a step down from the last.   This overall patterning leading up to the tones represents the unmarked form, but the series can be broken upwards or downwards to form a fresh flight of steps; in cases of marked tonality or tonicity, naturally, the series loses its tendency to be co-extensive with the sentence or clause.

Note
    The pre-tone step-structure of other kinds of sentence is well set out in O'Connor and Arnold (1961).

§75. While the stepped series of notes gives a characteristic pitch-movement in many cases to whole sentences, it is the Kinetic Tones (our *tones, tout court*) which make the difference of meaning between sentences of like composition.   If we merely list the possible range of phonetic forms they can take, these distinctive pitch-movements appear unmanageably complex ('In an article published in *Le Maître Phonetique*, No. 68, in 1939 I listed 60 possible stress-tone variants of the sentence *I can't find one*.   It now transpires that this number falls considerably short of the total possible.'   Kingdon, 1958_1, xvi).   In fact, the material is greatly simplified if we think of it as resulting from a fairly small number of independent variables, combined in a variety of ways.

    Thus, the voice-range available to any speaker may be thought of as structured into five layers, from low to high on the pitch-scale.   The middle one of the five is the normal range, within which the voice moves in tracing the tone-patterns.   Above and below it are bands into which the movement extends for extra emphasis; and above and below these bands are two more, into which the movement extends for special emotional effect.   Kingdon diagrams the layers thus:

Upper emotional range

Upper emphatic range

Normal unemphatic range

Lower emphatic range

Lower emotional range.

While the directional movement of the tones remains unchanged, there-fore, they may be stretched in pitch-coverage to operate over a wider range. The exploitation of this wider range is potential in any speaker, though the extent to which it is used seems to be a matter of group and personal style. Moreover, what *is* normal, emphatic or emotional is always relative, even within the speech of a single speaker; we respond, not to absolute difference of pitch-range, but to expansion and con-traction of the range of pitch-movement in a given stretch of speech.

§76. Leaving aside the variability of pitch-range, the tones that operate within the ranges can be reduced to five, and it is, as we have seen, the presence of one of these tones that defines a tone-group. They are identified by their characteristic direction, especially final direction, of movement, and can be symbolised by an appropriate slant-line before the syllable on which they occur (or begin). The first three are basic:

Tone I (rising) has a high variant, IH, as in, *Shall I come 'now? Do you want it 'now?* and a low variant, IL, as in, *I can't do it ,now. It isn't there ,now.*

Tone II (falling) occurs in, *I want it `now. Where is it `now? `Now's the time to do it.*

Tone III (falling-rising) occurs undivided in, *It'll be easier` 'now*; divi-ded in, *`I'll ,go.*

Note that although the rising element in I and III can be high or low, it is within the normal range; any of the tones can be extended into the emphatic or emotional range, by extra heightening or lowering.

Tone IV (rising-falling) occurs in *But you must do it' `now (without any further shilly-shallying).*

Tone V (rising-falling-rising) in (*You may think you can't but)' `'Try.*

§77. Exemplification of the tones begins to suggest something of their range of functions, but before we consider this subject further we must look at the remaining parts of the structure of tone-groups. A tone-group beginning on one or more unstressed syllables has a **pre-head.** Examples have already been given in §74. In the normal way a pre-head begins low, just above the bottom of the normal voice-range (as in those examples). The exceptions usually depend on special empha-sis, when a pre-head is selected which gives strong pitch-contrast with the following stress, as with the high pre-head of an emphatic pronun-ciation of *Good gracious!*

One or more unstressed syllables at the end of a tone-group constitute a **tail.** In the tones with final rise (the odd-numbered tones, I, III, V) the rise will be on the last syllable of the tone-group, whether it is stressed or (part of) the tail:

||I *Shall I* |*come to*|*mor'row* || III *It'll be* |*easier to ex*``'``|*amine*|| (with implication: *but perhaps less desirable in other ways*). ||V *Do*| '*try to*|| (with implication: *even if you think it's impossible*).

On the other hand in the tones with final fall (the even-numbered tones, II, IV) the fall occurs, of course, on the tonic, and the low pitch thus reached is maintained till the end of the tone-group:

||II *I'll* |`*wait for*| *you.*|| ||IV ,,*But you must* |*do it this*|'`*minute*|| In IV, however, the fall may not be completed till the syllable after the tonic: ||IV ``'``*He'd like some of them*||.

In the many cases where a tone-group includes more than one stressed syllable, it is useful to identify the first stressed syllable as the **head,** and the material between the head and the tonic the **body** of the tone-group.

Note

As a matter of course students should proceed from this summary treatment to its sources in the work of Kingdon and Halliday. To facilitate this further study, a note is necessary at this point on the correspondence between Kingdon's Kinetic Tones and Halliday's tones. This is not just a matter of equating symbols, since the symbols relate to somewhat different analyses, but there is some correspondence. The following approximate equivalences should be noted:

between Kingdon's IH (') and Halliday's (simple) 2; his IL (') and Halliday's 3;
between Kingdon's II (`) and Halliday's 1;
between Kingdon's III (`') and Halliday's 4;
between Kingdon's IV ('`) and Halliday's 5;
between Kingdon's V ('`') and certain cases of Halliday's 53 (i.e., 5 followed by 3).

Certain distinctions made by Halliday are treated by Kingdon not as tonal, but as devices for securing extra emphasis for the tonic; there are considerable differences between them in the treatment of compound or complex tones. On the other hand, Halliday notes that any tone can have, besides its normal form, forms with exaggerated or subdued versions of their normal form (symbolised + or −), and this interpretation can be related to Kingdon's view of the five-layer structure of the voice-range.

§78. We have already hinted that the meaning of intonation is of two kinds. Very clearly it is grammatical in the simple sense of the word— that much is involved in speaking of intonation-*systems*. We have suggested that it is also used to carry implications and convey attitudes;

if this role, too, can be described in terms of a finite number of mutually exclusive choices, then it is also grammatical, and we must be prepared to apply the term in an area in which it may strike us as unfamiliar. We shall find this to be the case; but we shall also find (as one would expect) systematic evidence in the language for our sense that two distinct kinds of meaning are involved. Grammatical differences of the familiar kind characteristically arise from the unmarked uses of the tones, and the differences of implication from the marked uses.

When, for example, tonality is unmarked (i.e., when the tone-group corresponds in extent to the clause) tone-choice is closely related to selection from the mood-system of clauses. Normally, affirmative clauses have tone II (see examples in §76). Other tone-selections in affirmative clauses are in marked contrast with it, the contrast normally signalling some special implication. Thus we have unmarked (plain statement):

//II , ,it's /not /going to be /ˋeasy//

But:

//III , ,it's /not /going to be /ˋ'easy// (with implication, "*But I'll try*") (glossed by Halliday as 'statement with reservation').

And:

//IL , ,he /might ,do// (uncommitted statement, often implying uncertainty or indifference).

And:

//IV of /'ˋcourse he /will// (committed statement, often implying assertiveness, superiority, rejection of doubt).

§79. The non-polar interrogatives also have tone II as their unmarked tone:

//II who are you/ˋlooking for//

The force of this tone II is, however, different, since it (necessarily) enters into a different range of marked contrasts from tone II as used in affirmative clauses. Perhaps this functional difference accounts for the widespread, but quite mistaken, belief that there is a general intonation-difference between statements and questions in English.

For non-polar interrogatives the only other tone which is at all common is IH, whose meaning varies according to its placing. Contrast:

//IH who are you/'looking for//

with

//IH 'who are you/looking for//

Halliday writes:

'If the tonic remains in its normal place . . . the clause is a question
accompanied by a request, as it were, for permission to ask: "may I,
or may I not, know the answer?" This variable, the strength or
degree of purposefulness of the utterance, operates with all moods,
though with different tones carrying the different degrees; I have
labelled it, perhaps rather unsatisfactorily, the "key", and distinguished the degrees of "strong", "moderate" and "mild". Tone
[IH] here thus represents the "mild key"; it is felt to be a tentative
enquiry, often described as polite, hesitant or diffident. If on the
other hand the tonic is on the "WH-" element, the clause becomes
the familiar "echo" question, meaning something like "I didn't
hear", "I've forgotten" or "I don't believe you"—"will you kindly
remind or reassure me?"'

§80. Polar interrogatives (which are what people think of when they
suppose English has a question-intonation) have IH as their unmarked
tone:

//IH , ,is it /'my turn//

Tone II also occurs, with the meaning *strong question*:

//II , ,have you / `finished it / yet//

Tones IL and IV occur with meanings rather like those they have in
affirmative clauses, meanings which Halliday labels *non-involvement* and
involvement:

//IL , ,would it /,matter//
//IV ' `would you /' `pay for it / though//

Alternative questions normally take tone IH followed by tone II:

//IH , ,is it /'mine or / II `yours//

but they can form a single group with tone II:

//II , ,is it / mine or /`yours//

Note

   Tag-questions enter into rather complex systems, both in their relations with the preceding main clause and intonationally (*You have,
haven't you?*; *you have, have you?*; *you haven't, have you?*; *you haven't,
haven't you?*).

§81. Concerning imperative clauses Halliday is not able to be more
than tentative. The following distribution is noted: tone II is neutral

for positive imperatives, with IV as a milder variant; tone I is neutral in the negative, with II marked as strong.

He distinguishes a further system operative in clauses of this kind, in which the unmarked term contrasts with, on the one hand, a term labelled *compromising*, on the other, a term labelled *insistent*:

Compromising—//III , ‚at | least | try to | ex | ` ′plain it ||
   //III , ‚well | don't just | run a | ` ′way ||
Insistent—   // IV , ‚well |′ ` tell him | then ||
   II IV , ‚in | that case | don't |′ ` give it to them ||.

Notes

1. The picture for imperatives is much complicated by the patterns occurring with *please*.
2. Non-finite clauses resemble affirmatives in their range of choices, but with additional possibilities.
3. Kingdon treats under the general head of *adjections* certain special forms with characteristic patterns of intonation—*temporisers* (such as *Well then, In fact*), parentheses, afterthoughts, vocatives, reporting phrases (such as *He said*); cf. Halliday's comments 'on the tendency for particular items in the language to be associated with particular intonation patterns' (1966, p. 130), citing such instances as *in any case, come to think of it*.

§82. Though I have omitted much from the accounts I have drawn on, the picture appears complicated. Yet the details do fall into some sort of broader pattern on which generalisation can be based. Halliday concludes:

> 'With regard to tone, I think we can see some sort of basic signifi-cance behind the falling and rising movements. We go down when we know whether something is positive or negative, and we go up when we don't know.'

In these terms, tone II means 'polarity known and stated'; tone IH 'polarity unknown'; tone IL, polarity known, but in a dependent or conditional sense; tone III suggests knowledge followed by doubt; tone IV, the reverse; ('you may think it's cut and dried, but it isn't against "you may think it isn't cut and dried, but it is"' [1966, p. 131]).

Note

Since stress, rhythm and intonation are highly interrelated it is useful to have the term *superfix* to refer to a suprasegmental pattern in which all three co-vary; of course the term must not be taken to mean that the pattern is just an addition.

EXERCISES

How many varieties of *I can't find one* can you transcribe and account for in grammatical terms? Further exercises can best be worked from the extensive materials provided by Kingdon and others.

FURTHER READING

Those without training in phonetics, or lacking expert guidance, should probably confine themselves to the source-works used in this chapter. Those confident enough to venture on other methods and transcriptions should consult Armstrong and Ward (1931), Pike (1943), Schubiger (1958), Lee (1960), O'Connor and Arnold (1961), Quirk *et al.* (1964), Crystal and Quirk (1964).

CHAPTER VII

Form-Classes
(I) Functioning in the Noun Phrase

(A) Head Words

§83. Form-classes can be treated under three general headings—those whose members function characteristically in the noun-phrase, those whose members function characteristically in the verb-phrase, and those whose members are not primarily associated with either kind of phrase. Within each of these large groupings we must distinguish open-class from closed-system items; otherwise the further sub-divisions depend on the varying things we find to distinguish.

§84. The words which act as head in noun-phrases constitute a distinguishable class, but by applying a finer or more delicate discrimination we can isolate several types amongst them, the chief being **noun, proper name** and **pronoun,** though there are various intermediate kinds for which no handy name is available. We shall class as **central nouns** words which comply with the following set of criteria:

(a) they constitute an open class—indeed, the most open of all, since any word (or other linguistic form) becomes (conforms to the criteria for) a noun if it is mentioned rather than used (as in, *There are too many ifs and buts about it, a certain je ne sais quoi*). It is a corollary that they have full lexical meaning, and, even if they are monosyllables, inherent stress.

(b) functionally, they can be the (or the head of the) subject or, without morphological change (cf. [d] below), the complement, of a sentence. Examples are *shopkeeper, boy* and *change* in *The shopkeeper gave the boy his change.*

(c) positionally, they can follow directly in minimal constructions (i.e., be head-word to) a closed system of words we shall call **determiners** (cf. §§105 ff.).   They can also follow directly in the same clause, and without change of form, the closed system of items we shall call prepositions (cf. §160). Examples of these positions are those of *house*, *top* and *hill* in *The house stood on the top of the hill*. They can stand in adjunct relationship directly before other nouns (as in *gold mine*, *retiring age*), and directly after nouns in the genitive case (cf. §90) (as in *a mare's nest*).

(d) morphologically, they are variables in respect of a two-term system of number and a two-term system of case.

For present-day English **morphological change** may be defined as change of form, normally at the level of the word; it is of two kinds, **inflectional**, if it involves relatively few variables in a closed system, and **derivational** if it involves variables, possibly numerous, in an open class. Thus, the change from *book* /bʊk/ to *book's, books, books'* /bʊks/ is inflectional; that from *book* to *bookish, bookman, booklet*, etc., is derivational. Inflectional change is a central concern of grammar; derivational change on the border between grammar and lexis.

Number can be defined as a system of special forms by which it is denoted whether one or not-one is spoken of (in English, according to 'style', *not-one* sometimes means *other than one*, sometimes *more than one*); in other languages other numerical distinctions are involved. The terms of the number-system are traditionally called **singular** and **plural**. The forms and their functions will be discussed in §§86–88, where it will become apparent that these terms are of limited appropriateness.

Case is 'any one of the varied forms of a noun, adjective or pronoun, which expresses the varied relations in which it may function' (*OED.* s.v., sb.[1]9). That is, it is a form to express relationship, not the relationship itself; and the kind of relationship is one that only certain sorts of word (those characteristically functioning in the noun-phrase) enter into—*case* and *noun*, etc., are to some extent mutually defining words. *OED.*'s definition is meant to apply to a wide range of languages; it does not of course imply that all these form-classes actually have case-systems in English (for adjectives clearly do not). For the two terms of the English noun case-system, the labels **common case** and **genitive case** are probably the most appropriate of those available. For the forms and their functions, cf. §§89–90 below.

(e) finally, nouns are sub-divided in terms of syntactical patterning into several **genders**, i.e., sub-classes capable of patterning with certain pronouns and not with others. *Gender* as a linguistic term generally relates to limited capacities for patterning with other linguistic forms, though the particular kind of limitation found in English is far from being the only one. The patterning is described at §91.

It is from all these features taken together that a family likeness arises, which is the source of the class-meaning of nouns. In the past, nouns have often been defined from the kind of class-meaning they have—it was said, for example, that a noun is the name of anything that exists or can be conceived. There is a good deal of truth in this— enough to have kept the idea alive for many centuries—but it is not wholly true. In any case it seems nowadays like putting the cart before the horse: it is the common formal features that fulfil a common function and so give rise to a common meaning in nouns as a whole. It happens in this case that the resultant class-meaning is relatively specific and easy to verbalise. But it is not the evidence that a particular word is or is not a noun.

What is characterised above is the central type of noun, and it is that that we shall proceed to examine next. But words and classes drift away from this complex standard in various directions, forming marginal types which can be examined once we are familiar with the norm.

Note

From now on much will be said of what will, must, may, can (and their negatives) happen. In this connection readers must bear in mind the sense we have given to the term *linguistic rule* (§24); we are not concerned to prescribe or to legislate, but to describe.

§85. Number (I) *General.* The distinction between singular and plural in English nouns is primarily morphological, though there are supporting features of limited collocation with other items, determiners, numerals and verbs (cf. §§105–113, 88). Thus, *a, one, every, much, this, that*, pattern only with singulars; numerals above *one, many, these, those*, only with plurals; so, in the case of central nouns, do groups without determiner (*Sheep grazed in the fields*) (some speak here of zero-determiner, since the determiner is not just absent, but by its absence contributes an identifiable meaning to the whole utterance). This restriction of patterning may, as in the examples just given, be the only indication of plurality. Those verb-forms which we may briefly label *-s* forms (cf. §123) pattern only with singulars (*The sheep is/was in the field*; *The sheep are/were in the field*)—and this may be the only sign of singularity (in marginal nouns and names, but not with central nouns). But in the great majority of cases number-variation is indicated by morphological change, and if there is only one indication, it is most often this one. That is why we speak of the distinction as primarily morphological; but equally we must recognise that noun singular and plural are established not by a single criterion but by family resemblances. The lack of an invariable criterion means that sometimes number is not clear (as in *The sheep ate up every scrap of* *grass*), but even internally ambiguous sentences are usually clarified by co-text or context.

Note

The collocations *these kind of, those kind of,* have established themselves as wholes (idioms) and cannot be covered by the generalisations appropriate to *these, those,* as single words; perhaps *a number of, the majority of,* followed by plural noun/name/pronoun and plural verb (if any), should be analysed in the same way.

§86. (II) *Forms.* Two types of morphological patterning must be distinguished in the pairing of singular and plural forms of nouns.

(A). The first constitutes, in any one idiolect, a virtually closed class, and consists commonly of the pairing of:

(i) *ox* /ɒks/ with *oxen* /ɒksən/

(ii) *man* /mæn/ with *men* /mɛn/ (similarly for the morpheme -*man* finally in compounds, if given contrastive stress, but cf. [xii] below; and *man-* as subjective element [cf. §§62, 190] in compounds [*men-servants,* but *man-eaters*])

(iii) *foot* /fʊt/ with *feet* /fiːt/

(iv) *tooth* /tuːθ/ with *teeth* /tiːθ/
goose /guːs/ with *geese* /giːs/

(v) *louse* /laʊs/ with *lice* /laɪs/
mouse /maʊs/ with *mice* /maɪs/

(vi) *woman* /wʊmən/ with *women* /wɪmɪn/ (note here the disyllabic change, obscured in writing)

(vii) *brother* /brʌðə/ (in the sense 'a fellow member of a Christian society' and related senses) with *brethren* /brɛðrɪn/

(viii) *penny* /pɛnɪ/ with *pence* /pɛns/ (generalising plural, cf. §88)

(ix) *die* /daɪ/ (in the sense 'a cube of ivory for gaming') with *dice* /daɪs/

(x) *child* /tʃaɪld/ with *children* /tʃɪldrən/ (again a disyllabic change obscured by the writing);

also of some patterns which can be described more generally, though the instances of them are still restricted:

(xi) a singular with plural having voicing of a final fricative and addition of suffix /z/:

(a) with labio-dental fricative:
calf /kɑːf/; *elf* /ɛlf/; *half* /hɑːf/; *knife* /naɪf/; *leaf* /liːf/; *life* /laɪf/; *loaf* /ləʊf/; *scarf* /skɑːf/; *sheaf* /ʃiːf/; *shelf* /ʃɛlf/; *thief* /θiːf/; *wife* /waɪf/; *wolf* /wʊlf/, in all of which singular /-f/ corresponds to plural /-vz/. *Dwarf* /dwɔːf/ and *turf* /tɜːf/ have this kind of plural along with open-class forms. Two words, also with alternative open-class plurals,

sometimes have this kind of plural combined with vowel change in the base, namely, *hoof* /hʊf/ : *hooves* /huːvz/ (occasionally *roof* is of this kind too), and *staff* /stɑːf/ : *staves* /steɪvz/. (This in turn has given rise to a distinct singular, a new word, *stave* /steɪv/—a process which is the measure of its oddity, its non-analogousness, among English noun-plural patterns.)

(b) with dental fricative:
bath /bɑːθ/; *mouth* /maʊθ/; *oath* /əʊθ/; *path* /pɑːθ/; *sheath* /ʃiːθ/; *wreath* /riːθ/; *youth* /juːθ/, in all of which singular /-θ/ corresponds to plural /-ðz/; often of this kind, though they sometimes have open-class plurals, are *hearth* /hɑːθ/; *lath* /lɑːθ/; *truth* /truːθ/.

(c) closely related is the pluralisation by voicing of a final sibilant and suffixing of /-ɪz/ in *house* /haʊs/ : *houses* /haʊzɪz/.

There is also a substantial group of nouns in which there is no morphological change in the plural:

(xii) always of this kind are *Chinese, deer, gross, grouse, Japanese, pike* (the fish), *Portuguese, salmon, series, sheep, species, superficies, Swiss, wildfowl*; sometimes *alms*. Morphemic unstressed *-man* is of this kind, though the spelling obscures the fact (*gentleman* /dʒɛntlmən/ : *gentlemen* /dʒɛntlmən/ except under conditions of contrastive stress, cf. [ii] above); non-morphemic *-man* has the open-class plural, as in *Roman* : *Romans*, cf. §87.

Limited use of this kind of plural (for generalising plural, or a special sense of the word, or in limited collocations) occurs with *brace, blues, cannon, cavalry, counsel, couple, craft, dozen, duck, elephant, fish, foot, fowl, head, horse, hundred, hundredweight, lion, million, sail, score, stone, thousand, ton, trout* (and in idiolects on the fringe of RP. occasionally in other words) (cf. also §112).

The remaining plurals form less fully closed classes; there is much idiolectal and 'stylistic' variation about their incidence, and some new words coming into the language conform to these types. The patterning is very varied:

(xiii) *stimulus* /stɪmjʊləs/ : *stimuli* /stɪmjʊliː/ or /stɪmjʊlaɪ/. Similarly for a number of words, especially fairly learned words, in *-us* /-əs/.
nebula /nɛbjʊlə/ : *nebulae* /nɛbjʊlaɪ/ or /nɛbjʊliː/. Similarly for a number of words, especially fairly learned words, in *-a* /-ə/.
desideratum /dɪzɪdəreɪtəm/ : *desiderata* /dɪzɪdəreɪtə/. Similarly for a number of words, especially fairly learned words, in *-um* /-əm/; at least one plural of this kind, *data*, is sometimes used as a new singular

(and in American English seems well established as such), and this development is a measure of the non-analogousness of the plural patterning involved.

criterion /kraɪtɪərɪən/: *criteria* /kraɪtɪərɪə/. Similarly for a number of words, especially fairly learned words, in *-on* /-ən/. At least two plurals of this kind (*criteria* and *phenomena*) are now being used as singulars, and this again is a measure of the non-analogousness of the plural patterning involved.

genus /dʒiːnəs/: *genera* /dʒɛnərə/.

crisis /kraɪsɪs/: *crises* /kraɪsiːz/. Similarly for a number of other words, especially fairly learned words, in *-is* /-ɪs/; this patterning is sometimes heard in *diocese* /daɪəsɪs/: *dioceses* /daɪəsiːz/ (in spite of the spelling and the history of the word). A common patterning for *species* is /-ɪz/ singular, /-iːz/ plural.

seraph /sɛrəf/: *seraphim* /sɛrəfɪm/. Similarly for *cherub* (optionally with open-class plural) when it means 'member of the second order of angels' but never when it means 'angelic child or depiction thereof'.

dilettante /dɪlɪtæntɪ/: *dilettanti* /dɪlɪtænti:/.

virtuoso /vɜːtjʊəʊsəʊ/: *virtuosi* /vɜːtjʊəʊsi:/ (and so for other words, but always with alternative open-class plural).

bandit /bændɪt/: *banditti* /bændɪti:/ (but only to give local colour and in reference to foreign characters; even in such cases the open-class plural is available).

The indeterminacy of membership of group (xiii) is closely related to the indeterminacy of English vocabulary as a whole.

Note

Even within RP. the existence of alternative noun-plural forms is greater than I have indicated above, for instance, some speakers have an open-class plural for *man-servant*, cf. A (ii) above; some use an open-class plural for *bath* except in the collocation *Public Baths*. It is probably impossible to be quite exhaustive in describing usage on this point. Furthermore, I do not attempt to record variant pronunciations which do not bear on the question immediately under discussion.

§87. *Form* (B). The second type of morphological change is much more common, but can be dealt with much more briefly, because a generalisation can be made about it. All nouns not catered for by the provisions of §86 have this second kind of pluralisation, and we have already frequently referred to it as the open-class kind. It is found, generally speaking, not only in the (literally) countless nouns already in the language, but also in the vast majority of newcomers being adopted. In this class the change for the plural consists of adding a final morpheme (suffix) realised in three distinct phonemic forms according to the character of the final phoneme of the base. These alternants are:

after sibilants (/s/, /z/, /tʃ/, /dʒ/, /ʃ/, /ʒ/), /ɪz/, as in *prince* /prɪns/ : *princes* /prɪnsɪz/; *judge* /dʒʌdʒ/ : *judges* /dʒʌdʒɪz/;
after voiced non-sibilants (including, of course, all vowels), /z/, as in *boy* /bɔɪ/ : *boys* /bɔɪz/; *moon* /muːn/ : *moons* /muːnz/; *food* /fuːd/ : *foods* /fuːdz/;
after voiceless non-sibilants, /s/, as in *cup* /kʌp/ : *cups* /kʌps/; *cuff* /kʌf/ : *cuffs* /kʌfs/.

The spelling change is usually the addition of *-(e)s*, but *-y* with syllabic value is replaced by *-i-* before *-es* (*ladies*, but *boys*). In a few words with open-class patterning in speech the spelling is unchanged or changes in a different way (*corps/corps; beau/beaux; flambeau/flambeaux; gateau/ gateaux*). In the overwhelming majority of cases, however, the spelling is regular, and what is linguistically interesting about the spelling is that its basis is morphemic, not phonemic; other grammatical morphemes are similarly treated in English spelling, cf. §§89, 123 and 124). An apostrophe is sometimes used before the *-s* in writing words that have recently (or for the nonce) become nouns by adoption from other classes, as in *The Four Mary's.*

Normally compound nouns with open-class plurals form them in the same way as simple nouns, but a closed class among them differs, either invariably adding the morpheme to their first elements, as in *hangers-on* or *passers-by*, or having it now on the first element, now on the second, as in *court(s)-martial(s), knight(s)-errant(s)*; a very few add it to both, as in *knights-templars, lords-justices.*

§88. (III) *Functions.* The functions of the singular-plural distinction in nouns have so far only been roughly indicated. They are primarily referential in character, and two concurrent systems must be distinguished. In formal speech and writing the distinction is most often between singular as referring to none or one, and plural as referring to more than one. But in informal and unself-conscious usage, the distinction is usually between one (singular) and other-than-one (plural). For instance, according to one's 'style', both the following sentences are possible in reference to the same situation: '*No children were there*' and '*No child was there.*'

It is important to be clear about what it is that is being referred to— not an object or concept single or not-single in itself, but one or other-than-one of the referent of the noun in question. Thus there is inherently no special problem about the singular of a word like *crowd* because a crowd is necessarily made up of a lot of persons, any more than there is about the word *person* because a person is necessarily made up of a lot of cells. But in practice a difficulty has grown up about words of this kind. Normally, the singular of a noun patterns with one set of verb-forms, the plural with another (indeed, we have used this to help establish the contrast, §85). Nouns whose referents are complex in such a way that we readily think, in using them, of the individuals composing their referents, sometimes depart from this type of concord. In the plural they present no difficulty; but in the singular they may pattern with either the singular or the plural form of the verb. So we find *The committee was/were planning* . . .

> *government*
> *team*
> *army*, etc.

(Normal patterning is restored if the noun is preceded by a determiner or numeral requiring singular concord:

A committee was planning . . .
One
Each
Every [but *this, that* are less effective in this way];

and these nouns in their singular forms cannot pattern with determiners requiring plural concord, or with numerals above *one*.)

Nouns having this peculiarity of concord are called **collective nouns**; they are sometimes said to have a third number, distinct from singular or plural, but their patterning suggests rather a blend category. For other exceptions to the expected concord-patterns, cf. note 2 below.

Within the ordinary functioning of the noun-plural for referring to other-than-one, we must notice further distinctions, notably between reference in which numbers of individuals are thought of, and reference in which a class, collection, species or type is thought of. The two are distinguished as **individuating** and **generalising** plurals; the resulting differences of form have been mentioned in §86.

In a limited class of nouns there is a special use of the plural form in reference not to number, but to scale. Examples are:

dews, heavens, sands, woods.

With these may be mentioned a few others where no such rationale can be advanced, notably *looks*, but perhaps also *fears, hopes, wishes*.

Notes

1. A general account of the functions of the plural cannot take notice of all idiomatic constructions. There is, for instance, a use of what looks like a noun plural in '*I'm not friends with you*', which is certainly not covered by our account. An overall description of English could place it in one of two ways: either taking *friends* as an independent adjective or adverb complementing the verb *be* (taking, in this case, syntactical

position as the principal determinant of form-class, and identifying the forms word by word as belonging to a form-class), or, more satisfactorily, as part of an indivisible **idiom** 'be friends with' + *person-referring complement* (noun, proper name or pronoun), which functions predicatively (verbally), and within which it is inappropriate to look for form-class membership.

2. Exceptions to the principle of concord described in this paragraph can be found not only in the patterning of collective nouns, but also in some cases where a noun-phrase directly preceding a finite verb is not its subject. In practice, however, failure of concord is extremely common in both speech and writing even in situations covered by this paragraph. See Strang (1966).

§89. Case. (I) *Forms.* The two terms of the case-system of English nouns are not on an equal footing. Formally, the one we have called common case is uninflected, while the genitive is inflected; functionally, the uses of the genitive are specific, those of the common case general, in the sense that a noun is in the common case unless there is reason for it not to be. In other words, both formally and functionally, the common case is unmarked and the genitive marked (cf. §73).

In the common case singular, then, the base of the noun is used. In the genitive a morphemic suffix is added, once again a sibilant suffix having alternants /ɪz/, /z/, /s/ in the same distribution as the open-class plural morpheme. There is, of course, a distinction in the written form, where the genitive has an apostrophe before the -*s*; and there is a difference in speech in those words that have closed-class plurals, since there are no exceptions to the spoken form of the genitive suffix—save in a few expressions where the next word begins with *s*-, and then only regularly in expressions that have become traditional as wholes, such as *Pears' Soap* /pɛəz soʊp/. (The uninflected form seems to have been more usual in earlier English and has sometimes survived in expressions where it is rhythmically fixed, like *St. Agnes' Eve*.) This degree of uniformity in distribution is unique amongst grammatical bound morphemes in English.

In the plural the common-case forms are those described in §§86–87. For those words that have open-class plurals, there is no formal case-contrast, though in writing a distinction is made by placing an apostrophe after the -*s* in the genitive. Nouns with closed-class plurals do have a contrast in speech, adding to the common-case plural the sibilant morpheme with alternants /ɪz/, /z/, /s/ in the now familiar distribution.

Notes

1. The uniformity of the genitive singular extends even to compound nouns which do not take their open-class plural morpheme in final position, thus *father-in-law's* but *fathers-in-law*; and beyond the bounds of units that can be pluralised as wholes, thus, *kings of Spain*, but *king of Spain's daughter*.

2. In spite of some asymmetries, it will be clear that for an immense majority of English nouns there is one marked form, the form with sibilant morpheme suffixed, covering a range of functions in contrast with the common-case singular. In this sense, the survival of two two-term systems, one of case and one of number, is vestigial; our strong sense of the two systems owes a great deal to the thoroughness of our training in the use of written English.

§90. (II) *Functions.* The value of grammatical contrasts is that they convey meanings and distinctions that the language is not well adapted to convey lexically; so any attempt to sum up 'the meaning' of the genitive is doomed. It is hard to get nearer to it than to say that it conveys a relationship, which may be of possession, origin, consisting of, extent of, association with or concerning (directed towards). Genitives commonly occur in collocation with another noun-like word, which provides the second term of the relationship, and may be classified according as the relationship is subjective (directed from the referent of the genitive noun to that of the other) or objective (directed towards the referent of the genitive noun). An example (adapting a book-title) is *my aunt's murder* (subjective if it refers to the murder she committed; objective if it refers to murder committed upon her). There is no formal difference, and this may lead to ambiguity, but generally the context and lexical probability make clear which is meant. Of the kinds of relationship expressed, that of possession is probably dominant, with the result that there is a tendency to avoid the genitive of nouns whose referents cannot possess (are not, or are not thought of as being, human or at least animate). So we readily speak of *a student's book*, but not of **a book's student* (=one who studies that book); and similarly not only for nouns with actually personal referents, but for others like *ship* and *car*, which have as referents things some speakers like to think of in human terms; but hardly **the typewriter's ribbon*. Possession is not the only relationship expressed by the genitive, however, and in expressions of a certain pattern the genitive of extent is very common (indeed, compulsory for the required relationship), e.g., *a day's work*, *a stone's throw*. For this reason, it is inadvisable to give the case a name like 'possessive', or indeed any transparent name, for it just does not correspond to any simple lexical notion in English, except in a special sense we shall now look into. Cf. also §174.

Naturally the genitive relationship in its full range needs to be expressed in connection with nouns not eligible, as we have explained, for genitive case-forms. In such words, a quite different pattern is used, namely the particle *of* followed by the noun in common case, the whole following the form for the other term of the relationship (as in *The Book of the Month*). *Of* therefore does have much the same 'meaning' as the case-form (though its distribution is different) and we might have used the name *of*-case if we could have been sure that that would not suggest that *of*-constructions themselves are case-forms. Though *of* is a word, it belongs not to lexis, but to grammar, since it is one of the closed-system items we shall call prepositions (cf. Ch. X).

There are two difficulties about describing the use of the genitive. That of saying what kind of relationship it expresses we have already met. The second is that of the relative distribution of case-constructions and *of*-constructions. The general principles outlined so far must now be restricted in application. First there are idioms, constructions functioning as wholes, internally invariable, such as *money's worth, harm's way, heart's content, mind's eye, wits' end.* Secondly, a genitive is used quasi-adjectivally in certain words which otherwise do not conform to noun patterning, as in *yesterday's rain, to-day's engagements, to-morrow's match.* Such constructions are not like the idioms, for their total lexical content is not fixed, but they do represent fixed patterns of usage. Thirdly, various forces combine to keep alive a sense of patterns formerly productive in the language; one such force is the analogy of idioms, another is the memory of familiar quotations (*mind's eye* is one of these, and one less fully assimilated is *the round world's imagined corners*), and a third is newspaper usage, especially in headlines, for which the compactness of the case-form is very convenient, so that it is often used where it would ordinarily be inappropriate, and so becomes increasingly familiar. Euphony is also a disturbing factor; except in set expressions (idioms, quotations and references) most speakers avoid the case-construction after final /s/, saying, for instance, *The Eve of St. Agnes* rather than *St. Agnes' Eve* (cf. §89; there is no need to distinguish nouns and proper names in respect of case). But the most important restriction of all is that our generalisation applies, as far as speech is concerned, almost wholly to the singular forms. As we have seen, the case-contrast in the plural is vestigial, and generally in the plural *of*-constructions are preferred. In writing the case-construction is more freely used, and some speakers follow the model of written English.

There are some instances, commonly in rather fixed patterns, in which the genitive is not associated with another noun-like word, but used absolutely, notably with locative force (*at the greengrocer's*); it may also occur, not alternatively with the *of*-construction, but in conjunction with it (*that boy of Smith's*).

Note

In the relative distribution of *of*-constructions and case-forms we meet a recurrent feature of English structure—the existence of alternative grammatical means to approximately the same end; the means in one case being the use of bound morphemes (inflections), in the other, a separate but grammatical word. In the second method, the total meaning is, so to speak, analysed into its lexical and grammatical components and each is expressed by a distinct word; so this type of grammatical structure is often called **analytical**, as contrasted with **inflectional**.

§91. Gender. B. L. Whorf wrote: 'A linguistic classification like English gender, which has no overt mark actualized along with the words of the class but which operates through an invisible "central exchange" . . . to determine certain other words which mark the class I call a COVERT class, in contrast to an OVERT class, such as gender in Latin' (1956, p. 58). Two things are important about gender in English: first, that it is a covert class, controlling the patterning of pronouns in relation to nouns, and second, that it is quite close to being natural, i.e., a reflex of the sex-distinctions of male, female or neither, but it is not entirely so. The pronoun-system with which it correlates is threefold, the terms being labelled **masculine, feminine** and **neuter** (cf. §98), but as there is not simply one-to-one correspondence between these terms and the conditioning classes of nouns, we find at least a seven-term system, thus:

(i) patterning with pronouns he/who, nouns like *man, bachelor*;
(ii) patterning with she/who, nouns like *woman, maid, ?hare*;
(iii) patterning with he/she/who, nouns like *person, doctor, parent, friend*;
(iv) patterning with it/which, nouns like *cake, box, insect*;
(v) patterning with it/he/which, nouns like *bull, ram, cock, horse*;
(vi) patterning with it/she/which, nouns like *cow, ewe, hen, car, boat*;
(vii) patterning with it/he/she/who/which, nouns like *child, baby, dog, cat*.
(There is some variation of usage; for instance, some will put *hare* under [vi] rather than [ii]; and where options exist they are not in free variation, but are controlled by factors which may or may not be linguistic—we may speak of a baby as *it* because we do not know whether it is a boy or a girl, but if we speak of a car as *she* it is to associate ourselves with a particular attitude to the car. There is also much complexity resulting from figurative and idiomatic uses; cf. the expression 'She's obviously one of the boys' [heard just after writing the above].)

Note

I owe this analysis of gender in English nouns to J. C. Catford.

§92. Departing more or less and in various ways from this complex standard of the central type of noun are other kinds of noun-like word. First come those that are not subject to number variation, often called **uncountables.** They are of two main types, those lacking a plural and those lacking a singular.

(a) Those lacking a plural can be sub-divided according to the kind of word-meaning they have, though it is not the meaning, but formal grounds that distinguish them.   There are, first, subject names, *phonetics, mathematics, classics, ethics*, etc.; second, names of materials, *wood, gold, rubber*, etc.; third, nouns expressing abstract ideas, *beauty, knowledge, progress*, etc.; and lastly a miscellaneous group including *news, billiards, measles, advice, information, furniture, game* (='animals to shoot').

The special patterning of these words is not just a matter of lacking plurals.   They are also virtually without case-contrast; and unlike central nouns they can function in singular constructions without determiner, adjective or numeral.

Three things should be noted.   The special patterning of these words is a feature of English structure and does not in any sense reflect 'the nature of things'—in other European languages, for instance, the word for *information* is often plural.   Next, it does not matter for the special patterning of these words whether the one form they have 'looks like' a singular or a plural; the permitted collocations show that in this class we are dealing with words whose one form is a singular.   Lastly, the words in this class must be distinguished from similar words which are central nouns—there is a central noun *ethic* as well as the uncountable *ethics*; many of the material-name uncountables have countable homonyms with different referents ('*a fine set of woods*', for instance) and so have many abstract-noun uncountables ('*a real beauty*').

§93. (b) Lacking a singular are (i) a large number of words evidently plural in form, such as *annals, bellows, bowels, braces, dregs, glasses, greens, munitions, oats, scissors, trousers*; (ii) a few words of closed-class plural types, *cognoscenti, magi, antipodes*, etc.; these must be preceded by *the*, and are therefore akin to some proper names of which *the* is a part, cf. §95; (iii) a few that do not 'look plural' at all, *cattle, clergy, folk, gentry, police, swine* (=pigs [generalising plural]); cf. also *intelligentsia*, with which *the* is compulsory.   Here too it must be remembered that the special patterning is a feature of English structure, not of 'the nature of things' (why *oats* but *wheat*?); and the relevant words must be distinguished from near-homonyms with number-contrast ('*The only greens I like are sprouts*' has not got the same word *greens* as in '*I prefer the paler of the two greens*').

Within this group there is a structural difference between those that 'look plural' and those that do not.   Those that do are naturally, especially in spoken English, free from case-contrast (we do not say **the trousers's press*); the others do make use of the -'*s* forms (some more than others; we would say *the cattle's byres* more readily than **the police's houses*).   Those that look plural are unique among noun-like words in having a special form for noun-modifying (sc. **attributive**) use, namely, the form corresponding to their otherwise missing singular, as in *trouser press, munition factory* (an exception is *glasses case*, where the 'singular' would be ambiguous). Many words in this class can be preceded by **numeratives**, such as *pair of, head of*, which enable them to function in a way similar to countables in spite of lacking their morphological patterning.

§94. The next groups are partly like nouns, partly like adjectives in their patterning (for adjectives, cf. Ch. VIII). First come words that I shall call **de-adjectival class nouns**. This is because they are homonymous with adjectives, function roughly like nouns (but without number-contrast or any freedom about preceding determiners) and have the general meaning 'the class of things, people, etc., having the attribute x.' Such forms are always plural (the only formal sign of this being collocation), must collocate with the determiner *the*, and if they have other modifying words, take only those that collocate with adjectives; they are virtually without case-contrast. Examples are *the poor, the first of the few, the very rich*. Like all the others, this class is isolated on formal grounds; we might say that the forms look as if they have moved half way along the road from being adjectives to being nouns, and strayed a bit as well as not going all the way. For this state of affairs and others roughly similar, I use the term **partial conversion.** Conversion is a historical process, not of itself the affair of the descriptive grammarian. For instance, the adjective *first* has given rise to a noun *first* used in such sentences as ' There were two firsts in that year'. But in descriptive study we do not say that the noun *first* is converted from an adjective; it behaves like any other noun, and it is not our business to reflect on its origins. But when a class of forms, primarily associated with one important form-class, shows a measure of conformity with a different class, such a marginal case may well be described as a partial conversion, as long as we read the term descriptively, not historically.

The second special group to be considered here we may label from their lexical meanings **colour-adjectives.** They are fully like adjectives in all positive respects (cf. Ch. VIII), but in addition they take on sentence-functions of nouns (cf. §84[b]) of which other adjectives are not capable. Thus they are subject, complement and preposition-follower in: '*Red is a nice colour*', '*I don't like green*' and '*That shade of blue doesn't suit me*'. (For the impossibility of this with other adjectives cf. *' Warm is nice*', *'I don't like uncomfortable*', *'The degree of hot was unbearable*'.) There are, of course, 'fully converted' nouns from adjectives ('*the reds and golds of autumn*') but these are like any other nouns descriptively and do not require special mention (cf. §93).

A third class of partly noun-like words consists of forms derived from

temporal adverbs—*yesterday*, *to-day*, etc. They have noun-like sentence-functions and positions (subject, attributive and post-prepositional in the following examples: '*To-morrow is another day*', '*Yesterday afternoon I went to the cinema*', '*The day after to-morrow is my birthday*'), and noun-like case-contrast ('*To-day's game should be decisive*'). But they have only singular number and cannot collocate with determiners, adjectives or numerals (though there are 'fully converted' nouns from them that do ['All our yesterdays...']). As always, this class is delimited from its formal properties, not because of its typical meanings; on it cf. also §90.

Note

There is also a class of **determiner-pronouns** patterning rather like the words considered in this paragraph, but lacking case-contrast; they will be considered under the heading of determiners in Chapter VIII.

§95. Next comes the large and important open class, for which a traditional term exists, **proper names.** These are noun-like in sentence-functions and case-system, but they do not have number-contrast or pattern with determiners. With adjectives, to a limited extent, they can collocate; complex ones often have parts in apposition. Examples are *John Brown*, *Queen Elizabeth*, *Croydon*, *Europe*. A determiner may be part of a proper name (*The Thames*); and a proper name may be plural as opposed to singular (*The Mendips*); and of course, homonyms of names may be ordinary nouns with the ordinary contrasts and patterning (*The Joneses*); but these observations do not invalidate the account given above. When we have examined pronouns, it will become clear that proper names are a class intermediate between nouns and pronouns, akin to pronouns in all but their case and number system.

Outside the traditional proper names there is a closed class of words which pattern similarly, *someone, somebody, anyone, anybody, no-one, nobody, none, everyone, everybody, people* (as in '*People are so unpredictable*'). Amongst them, *none* is rather marginal between this class and the determiner-pronouns (like them it fits the frame '*There are . . . here*', which most of the other words listed do not; and although it can fill positions like *none came*, it is in them something of an intruder into informal spoken usage, where *none of them/it* would be more usual). All our list except *none* have case-contrast ('*anyone's bicycle will do*'); each is placed in relation to the number-contrast, singular or plural, but none of them are both singular and plural (*none* has singular or plural concord according to 'style' but not number-contrast [except as in §97 Note]). They have noun-like sentence functions and positions, but do not collocate with the form-classes associated with nouns (cf. Ch. VIII).

Notes

1. Though *everyone, everybody*, consistently collocate with singular verbs, they vary in patterning with pronouns. In a recent (November, 1961) comedy broadcast satirising linguistic fads Barbara Kelly produced for Bernard Braden (defending the pedantic position) the sentence '*When everybody had finished eating I took away his plate*'; and a friend of mine, entering a Post Office laden with Christmas parcels, was addressed with the remark '*This is the season when everybody should help one another.*' Swift's '*This October club renewed their usual meetings*' is a type of pattern still possible. A comparable blend-patterning can be observed with *no-one* and *nobody*.

2. An exception to the generalisation that the closed-class items treated in this paragraph do not collocate with the same forms as nouns is the use of adjectives following the name-like word, as in:

'*Someone nice came to see me to-day*';
'*Something rather strange/nothing unusual has happened*'.

§96. With proper names we have reached a stage part way between noun and pronoun. Before we complete that transition, a point of a different kind should be noted. Countable nouns are one of several kinds of form in English having a **generic substitute**, that is, a single lexical form which may stand for any member of the class clearly specified by the co-text or context. The substitute occupies the territory of the ordinary class member, fulfilling its grammatical function without lexical repetition. For countable nouns the word is *one*, behaving as any other countable noun would do, syntactically, morphologically and positionally. Two examples are found in:

'*I want some carnations—have you any red ones? . . . Oh well, I'd better take a bunch of roses—that one at the front looks fresh.*'

For other generic substitutes, cf. §§150, 154, 156.

§97. **Pronouns** are like nouns in syntactical function and in their capacity to follow prepositions, but they differ in their other collocations, in morphology, and in being a closed system. They do not collocate with the characteristic adjunct-words of nouns (cf. Ch. VIII), but have **intensifiers** of their own (cf. §100). In morphology the differences are multiple: first, they have a three-term instead of a two-term case-system, in which a genitive corresponds to a genitive in nouns, but two cases cover the range of the common case in nouns; I shall call these cases **subject case** and **unmarked case**, cf. §99. Second, they have, ostensibly like nouns, a two-term number system,

5+

but it turns out actually to be considerably different. Third, gender is in them to some extent an overt system. Fourth, pronouns are subdivided according to a grammatical category, that of **person**, not relevant to nouns. *Person* is a way of classifying referents in relation to the speaker; it can take various forms, but the one found in English pronouns is traditionally interpreted as distinguishing between speaker (**first person singular**), person(s) addressed (**second person**), and referent (personal or otherwise) spoken of (**third person**). It will immediately be clear that the difference of number-system between nouns and pronouns is related to the person-distinctions. In the first person the usual functional plural contrast is impossible, and in fact the distinction English makes is between (singular) speaker and (plural) speaker plus any one or more others, present or not; in second person the distinction of one or more than one is perfectly feasible, but English pronouns do not make it, having one form, with one set of verb-collocations, for singular and plural—though the appositional forms *all*, *both* or a numeral will serve as a plural marker ('*You all/both/two go on ahead*'); in the third person the distinction is marked formally, and is of the kind functionally in which one contrasts with more than one (there is no single form for less than one, but notice that the construction *none of it* collocates with a singular, *none of them* with a plural, verb). The anomalies of the traditional view can be avoided if the person-system is re-stated in terms of several binary choices (Thorne, 1966). The first is between presence (+) and absence (−) of the feature **egocentric** (i.e., involving the speaker); the second is between presence and absence of the feature **non-egocentric** (i.e., involving someone or something other than the speaker; it is not, therefore, merely the negative of the first choice, and presence of both features in combination is feasible); the third depends on the presence of the feature non-egocentric, since that is a condition of presence of **vocative** (i.e., involvement of an addressee); ± vocative need only be marked, therefore, if non-egocentric is present. In these terms,

I is +*egocentric*, −*non-egocentric*;
you is −*egocentric*, +*non-egocentric*, +*vocative*;
he, she, it, they, are −*egocentric*, +*non-egocentric*, −*vocative*;
we is +*egocentric*, +*non-egocentric*, ±*vocative* (since it may or may not involve the addressee).

This analysis clearly brings out the relationship between *I* and *we*, and the dual function of *we*; the re-statement in binary terms is not mere playing with variant presentations, but explicates what had hitherto appeared unsystematic.

As a closed system, pronouns have grammatical rather than lexical meaning, and generally lack inherent stress except in the genitive; neither their forms nor their functions encourage us to analyse them morphologically, presenting them in paradigm form; rather they should be seen as making up a complex system operating in several dimensions; the first four dimensions are those of person, gender, number and case, but the lack of inherent stress means that they have distinct forms for normal functioning and for functioning in conditions of contrastive stress, so that in effect stress forms a fifth. Of these dimensions, number is not internally marked in second person, and gender is only marked in third person singular. I take as the central pronouns of English the system of forms describable in terms of this set of dimensions; these forms are traditionally called **personal pronouns**, from the relevance to them of the category of person.

Note

Where *none* is plural in referential function (sc. could without change of meaning be replaced by *none of them*) it normally collocates with a plural verb-form, and the use of a singular verb gives rise to ambiguity, cf. *Daily Telegraph*, Wednesday 28 March, 1962, p. 15, col. 1: 'There are 20 types in all. None has identical furniture.'

§98. It is one thing to decide that multi-dimensional representation would be best for pronouns; another to find a way of carrying it out on the two dimensions of paper. The way the material is set out below is largely traditional, but it should be read in the light of the model presented in §97.

FIG. 5

'First person'			'Second person'	'Third person'		
				Masculine	Feminine	Neuter
sg.	sb.	I/aɪ/	you/juː)/, /jʊ/, /jə/	he/hiː)/, /hɪ/	she/ʃiː)/,/ʃɪ/	it/ɪt/
	un.	me/miː)/, /mɪ/		him/(h)ɪm/	her/hɜː)/, /(h)ə/	
	gn.	mine/maɪn/	yours/jɔəz/	his/(h)ɪz/	hers/hɜːz/	its/ɪts/
pl.	sb.	we/wiː)/, /wɪ/	you	they /ðeɪ/		
	un.	us/ʌs/, /əs/, /s/		them, 'em /ðɛm/, /ðəm/, /əm/		
	gn.	ours /aʊəz/	yours	theirs /ðɛəz/		

(sg. = singular; pl. = plural; sb. = subjective; un. = unmarked; gn. = genitive.)

A few explanations are required. Alternative spoken forms are given, in general, where the emphatic form is phonemically distinct from the normal one, but to do this at all we have to go outside our usual range of phonemic symbols, and even so the account is much oversimplified. This is because the whole conception of the phoneme as we have presented it is an over-simplification. There is not just one set of sounds for English, but different sets for structurally different functions, including a different one for stressed and unstressed syllables. In general terms this difficulty was anticipated in §4 Note 2 when, to avoid the danger of confusion, we adopted the policy of analysing in terms of one system. This is the first issue that has exposed the weakness of our compromise, and students who wish to proceed further will need to start thinking in terms of more than one sound-system. Two minor points requiring comment are that in the forms for *her* potential linking-*r* has not been included, and that the /s/ form of *us* functions characteristically after the verbal element *let* (cf. §149).

The incidence of stress on the genitive forms indicates that they are rather different from the rest, and in fact they are not altogether parallel to genitives in nouns, since they are used absolutely, but not before a noun. With noun genitives we say: '*The house is Peter's*' and '*It's a mare's nest*', but with pronouns, '*The house is hers*', not *'*it's hers nest*' (instead, in the pre-noun position we use a determiner [cf. §109], *her nest*). But the distinction is somewhat blurred since (a) in the form *his* pronoun genitive and determiner coincide ('*The house is his*', '*it's his nest*') and (b) there is also no difference of form with *its*, but in that case the pronoun use is rare in Standard English), though the determiner use is common.

In addition to the forms charted above, in certain 'styles', notably for public worship, there are distinct singular forms for second person *thou* /ðaʊ/, *thee* /ði:/, *thine* /ðaɪn/; the plural can then be *ye* /ji:/ or *you* subjective; *you*, occasionally *ye*, unmarked. The second singular form collocates with special verb-forms (cf. §123 Note 4). *Ye* has wider currency in the interjective phrase *Ye gods!* Royal and editorial *we, us, our* removes the number-distinction in first person.

Note

The forms *it, we, us, you, they, them* can pattern with the following adjunct-word *all* in constructions like '*They all hated us*', '*I gave it all to them*'. *Alone* may pattern in post-position with the subjective or unmarked case of any of the pronouns; in larger syntactical units the numerals above *one* pattern with those having plural reference.

§99. There remains an important question of function, namely, what is the relative distribution of the forms we have called **subjective** and **unmarked**. These names are unusual, and are meant to embody a view about the forms. For British English we await a frequency survey of the forms in various positions, and can only speak impressionistically. One thing is clear, that in RP. the forms I have labelled *unmarked* do not occur in manifest subject relationship, i.e., directly before and governing the finite verb (except in constructions introduced by *none of* . . ., which are not manifestly subject, but rather are blends to which relationship both with the preceding preposition and with the following verb contribute). Here, then, is a well-marked territory which is the province of the *I*-series. There is an equally well-marked territory of object which is the province of the *me*-series, but *me* is widely distributed in other functions too, for instance, always after prepositions (cf. Ch. X). It does look as if we are dealing with a case of functional marking—the *I*-series functions being marked off from the rest, and being characteristically subject-functions. Hence our terms. But what of the uncertain territory?—What of absolute uses ('*Me? It's not my idea!*'), non-object complement uses ('*It's me you're hurt-ing*'). Certainly members of both series are heard in both functions; certainly the *me*-series fits better into the kind of English we are taking for analysis in this book—educated, not too formal, speech. Without precise numerical information, more cannot be said.

There are conventions about the order of pronoun-forms when they occur together, second person before third, and both before first singular; first plural, however, often precedes the other two, especially third person. Perhaps approaching Standard is a usage in which *you and I* functions as a unit in which both elements remain unchanged ('*He has invited you and I to dinner*').

§100. The system just examined is one of pronouns in the fullest, most central sense. There are, however, various kinds of words similar, but not identical, i.e., pronoun-like words. Not the closest, but most conveniently treated near the central pronouns, are **reflexives**, formally invariable words functioning as complement when the complement has the same referent as the subject of the sentence. The forms are *myself, ourselves, yourself, yourselves* (here is a number distinction in second person, and one that can establish it for the subject-form too), *himself, herself, itself, themselves*. All have inherent stress on the second syllable. The same set of forms has a distinct function as **intensi-fiers**, functioning immediately after the related central pronoun, or at the end of the clause, or occasionally in initial position (in the third person, also after nouns and names). At the end of the clause the intensifiers are distinguished from reflexives by a different superfix. Examples are:

Reflexive	Intensifier
I hurt myself	*I myself gave it to you*
	I gave it to you myself
	Myself I gave it to you
They washed themselves	(*Not only did they expect others to wash but*) *they washed themselves.*

These forms may therefore be adjuncts either to the subject or to the whole of the object.

With them may be mentioned two **reciprocals**, *each other*, *one another*, found only as complements, and in plural constructions (but cf. §95, Note 1).

§101. Also closely related are those forms used, especially in subject-function, with reference either to an unspecified person or to people in general. One such form, *people*, has already been mentioned (cf. §95); the others are *you*, *they*, *one*, the first two collocating with verbs in the same way as if they were the central (personal) pronouns, the third collocating like *he*. The first two are contrasted in normal spoken English, *you* in reference to the speaker or those with whom he identifies himself, *they* in reference to people with whom the speaker does not identify himself; *they* also collocates with preceding *anybody*, *-one* ('*Anyone could come, couldn't they?*'); *one* corresponds, in a rather stiffer 'style', to *you*. By contrast with the central pronouns, these are usually called **impersonal**. A further, rather informal use, is inherently stressed *they* for people one dislikes or condemns, and this more often has non-subject uses, with the usual formal patterning (*them*, *theirs*).

Impersonal in another sense is the **spot-filling** use of *it*, *there*, as in '*It's raining . . . a pity*'; '*There* /ðə(r)/ *isn't enough!*' *There* in this introductory-subject use is always unstressed; *it* can spot-fill for object as well as subject ('*Hop it!*').

§102. Closest in syntactical functioning and morphological patterning to the central type of pronouns are the **relatives** (which we have already used with the central pronouns to establish gender in nouns, cf. §91). The relatives are clause-linking, pronoun-like elements relating back to an antecedent term in the utterance. It is necessary to distinguish between the relative function and relative forms, since under certain conditions the function may have no (word) form to express it, but may be indicated by the juxtaposing of clauses without pause or break in the intonation pattern; this may be spoken of as the **zero-relative**, as long as we understand that zero only means there is no separate word to express the relative function; there is a patterning of clauses which only occurs in that function ('*The man I spoke of . . .*'). If there is a form, it may be one of two, one variable, the other invariable. The variable has a paradigm with contrast of gender and case (not number). From its written form this relative is known as the *wh*-relative. The gender-distinction here is different from that we have met so far, being a contrast between what is thought of as human and what is not so thought of. The, in this sense, '**human**' gender has **subjective** form *who* /hu(:)/, **second case** *whom* /hu(:)m/ (this is commonly unstressed, and then in some speakers has variant /hʊm/), and **genitive** *whose* /hu(:)z/. The '**non-human**' gender has the case-invariable form *which* /wɪtʃ/ or /ʍɪtʃ/. The three-term case system links the 'human' gender *wh*-relative closely with the central type of pronouns, but, as we have already hinted, the cases are not identical. In straightforward instances of subject-relationship the *who* form is used; it also occurs in other uses, but so does the second form; the second form is not, however, consistently used in any one function (not even object-relationship), and so is not on a par with the *me*-series (nor need they all be on a par with each other). The title *second case* is meant to indicate that it is the less favoured form and has no clear area of exclusive use. The situation is complicated by the existence of another relative, the invariable *that*. *That* and *wh*-forms are generally felt by English people to be in free variation, and it is only recently that a painstaking frequency-survey by Randolph Quirk has shown up the complicated network of conditions operating to favour one relative or the other (or zero) in a given utterance. Summarising this analysis will lead us to the treatment of syntactical patterns larger than most considered in this chapter, but there is every reason to go outside our normal limits on a topic where so much has become known so recently, especially when the patterns revealed are of a delicate intricacy which, as speakers, we may reasonably be proud to control.

The first point to be made is that the survey was carried out on three kinds of spoken material, from unself-conscious, informal talk to an unscripted broadcast discussion, and that in respect of relative-usage, no differences were found in the three sorts of material; what is described is not, therefore, the merely colloquial or the unduly formal. The second is that the patterns emerging here as dominant in spoken English do not wholly correspond either to what occurs in modern writing or to what, in a substitution-test, speakers are prepared to accept as idiomatic. The third is, that to unravel the strands, one needs to equip oneself to make a number of subtle distinctions, part referential, part formal, about the nature of the clauses linked by the relative, and about the immediate environment of the relative.

The primary distinction concerning the relationship of the clauses is between the relative clause as **restrictive**, i.e., indicating a limitation on the possible reference of the antecedent, and **non-restrictive**, i.e., characterising the antecedent without limiting it. This is a formal distinction in the clauses themselves, independently of the choice of link between them. 'Restrictive clauses ... are linked to their antecedents by close syntactic juncture, by unity of intonation contour, and by continuity of the degree of loudness. In contrast, non-restrictive clauses are characterised by open juncture (recognised, together with

the following features, by a comma in writing), a fresh intonation contour, and a change (especially a diminution) in the degree of loudness'
(1957, p. 101). In non-restrictive clauses *wh*-relatives were used in 173
out of 174 cases. Examples are:

'*the office administration department—which is the department I mean—
comes in very much*' and '*it's all based on violence—which I hate*'.

The only exception had *that* (i.e., there were no zero-forms), and was:

'*all he'd got in his tummy was raw turnip—that he'd taken from the
fields*'.

In general, then, *that* is hardly ever freely produced in a non-restrictive
relative clause, and yet in a substitution-test it is not rejected. The
antecedent may be, not a word or phrase, but a whole clause, and then
only *wh-* is possible:

'*we may have exploded the Canal at the same time—which is going to be
very unfortunate.*'

Restrictive clauses are very much commoner than non-restrictive,
and in them *wh-*, *that* and zero are all common, but in that order of
frequency (the figures being 524, 372, 228); *wh-* is especially favoured
where the antecedent is complex, or the relative clause itself lengthy.
'Non-human' gender is much commoner than 'human' in the antecedents, but even in restrictive clauses the great bulk of 'human'-
gender relatives are of *wh*-type; in other words, speakers exploit the
gender-distinguishing forms in preference to the less differentiated
ones. Where the relative is the object, however, there is a striking
preference for *that-* or zero-relatives; in other words, speakers tend to
avoid the case-distinguishing forms (*who/whom*), except in clearly
subject function, where *who* is selected. Elsewhere, if *who(m)* is used,
there is a good deal of overlap of distribution.

§103. The *wh*-forms also belong to a closed-system of sentence-intro-
ducing words which serve to mark one kind of question (cf. §68), and
hence are called **interrogatives**. The other items belonging here are
what, why, when, where, how. All may be made emphatic by use of the
intensifier (-)*ever* in post-position, though that rarely collocates with
whom, and in the genitive the case-mark is transferred to the intensifier
(*who ever's* not **whose ever*).

The interrogatives are also used as clause-linking words, as in:
'*I don't know what to do*'; they enter into idioms, such as *who's who,
what's what*; and occur finally in curtailed constructions which, if they
were realised in full, would be of the kind introduced by these words,

as in: '*I don't remember where or when*'. With this function we have passed right away from noun-like functions, and are on the borders of adverbial and subordinator uses to be treated in Chapter X.

The interrogatives, unlike those relatives that are homonymous with them, are inherently stressed; it follows that the form *whom* does not have variant pronunciation /hʊm/ in interrogative function. It is in any case somewhat marginal in that use in spoken English.

§104. Lastly, in respect of sentence-functions and syntactical patterning several determiners resemble pronouns. The matter will be treated in the next chapter in the account of determiners, and here it need only be said that examples are *that*, *these* and *three* in the sentences:

'*That'll do*'; '*I prefer these*'; '*Three should be enough.*'

Members of this closed class of noun-phrase head-words may be called **determiner-pronouns**.

EXERCISES

1. 'As time passed, people leaving, others arriving, I began increasingly to suspect that Members was not going to show up. That would not be out of character, because cutting appointments was a recognised element in his method of conducting life. This habit—to be in general associated with a strong, sometimes frustrated desire to impose the will—is usually attributed on each specific occasion to the fact that 'something better turned up'. Such defaulters are almost as a matter of course reproached with trying to make a more profitable use of their time. Perhaps, in reality, self-interest in its crudest form plays less part in these deviations than might be supposed. The manoeuvre may often be undertaken for its own sake. The person awaited deliberately withholds himself from the person awaiting. Mere absence is in this manner turned into a form of action, even potentially violent in its consequences.' (Anthony Powell, *The Acceptance World*, 1955, p. 35.)

   (a) make separate lists of the central nouns, proper names, pronouns and other noun-like words in the above passage.

   (b) is there anything striking about the proportions of entries you have in different columns—or about the proportions of case and number forms?

   (c) are there any forms you find it difficult to place, or any that function as noun-phrase heads but are not covered by our survey? If you answer yes, explain your reasons.

2. What English uncountables are translated by number-variable words in another language you know?

CHAPTER VIII

Form-Classes
(I) Functioning in the Noun Phrase

(B) Adjunct Words

§105. Of the three main types of word examined in Chapter VII it is only nouns that pattern freely with a large and characteristic range of adjuncts. These adjuncts may be divided into two main classes, closed-system items, which we shall call **determiners**, and open-class items, which we shall call **adjectives**. Within both classes we shall also need to make finer discriminations.

The name *determiner* is appropriately given to words which, functioning as adjuncts, show their head-words to be nouns. The most central type of determiner is that to which traditionally the name **article** is given; it is so central because its only function is as adjunct to a following noun or noun-like word or sequence which is its head; it is therefore a marker of the following noun; lexically empty itself, it indicates the 'noun-ness' of its head and contributes to its meaning as a noun. There are two mutually exclusive articles. One has the form *the* /ðə/ before consonants, /ðɪ/ before vowels, lacking inherent stress but taking the form /ðiː/ under conditions of contrastive stress; it is invariable and used before singular and plural nouns, though its contribution is different in the two cases; it is known as the **definite article**. The other has the form *a* /ə/ before consonants, *an* /ən/ before vowels; it lacks inherent stress but takes the forms /eɪ/ before consonants, /æn/ before vowels under conditions of contrastive stress; it is used only before singular countable nouns, and is known as the **indefinite article**. With absence of article (sometimes referred to as the zero-form) also functioning as a term in the article system, we have five possibilities:

1. zero+noun singular (*cake*)
2. *the*+noun singular (*the cake*)
3. *a*+noun singular (*a cake*)
4. zero+noun plural (*cakes*)
5. *the*+noun plural (*the cakes*)

But there is an element of sleight of hand here, because to get the same example throughout we have chosen homonymous forms, one countable, the other uncountable (type 1 must have an uncountable, type 2 may have).

The kind of meaning contributed by any one term is determined in relation to the other terms available with the given noun-form. 1., in fact, indicates that the noun is an uncountable; it is a pattern that does not occur with what we have called the central type of noun. 2. does not distinguish countable from uncountable, but adds one of a range of specifying meanings, which will be examined in §106. 3. indicates that the head is a countable, and adds one of a range of specifying meanings to be considered in §107. 4., which occurs only with plurals, does not distinguish countables from uncountables, and points a purely lexical contrast (*cakes, not sugar, bread, biscuits, etc.*). 5., mostly used with countables, adds a specifying meaning (in contrast with 4.) to be considered in §106; it is also used with plural uncountables, and with a few uncountables it is indispensable (e.g., *the intelligentsia*)—where this is so the *the* cannot be contrastive, and so is more like a part of a name than a true article.

Not only do the articles uniquely function as markers of the noun-phrase, but they also have a special place in it, occurring, with very few exceptions (cf. §108) at its outset.

Notes

1. There are two main sources for the study of the articles in English, the *OED.* entries for the two words, and Christophersen (1939). My §§105–108 draw heavily on both, though with modified terminology; for more detailed treatments, students should consult these two sources.
2. The generalisations above are chiefly derived from characteristic patterns in subject function. Predicatively the zero-form is more freely used, especially in words for occupations ('*more artist than businessman*'; '*he was (the) headmaster of Rugby*'—both examples from Christophersen); also with certain other characterising words, usually predicative ('*more knave than fool*').

§106. *The Definite Article* has two main kinds of use:

(i) in relation to an individual instance, or individual instances of the referent of a noun, marking it or them as before mentioned or already known or contextually particularised, as in:

'*We keep a dog. We are fond of the dog.*' '*The Queen.*' '*The poet Virgil.*'

The expressions 'before mentioned' and 'already known' are clear enough, but 'contextually particularised' can do with some explanation. Among the forms the particularisation can take are subsequent specification in the utterance ('*The passage I have quoted*'), implicit reference to immediate surroundings ('*Pass the butter*', '*Keep off the grass*'—sc. the butter now on the table, the grass cultivated in the enclosure where the notice stands), or to the total situation of the speech-community ('*The Queen*'—sc. the present Queen of the United Kingdom), of the person concerned ('*To be hanged by the neck*'), or mankind in general ('*The sun, the world*'). With this last group we have also come to name-like expressions, since this sort of *the* is only used where the referent is being thought of as unique (of course, we now know that the sun is not unique, and we refer to *suns* and *moons*; but we cannot speak of *the sun* without implying that it is alone of its kind—*sun* is therefore two homonyms, one a unique, one a countable, and when we use it as the former our language keeps alive a fragment of an astronomy we well know to be no longer valid).

Another type of particularising is found in expressions where *the* is followed by a superlative adjective (cf. §115) in noun function, as in '*He's the best*'. Here the implied context is all that exists or could be considered relevant. Note too the use in apposition, in such constructions as '*Alfred the Great*'. All the uses noted under (i) may be briefly labelled **particularising** uses.

(ii) in relation to a noun used generically or universally, or as a type of its class; or with a plural noun used universally or a de-adjectival class-noun (cf. §94). Examples are:

'*The whale is threatened with extinction.*' '*Playing the piano.*' '*The World, the Flesh and the Devil.*' '*The sublime.*' '*The French.*' '*The Joneses.*'

This may be called the **non-particularising** use. A sentence exemplifying the particularising followed by the non-particularising use is:

''*Tis the Voice of the Sluggard.*'

In addition, there are several minor uses, which can only be briefly mentioned here, the now rather marginal use in stating rates ('*Two shillings the pound*'), the correlative use in patterns like *the one ... the other* and in linked comparatives (cf. §115) ('*the more, the merrier*'), with single comparatives ('*the worse for drink*'), the quasi-superlative use, always stressed ('*Ulanova was* **the** *Giselle of her day*'). But even to give an account of the principal uses would mean moving out to larger syntactical units. For instance, we can say, without definite article before the first noun:

'*In spring I take a week's holiday*' or (quite differently) '*In spring I shall take a week's holiday*',

and so far we might wish to claim that the difference between the **two** is due to the difference of verb. That is simple enough. But if we put in the article, saying:

'*In the spring I take a week's holiday*' or '*In the spring I shall take a week's holiday*',

then the first *the* is non-particularising (referring to an annual event) and the second one is particularising (referring to the coming year). So we cannot describe the functions of *the* simply in terms of how it contrasts with other possible occupants of the same position, but must take account of particularising factors in a larger environment; we should look at contrasting patterns rather than contrasting forms. In this book we have not scope to do more than lay a foundation for such wider-ranging analysis, but from time to time it is salutary to issue a reminder that the further goal exists.

§107. *The Indefinite Article* can only be used with a singular of a countable (central) noun as head. It indicates that that noun is being used of *one*, or *some(one)*, or *any(one)* or *a particular instance* of the referent of that noun. Examples are:

'*A pound isn't enough*'; '*A child turned the corner and came into view*'; '*A child could do it*'; '*They were talking to a man I know well*'.

(Consider what difference it would make to replace *a* by *the* in these sentences; observe that it is not always the same difference.)

This, too, has idiomatic uses, for instance in stating rates ('*A shilling a pound*') and in the formula *to a* . . . = 'without exception' ('*they* all gave their permission—*to a man*').

§108. The definite and indefinite articles are unique in being lexically empty forms only occurring in a fixed place in relation to noun-like heads. But very similar is *no*, linked with them in the sense that the three form a mutually exclusive system (no one head can have more than one as adjunct), and in the sense that it shares their special position in the noun-phrase—indeed, not even the few forms that can precede the other two can precede it. It differs from them, perhaps, in not being wholly tied to the noun as head. It belongs to a functional class of items we may call **negators**, and it may perform its function of negating in relation to either the noun-phrase or whole clauses or sentences. It is a **noun-phrase negator** in:

'*No really sweet and sound eating apples have been available all the week*';

and a **sentence-negator** in:

'*Can you come at nine?*' '*No.*'

I say *perhaps*, because another way of looking at the matter would be to treat *no* in the two functions as two distinct words. Either way, it is not so restricted in patterning that when we hear it we know a noun-phrase is being ushered in. But when it does function in the noun-phrase it is so like the articles that we may call it the **negative article**; it can have singulars, plurals and uncountables as its head-words.

Note

It may be said here once for all that generalisations made about a unit functioning at word-rank will not necessarily cover its functioning at other ranks. For instance, our account of *no* will not help us to place the bound element *no* in ' *You no-good layabouts!* '

§109. Also very close to the definite and indefinite articles are the forms *my, our, your, her, their,* and marginally *his, its.* They have a class-meaning corresponding to that of the genitive case, and they have it each in relation to one of the (central, personal) pronouns, but they pattern not like pronouns, but like determiners, and more specifically, like articles. They form a system mutually exclusive with the other articles (we cannot say **the my apple,* etc.), they share the special position of articles in the noun-phrase, being preceded only by the noun-phrase initiators (cf. §113) (as in '*our own lovely new house*', but '*all our yesterdays*'). For these reasons it seems best to class these words as **genitive articles**, some central because like true articles they have no other sentence-function and so signal the onset of noun-phrases, others (*his, its*) marginal because they do have another function (the homonymous forms being pronoun genitives, cf. §98; though *its* is hardly standard in that capacity).

This class of forms has its own reinforcing word, *own,* which has both attributive and predicative functions, but can only be at best marginal as member of the adjective or determiner classes because of its limited collocation with the genitive in articles or other parts of the noun-phrase. It is best treated as a post-positional **genitive intensifier** patterning with these genitive forms. Examples are:

'*His own house*'; '*the house is his own*'; '*Sheila's own writing-desk.*'

Note

Of the marginal noun-phrase initiators (§113) the only one that can collocate with the genitive article is *many*, but when it does so it patterns like an ordinary adjective, following, not preceding the article—thus, '*many a slip*' but '*her many triumphs*'.

§110. The remaining determiners are of a different kind, since they function not only as adjuncts in the noun-phrase, but also as pronoun-like head-words (cf. §104). They may therefore be called **determiner-**

pronouns. They fall into three classes, and only one from any given class can occur in a single noun-phrase. They have a fixed position at or near the beginning of the phrase. The first class has only two members, *this* /ðɪs/ and *that* /ðæt/, and is singled out primarily because it alone among noun-phrase adjuncts has number-variation. The number-variation is of the two-term kind (*one* or *more than one* in this case), selection between the terms being governed by the number of the head if there is one and by referential considerations if the determiner-pronoun itself is head. The plurals are formed by processes without analogy elsewhere in English grammar, *these* /ðiːz/ and *those* /ðəʊz/ respectively. Though the class is identified on formal grounds, it is labelled, as so often, with reference to the kind of lexical meaning its members have, as **deictic** or **demonstrative.** As the two members are contrasted in a closed system it falls to the grammarian to try to describe their relative values in the system. Bearing in mind the dangers of such attempts we may perhaps risk saying that *that* is generally the unmarked term of the opposition, *this* being the member used to draw attention to the immediacy or nearness of the referent in terms of some implied standard, probably unspecified. In recent years, in some 'styles', *this* has been encroaching on *that* territory, making the border even harder to draw. A full study of the subject is awaited from M. A. K. Halliday.

Both members of this class can be preceded by noun-phrase initiators. Examples illustrating the characteristic positions and contrastive functioning of the two items are:

(*All*) *this* ([*lovely*] [*hand-worked*] *embroidery*) *is for sale.*'
'(*Half*) *that* (*quantity*) *would have been enough.*'

Observe that *much, many* can be heads to this pair of forms, though not to the other determiners (except when *many* changes form-class to become a noun-like word, as in *the many*).

Notes

1. On the concord of *these/those kind of* cf. §85 Note.
2. Though *this* and *that* are mutually exclusive in a series of noun-adjuncts, they can function together in a noun-phrase if linked by the co-ordinator *and*; so, as head '*this and that remains to be done*' (the usually singular concord here indicates how far the collocation has become a unit), and as adjunct, '*he was fussing about this and that concern of the partnership*'.

§**111.** The second class of non-article determiners also has dual function, as adjunct in the noun-phrase and as independent pronoun-like head-word. It has no number-variation. It forms a system mutually exclusive with the articles and the central noun-phrase initiators (cf. §113), and so, if it is in a noun-phrase, must introduce it. The members

of this class are *any, each, either, enough, every, many, more, most, much,*
neither, some, such, what (but of these *many, such* and *what* are marginal
with the noun-phrase initiators and will be considered with them in
§113). In the adjunct function, these items are in complementary
distribution with the articles in initial position (or next to it); consider:

'*The good eating apples . . .*'
'*Some* "   "   "   "'
'*Any* "   "   "   "'

As heads they are in complementary distribution with each other in a
function the articles cannot share, as in:

'*Would you like some/any/more?*' but not **would you like the/a/my?*
'*Some are ripe*' but not **the are ripe.*

The class once established, we can make finer distinctions within it.
For instance, *any, enough, more, most, neither, some, such, what,* pattern
with singular or plural constructions ; *each, either, every, much,* only
with non-plural constructions; and *many* only with plural constructions.
Again, within the non-plural group, all pattern only with singular
countables except *much*, which patterns only with uncountables. Another kind of limitation, functioning in larger syntactical units, is that
affirmatively predicative *some* occurs only in positive constructions,
while *any* has the corresponding function in negative patterns (the two
answers '*I've got some*', '*I haven't got any*', both function in relation to
the two questions, '*Have you got some?*' '*Have you got any?*'). Yet
another is that *either* and *neither* occur only in connection with reference
to one out of two, they being the only grammatical sign of 'twoness', and
so forming a sub-system of **duality** (a numerical category in contrast
with both singularity and plurality) (cf. §113 on another dual *both*); the
correlative co-ordinators *either . . . or* and in some 'styles' *neither . . .*
nor constitute a similar sub-system, but in spite of lexical similarity
belong in Chapter X rather than here (cf. §161).

Members of this class may be called **invariable determiner-**
pronouns, by contrast with those described in the last paragraph, the
variable determiner-pronouns.

§112. The third group consists of determiner-pronouns with the usual
functions and no number variation; where they differ is that they can
collocate with the articles and two of the noun-phrase initiators (cf. §113),
following them directly, and in their absence starting off the noun-
phrase. Here belong *few, fewer, fewest, least, less, little,* and the cardinal
numerals (i.e., those in the series starting *one, two, three*). Of these,
one, least, less, little occur only in non-plural constructions, *one* with

singular countables, in complementary distribution with the indefinite article though it can collocate with the definite; *little, least, less,* with uncountables, which cannot have the indefinite article (though there is a unitary expression *a little*).   These three determiner-pronouns follow the definite article in such constructions as '*The little food there was in the house was stale*'; the determiner-pronoun *little* must not be confused with the homonymous open-class adjective in such constructions as *the little house*.   *Few, fewer, fewest* and the numerals above *one* occur only in plural constructions.   Marginal between these and the determiner-pronouns described in the last paragraph is *several* (in the sense 'more than two or three but not very many' *OED.* 4), since it usually collocates with the genitive articles and the noun-phrase initiators (except *both*, which is a dual), but not with the other, the most central, articles.   Since it occurs in plural constructions the indefinite article is ruled out; after *the* it is possible, but not common, in such patterns as '*the several houses along the road were all closed*'—perhaps the reason for its unpopularity in such patterns is the possibility of confusion with the homonymous open-class adjective (=*separate, distinct*).   Ordinal numerals (those in the series beginning *first, second, third*) behave in general like members of this class, but in the singular, in full sentences, generally require the presence of a preceding article, as in:

'*The first (person) to come was served first*' (but in an aphoristic minor sentence, '*First come, first served*'); '*The first edition was in 1878*' (but in disjunctive grammar, '*First edition, 1878*'); plural, '*There's no time for second shots*'.

The following examples illustrate the adjunct and head functions and the positions characteristic of the class:

'*One (dress) they saw was suitable.*'   '*All the little (stock) they discovered was contaminated.*'   '*Half the few (rooms) available faced due north.*'

With the adjunct use only of this class we may compare the number-invariable use of numeratives and other measure-words, *dozen, hundred, score, stone, pound,* etc., when preceded by a cardinal numeral (cf. §86 [xii]).

Note

To the warnings already given about avoiding confusion of these items with homonymous open-class adjectives, should be added one about **age-denominators**.   These are open-class adjectives used only predicatively after linking verbs and are identical in form with the cardinal numerals; an example is *three* in '*She'll be three to-morrow*'; the corresponding attributive form is [*numeral*]-*year-old*, as in '*a three-year-old filly*'.   The cardinal numerals are just possible as predicative heads ('*We are six*'='*There are six of us*') but the favoured use of this series of forms in that position is as age-denominators.

§113. Lastly, we come to the small group of determiners capable of preceding even the articles (cf. §105); they can be called **noun-phrase initiators**. The central members of this class are *all, both, half*. *All* collocates with either plural or uncountable head-words; it therefore could not precede the indefinite article, but does precede the definite, as in:

'*All the nice trim little schoolgirls.*'

(But in earlier English *all* could pattern with the indefinite article, where now we would use *whole* following the article, or *all of* preceding it, and familiar phrases from literature keep alive a sense of the older pattern, as in *all a summer's day*.) *Both* can only have dual function, that is, its head must be two singulars ('*Both Mary and John*') or a plural with referents two in number ('*Both the crumbling, gnarled old elm trees*').

Half can have singular, plural or uncountable head-words, and so can precede the definite or indefinite articles, as in:

'*Half (the people there) were in evening dress*' or '*Half (an hour) is plenty long enough*'

(the bracketed forms removed, we see the operation of *half* as a head).

Marginally belonging here are *many, such, what, not*, all of which can precede the indefinite article, as in:

'*Such a pity.*' '*What a nuisance!*' '*There's many a slip.*' '*There I was, not a penny to my name.*'

Two things make these marginal. In the first place apart from *many* they hardly function as heads (*such* is just possible, especially preceded by *any* or *some*). In the second, although they can have as heads words which collocate with *the*, three of them are in any given construction in complementary distribution with *the*. So we have, '*Such nice people*', '*The nice people*', but neither **Such the nice people*, nor **The such nice people*. Similarly for *what* and *not* (except [a] in idioms such as *What the devil*, where in any case *what* is an interrogative [cf. §103] introducing the clause, not part of the noun-phrase, or [b] in constructions like '*not the nice people we met at your party*', where *not* is a **phrase-negator** operating in relation to the whole phrase and not in relation to the noun as its head; as a noun-phrase negator it has inherent stress, as a verb-phrase negator it does not, cf. §130; in cases of doubt, such differences can be shown up by constituent or transformational analysis; cf. Ch. XI). *Many*, of course, is not mutually exclusive with *the*, but if they collocate, *many* follows *the* in ordinary adjective position ('*the many happy meetings we have had in the past*'). *Many* is on both counts marginal in a different way from the others.

Note

Another form which functions in the same position, but in relation to the whole phrase, not to the noun as head, is *only* ('*only the best will do*', '*only a nincompoop would say that*'); as confirmation of the difference of function note that *only* can collocate with *the*, and then has ordinary adjective position ('*The only man who has executed an entrechat dix*').

§114. We have now examined the different kinds of determiners functioning in the noun-phrase, but before we move on to adjectives another point, already implicit, should be drawn out. For these two kinds of word are distinguished not only in terms of the fairly clear dividing line between closed system and open class, but as the extremes on two clines. At one terminus of one cline are those words occurring only as adjuncts, at the other those occurring only as heads; the other cline is one of positional behaviour. The functional cline (head～adjunct) requires a little comment. Most of what has been said in this chapter so far has been most directly relevant to subject-function, in which the distinction between adjunct and head is clear. But predicatively the distinction is much less clear, since two different functions coincide positionally. We say:

'*I bought some*' but also '*You do look miserable*'.

And we distinguish the first post-verb position as that of a pronoun-like word, the second as that of an adjective-like word. The relationship of subject to complement through the verb is different in the two cases, as transforms show, cf. § 171; but after some verbs it is impossible to distinguish the two functions in this position, cf. '*It is red*' and '*It is mine*'. So in keeping, as we do, to the traditional distinction between adjectives and pronouns in this position, we draw, not on anything in the structure before us, or any possible transforms of it, but on our sense of the total patterning of the words, distinct except in this one position.

§115. As a whole, adjectives function characteristically in two ways, as adjuncts in noun-phrases, and as predicatives, examples being *good* in the two sentences '*He is a good man*' and '*He is good*'; indeed, so characteristic are these two uses that we may take it in the first instance to be the criterion of adjectives in the most central sense that they have these functions and not others. Within the general class so established we need to make sub-divisions on two independent lines—first the morphological (whether the word is a variable or not), and second the positional (where, in a sequence of adjectives, a particular form belongs). We have already taken position of adjectives as a whole, as contrasted with determiners, to be another criterion of the class (cf. §105).

If we wish to speak of morphological change in adjectives, we must realise that we do so in a sense quite different from that in which the term is used elsewhere in English. For unlike the contrasted forms of nouns, pronouns and verbs, morphologically varied forms of adjectives are found in only a small proportion of adjectives, so that we have with them no strong sense that one form has been selected to the exclusion of others intimately bound up with it; and, unlike most other inflectional variants in English, those of adjectives present a choice referentially, not grammatically determined. Anyone looking at the sentence *The small girl are presenting a bouquet* knows that there is an error, and that it is grammatical—I must have meant to say either ' The small girl is presenting a bouquet' or ' The small girls are presenting a bouquet'; at a second stage, when they wish to determine which error I have made, they will have to turn to referential considerations. If they then establish that one girl was involved they will claim that I should have said ' The small girl is presenting a bouquet'. When they have got that far, I may say, ' You think you have been very clever, but you still haven't got it right; what I wanted to say was " The smaller girl is presenting a bouquet"'. At that, my critics will very properly be indignant and point out that they could not spot such an error—any more than if I had meant to say *the tall girl* or *the girl with yellow spots on her dress*. The selection of items from the series *small-smaller-smallest* is like the selection from a lexical series, not like selection from a paradigm of grammatically contrasted items. Formally, the suffixes involved are like inflections, but functionally, they are like derivational morphemes (on this contrast cf. §84[d]). There are, however, some patterns in which prediction could be made about the form to be selected, for instance if I say, '*Jane was chosen to present the bouquet because she was . . . than Mary*'; in such a frame lexical prediction is not possible (I might have meant *smaller, younger, prettier, bolder,* etc.), but grammatical prediction is possible, namely that I intended something like an *-er* form and not a zero-inflected (uninflected) form. We may say that this kind of change just qualifies as inflectional, but it is not very characteristically so.

The pattern of morphological change we have been discussing is that of **comparison**, and the three terms of it in English are labelled **positive** (uninflected), **comparative** (*-er* form) and **superlative** (*-est* form). Phonemically, the comparative is /-ə/ with potential linking-*r*, and the superlative /-ɪst/; between the base and either inflection there may be modifications of boundary phonemes, for instance, /ŋ/ becomes /ŋg/, linking-*r* is realised, syllabic /l/ becomes consonantal; cf. *long* /lɒŋ/, *longer* /lɒŋgə/, *longest* /lɒŋgɪst/, *poor* /puə/, *poorer* /puərə/, *poorest* /puərɪst/, *able* /eɪbl/, *abler* /eɪblə/, *ablest*, /eɪblɪst/. The adjectives subject to this kind of change are a virtually closed class, consisting of monosyllables, disyllables ending in a syllabic consonant or a vowel or stressed on the second syllable, and one or two others. All the adjectives so far given as examples in this paragraph belong to the type we are considering (but for *good* cf. the next paragraph below), and others are *nice* /naɪs/, *green* /griːn/, *tender* /tɛndə/, *sober* /səʊbə/, *profound* /prəfaʊnd/, *pleasant* /plɛznt/, *handsome* /hænsəm/. This class of adjectives is very largely phonologically determined.

Another, much smaller, class conforms to the patterning of having three terms of degree, but changes suppletively to form the three terms (on **suppletion** cf. §125[f]). The members are *good* /gʊd/ (for *well*, which has the same terms of comparison, cf. §120), comparative *better* /bɛtə/, superlative *best* /bɛst/; *bad* /bæd/ (for *ill*, which has the same terms of comparison, cf. §120), comparative *worse* /wɜːs/, superlative *worst* /wɜːst/; *far* /fɑː/, comparative *farther* /fɑːðə/ or *further* /fɜːðə/, superlative *farthest* /fɑːðɪst/ or *furthest* /fɜːðɪst/. A number of the closed-system items described in §§111–112 could be regarded as forming sets of comparatives, 'regular' or suppletive; they pattern partly like independent lexical variables, partly like grammatical alternatives. As in *than*-constructions we have to select the comparative of an adjective, so we have to select *more, fewer, less* rather than *much/many, few, little* from the list of determiners; and as in . . . *of all* constructions we have to select the superlative of an adjective, so we have to select *most, fewest, least* among the determiners.

Notes

1. As in other reaches of English grammar where an inflectional category is relevant only to a sub-division of the form-class it concerns, there is an alternative, analytical means of expression available, which renders the same relation for the invariables (cf. §90 Note). Those adjectives which do not inflect have analytically constructed comparison, using the forms *more, most* preceding them for comparative and superlative respectively. These are two items from a closed class of adjective modifiers for which see §157.
2. Those adjectives that do inflect are not inhibited from expressing degrees of comparison by analytical means. As in other reaches where such alternatives are available, significant use can be made of the choice between them. The inflectional form is more compact and will be used where it is adequate; but the analytical form gives the opportunity of contrastive stress-placement. Stress on the comparative particle will focus attention on the notion of degree, and stress on the adjective will focus attention on the lexical content. Consider the two pairs of sentences:

   '*She seems happier than she used to be.*'
   '*She seems, if anything, even more happy than she used to be.*'
   '*He is wealthier than before.*'
   '*He is more wealthy, but less contented.*'

   The last example illustrates the principle that though there may be parallelism between inflectional and analytic constructions, the analytic constructions should not be brought into the grammar as equivalents wholly on a par with the inflectional forms. For if we did that with *more, most,* we should also need to do so with *less, least,* and fresh analogies would come to light, extending the process indefinitely.

3. We have sounded very often a warning against attempting to cover the ground of a grammatical distinction in a paraphrase. About differences of degree, notice that the formally parallel terms conceal at least two kinds of meaning-difference. Some adjectives have 'gradable' meanings, others 'absolute' meanings. A thing can, for example, be more or less big, and *big* is a gradable adjective, for which the *-er* and *-est* forms can properly be paraphrased as *more big, most big*; but *pure, real, right, perfect, equal, unique, white, black* etc., are, in their referents, incapable of such gradations. Unmodified, they mean the absolute of what they say; with *more, most,* or the inflections of comparison, they mean *more nearly pure, real,* etc., *nearest of all to being pure, real,* etc.— in other words, they are weaker in effect than the positive term. (For some reason, popular pedantry has picked out just one of this group, *unique,* and without realising that it is merely one of a whole class in which the comparative cannot be paraphrased by *more in degree* and the superlative by *in the highest degree,* tried to warn speakers off comparing it.)

4. One monosyllabic adjective, *like,* is not nowadays inflected for degrees of comparison; but it is peculiar in patterning in other ways too, and is not felt as being fully a member of the adjective class. It is nearly always predicative (cf. §109), and functions often in predicates as much like a preposition as an adjective ('*Do you think she is like her mother?*') (cf. §160); it also has a pronoun-like use ('*Like answers to like*'), a coordinator-like use, cf. §161, and a noun-like use ('*gardening and the like*'—but this lacks case and number variation, the ordinary article-contrasts and patterning with characteristic noun-adjuncts). An ordinary attributive use is possible in some 'styles': '*The like reasons persuaded me . . .*'.

5. There has been considerable interest in comparative constructions in recent years; see Huddleston (1967) and references there.

§116. Less known analytically, but probably more important structurally, is the positional classification of adjectives. This occurs only in their functioning as adjuncts. Predicatively, a sequence of more than one adjective will have its last two members separated by the co-ordinator (cf. §161) *and*; there are some habitual orders, but no structural change results from infringing them (for instance, we would more often say '*The checks were red and white*' but '*. . . white and red*' is equally possible; there is no structural change, though we tend, in a case where the meanings of the two adjectives are mutually incompatible, to mention the predominant one first in this pattern). But what concerns us at the moment is the attributive or adjunct function in which the structural positional classes are fairly well defined, and contraventions effect a structural change. There is no overt clue to the positional groupings—perhaps this is what concealed from English speakers for so long that these intricate patterns exist, and exist because they create them. B. L. Whorf wrote: 'We say "a large black and white hunting dog".... How is the speaker of a radically different tongue supposed to know that he cannot say "hunting white black large a dog"? The English adjectives belong to cryptotypes having definite position assignments' (1956, p. 83).

Confining ourselves to what we are counting as central adjectives, it is still a complex problem to establish and describe the **positional classes.** As a preliminary, we may get certain general considerations out of the way. First, the classes now to be described all follow those we have described under the heading of determiners earlier in this chapter. Second, the rules described here are not inviolable (in the way that the placing of, say, *the* is), but concern only what may happen within a single intonation contour and without change of structural meaning (consider the 'tweeness' of '*a nice little, white little house*', with a fresh superfix starting on *white*); alternative positional class membership is possible for adjectives, but not without lexical change, for instance, *little* is an adjective of size in *a little white house*, but not, or not necessarily, in *a dim little old man*. Lastly, we must recognise that some adjectives do have an inherent positional grouping and others do not. Roughly speaking, the longer, less everyday adjectives, like *bombastic, monocotyledonous,* do not; the shorter, very common ones do. This is not to say that the placing of the longer adjectives is immaterial, but that it may be governed by factors external to them—either that the adjunct nearest the head is the one most closely associated with it, or that characteristics are named in decreasing order of generality. Thus one can say that '*the bean has a pale green dicotyledonous seed*' or that it has '*a dicotyledonous, pale green seed*'; but if we look at the *OED*.'s definition of a bean we find that the adjuncts cannot be in any order but the one used: 'A smooth, kidney-shaped, laterally flattened seed ...'. The movable adjectives may be called **inherently unplaced,** by contrast with those that inherently belong to positional classes and may be called **inherently placed.**

For the inherently placed adjectives we may distinguish three positions, 1. nearest the head, 2. next, and 3. furthest from it; before that again, come the determiners. 1. is the position of adjectives of age (*young, old,* etc.), 2. of colour adjectives and diminutive *little* (see footnote, and the example *a dim little old man* above), 3. of general characterising adjectives (*tall, pleasant, horrid, nice*). The placings are not absolute; we are describing the relative order of elements in a maximal noun-phrase. In *a dim little old man* any one or more adjectives can of course be omitted. The positions can be occupied by more than one 'filler' at a time. Thus prenominal items may be parallel or successive in their relation to the noun-head, a distinction indicated in both speech and writing. Compare *a nasty, irritable, selfish man,* with *a nice little old man.*

Note

We have distinguished *little* as an adjective of size from *little* as a **diminutive**, and this term should be explained. Diminutives are usually forms that have begun by meaning 'a small one of its kind' but have undergone a development whereby they come to express not merely an assessment of size, but also, or even exclusively, the speaker's response to small things, a response ranging from affection through condescension to contempt; we might say that a diminutive is mature when it carries only this 'response'-meaning. It is often said that English lacks diminutives; in fact *little* (position 2) is a diminutive as contrasted with *little* (position 3).

§117. The structure of the noun-phrase as we have analysed it so far can be represented thus:

III	II	I	HEAD

Noun-phrase/Determiner/Adjectives, inherently placed/Noun
Initiator   or unplaced
                             /Placed Adjectives in Positions/
                                       3   2   1

But we have not yet taken account of one of the defining characteristics of the noun (cf. §84[c]), that another noun can stand directly before it in minimal constructions. Such a preceding noun may be in the genitive or the common case. If it is in the genitive, it will stand at the beginning of the collocation, possibly with its own adjuncts about it, as in *The Queen's African tour*; in such cases analysis is simpler if we take each noun as head of a distinct noun-phrase. If the preceding noun is in the common case, it will directly precede the head, as in Whorf's example (§116) '*a large black and white hunting dog*'; cf. also *a veritable gold mine, a disastrous accident rate*. In that case, the only possible analysis is as a single unit with one head and the rest adjuncts. We should therefore revise our scheme to read:

([Adjuncts] Genitive head)/ III / II / I / Adjunct-noun/Head.
                                     /3, 2, 1/   common case/

Notes

1. Adjective modifiers and noun modifiers are characterised by different stress-tone patterns. Minimum contrasts are freely provided by those segmentally identical words formed from a verb-base + *-ing* (cf. §§129, 147, 148), which can be either adjective-like or noun-like; the adjective appears in *dancing feet* and the noun in *dancing shoes*. The title of John Dickson Carr's novel *The Burning Court* is often misread by those who do not realise that witchcraft is a theme of the book, and take *burning* as adjective-like rather than noun-like. Outside this class of words there are plenty of other examples; for instance, Dorothy Sayers' title *Gaudy Night* is sometimes misread by people who are ignorant of Oxford customs and take *gaudy* as adjective rather than

noun. A further example of the use of stress-tone patterns to distinguish between form-classes is found in the difference between *Oxford Road* (adjective followed by head-noun) and *Oxford Street* (in spite of the parallelism of written form), which in speech is modifying noun followed by head-noun (cf. §148). There is in some cases a parallel distinction between other homonymous pronominal modifiers in their primary and denominal forms. Compare *Forty-five sheep were grazing in the field* (primary cardinal numeral) with: *Forty-five bullets sprayed the room* (denominal; bullets from a ·45 calibre revolver).

2. There is a further complication of noun-phrase structure in that the adjuncts in such a phrase may also have their own adjuncts; this form of patterning must be mentioned here, but what the adjuncts are will be considered in Chapter X, cf. especially §157. The phrase '*a very pretty, rather charming old lady*' illustrates the patterning through the placing of *very, rather*.

   Certain modifiers, unlike those just mentioned, function exclusively as adjuncts to adjectives, and should be included here. They precede their heads. Examples are *pale* and *dark* modifying colour-adjectives, and colour-adjectives themselves modifying other colour-adjectives, as in *pale green, dark red, blue grey*.

3. There is nothing to prevent more than one member of an adjective positional class being present in the same noun-phrase; in such cases, any two will be separated by a pause or *and* and each item will have a fresh intonation contour; if there are more than two they will be separated by pauses except the last two, which will be separated by *and*, cf. Whorf's example with *black and white* above, which could be expanded to *black, brown and white*.

4. For purposes of description, it is simpler to analyse a genitive noun-phrase followed by a common-case one as two separate phrases, but the common-case one is in fact limited by the presence of a related genitive before it, and cannot have separate standing in relation to article-determination. To this extent, though there are two noun-heads, they coalesce into one phrase. Thus, we have *the Queen's uncle* (two-headed phrase) involving a measure of ambiguity which is resolved when two separate phrases are used (*the uncle of the queen, an uncle of the queen*).

§118. Among the preceding adjuncts of the noun-phrase there is a fairly small group of words partially converted from adverbs (cf. §94, 156). They show that they are not fully assimilated to the class of adjectives by their relative intolerance of collocation with other non-determiner adjuncts; where there is such collocation, the 'adverb-adjective' takes the position nearest the head, overriding the adjective positional grouping. Examples are *down, upstairs* in *the down line, the cramped little upstairs flat*. However, such words, if their function is to limit rather than to characterise, follow their heads, as does *upstairs* in *the cramped little flat upstairs, down* in *the train down from London*.

There is also a pattern in which ordinary adjectives follow their head, but in that case the positional classification does not seem to function, and each adjective is followed by a pause and has a separate intonation contour; consider, '*The judge, solemn, upright and stately, entered the silent courtroom*' (a pattern from written, not spoken, English).

Note

Where the adverb-adjective has the same form as a central adjective only the central adjective can occur in predicative, non-attributive position. Contrast '*The line is down*' with '*That is the down line.*'

§119. A noun may also have larger syntactical structures as adjuncts—other phrases or whole clauses preceding, as in '*his man-of-the-world look*' or '*that guess-what-I'm-going-to-say-next expression*'; and prepositional phrases (phrases consisting of preposition [cf. §160]+noun or noun-phrase) following, as in '*men at work*'. A superlative antecedent with its dependent relative clause with noun as head will occur in broken or discontinuous order, the head-word following the antecedent of the adjunct ('*the wildest landscape I have ever seen*').

Note

The noun-phrase may also be interrupted by forms which are not part of its structure (grammatically, and as shown by the superfix), cf. in §102 my expression, "The, in this sense, 'human' gender . . .".

§120. A small marginal class of adjectives has only one of the two characteristic adjective functions, occurring as predicatives, but hardly as attributives. The two items chiefly in question are *well* and *ill*; compare also *alive, abroad*, etc., and cf. §173. We say '*The man is well (ill)*' but not in 'straight' usage *The well (ill) man . . .*'. *Well* represents a coincidence of adjective and adverb functions, since it occurs predicatively not only after linking verbs (a test position for adjectives) but also after non-linking verbs ('*She dances well*') (a test position for adverbs); but it does not extend into the full range of adjective functions. *Ill* is hardly current adverbially in spoken English except in fixed patterns such as *to speak ill of*. For *like*, which is marginal in this and other ways, cf. §115 Note 4.

EXERCISES

'She opened her eyes, and saw how she lay in the twilight dawn on the mossy, leafy floor of a grey stone temple; a temple into which, down the centuries, the forest had flowed, so that trees and shrubs were rooted in its floor, and, thrusting up, had broken through the crevices of its stuccoed roof. The nearest of these trees stretched a bough just over Isie's head; it was laden with small pale-green fruit like apples. It was from this tree that the fluting came, for high on a branch among the fruit a golden bird was trilling a song to the dawn. An oriole, thought Isie, half-asleep. She sat up, and shivered. She was wet through and stiff, swollen with bites, torn by savage plants, lost and alone in the jungle. The night of storm was over; a still, grey dawn lay like evening on the soaked and littered forest. Isie crouched against a carved and lichened wall, while land-crabs scuttled about her with their earthy smell, and little snakes uncurled themselves from the crevices of the walls and wriggled about the floor.' (Rose Macaulay, *Staying with Relations*, Pan Books edition, pp. 87–88.)

1. Make a list of the noun-phrases in this passage and describe the structure of each.

2. Make a list of the adjectives and adjective-like words not in noun-phrases and describe their functions.

3. Do you find any forms which you are not sure whether to include as noun-phrases or as adjectives? Explain the reason for your uncertainty.

CHAPTER IX

Form-Classes (II) The Verb Phrase

I

§121. We turn now to those classes of words which characteristically function in the predicating part of the sentence. We may begin by using for them as a whole the traditional name, **verb**, but later we shall find it necessary to distinguish two major kinds of word within this general class, and our use of the term *verb* will have to be narrowed. Not surprisingly, since their sentence-function is so different, the class-meaning they carry is quite different from the class-meanings we have encountered so far, and the grammatical categories in relation to which their members must be placed are equally distinct. The class-meaning has, as with nouns, traditionally been made a starting-point for defining the class, but (for the same reason as with nouns, cf. §84) we shall depend on other criteria, regarding the class-meaning as a consequence of the total functional peculiarities of the class. All the same, it is of practical use when discussing verbs to have a term for the cumbersome expression 'the kind of meaning verbs have'. There is in ordinary English no single word for this notion, but as many verbs are *action*-words, it is common to refer to their meaning as verbs (not their lexical meaning) as '*the action denoted by them*'. This is a convenient formula, and I shall use it; but in using it one must always remember that 'action' here is a technical term for the class-meaning of verbs—it does not have its ordinary value or imply that every verb names, denotes or expresses an action. As a reminder of this, I use the term between single inverted commas, thus, 'action'.

In fact, the appropriate grammatical categories constitute the best point of departure for making more precise the definition of these classes, continuing the process of identification that began by specifying their characteristic sentence-function. The forms of the verb varied in accordance with these criteria together make up the **conjugation** (i.e., the kind of paradigm verbs have) of the verb. There would be relatively few marginal cases if one defined the verb as a member of the class of words subject to conjugation, in the sense explored below.

§122. The seven grammatical categories in relation to which verb-forms must be placed are as follows:

(a) **Person**, which we have met in a similar technical sense in relation to the pronoun (cf. §97). Indeed, it is a category rather of *concord* between subject-form and verb than one appropriate to a single sentence-component. Its range in modern English is very limited (cf. §123).

(b) **Number.** The sense, once again, is technical, and it is different from the sense of number in relation to nouns, etc. (cf. §84[d]). In verbs, it is a dependent grammatical function, a feature of concord, since it depends on the number of the verb's subject, and not on anything inherent in the verb. Like person, its range in modern English is very limited (cf. §123, 123 Note 2), but the two together form, with position, the principal ways of showing what is the subject of the sentence.

(c) **Mood** is defined by the *OED*. as 'any one of the several groups of forms in the conjugation of a verb which serve to indicate ... whether it expresses a predication, a command, a wish, or the like' (sb.²2).

(d) **Voice** can be defined (adapting the *OED*., sb. 5) as any one of the forms by which the relation of the subject to the 'action' is indicated.

(e) **Tense** (adapted from the *OED*. sb. 2) is any one of the forms in the conjugation of a verb which serve to indicate the different times at which the 'action' *is viewed as happening or existing*. The italics here draw attention to the fact that tenses do not refer directly to 'real', i.e., extra-linguistic, time, but to a speaker's subjective use of distinctions of time drawn (in general, compulsorily drawn) in accordance with the conventions of his language; the language may even use these distinctions for grammatical purposes that have nothing to do with time (for English examples, cf. §126). More strictly, tense-differentiation should not be thought of as a property of the verb acting alone, but as a system signalled by patterns of co-occurrence between verbs and adverbials. Crystal (1966) has shown that in 70% of cases where tense-differentiation is clearly made an adverbial is not merely present, but required; in yet other cases absence of adverbial contrasts with presence of adverbial for the signalling of tense. The same principle holds for the signalling of *aspect* (see below). For a full analysis see Crystal's article.

(f) **Aspect** is any one of the several groups of forms in the conjugation of the verb which serve to indicate the manner in which the 'action' denoted by the verb is considered as being carried out.

(g) Lastly comes a category marginal to the verb as we are defining it, that of **finitude**—marginal in the sense that one of the two terms involved, that of **non-finitude**, characterises forms belonging to the verb conjugationally, but not usually sharing the typical sentence-functions of the verb. *Finitude* is the property of being, or not being, subject to limitation in respect of the two concord-categories of person and number.

Two general observations are necessary before we begin to examine the conjugation of English verbs in the light of these categories. The first is that in actual verb-forms the component grammatical meanings are often not so separable as this analysis might suggest. In particular, tense, mood and aspect are often inextricably entwined, and one's terms may need to take account of this by combining to form tense-aspect, tense-mood, etc. Since the categories represent, for the most part, independent variables it is, however, an advantage to have the terms available for separate use.

The second observation is that the use of *form* and *conjugation* in the sections above begs a lot of questions. Neither must at this stage be thought of as confined within the limits of a single word; the nature of the variations will be examined at length in subsequent paragraphs. The issue is closely bound up with another: while the English verbal system forms a unity in the sense that its components fulfil a common sentence-function, from other points of view it divides into two distinct classes, one open, one closed, with some overlap of membership between them. It is the open class that most simply exemplifies the principle of conjugation described above; with it we can begin, and to its members I should like to restrict the name **verb**. However, as the wider use is so firmly established in current speech, I shall where necessary use the more explicit term **lexical verb** as a reminder of our special sense for the word. As is usual with open-class words, these words have full lexical meaning—that is why our term is appropriate. With one exception (cf. §123, Note 2) each member of the class can have three finite and three non-finite forms, though some of the forms may be undifferentiated. The dictionary form of verbs, without any inflection or other modification, may be called the **base** (cf. §86), and other forms described in terms of their departures from it. It is necessary to distinguish between **simple conjugation**, in which formal variation is confined to the limits of the word, and **complex conjugation**, in which it is not. We shall begin with simple conjugation.

II

§123. The base is used to constitute the first tense-aspect-mood. Though often called **present**, this can best be characterised negatively— it is the form used when there is no positive reason for the use of the past, or the subjunctive, or any complex conjugational form. It is— formally and functionally—the unmarked term in the conjugation; it could well be called the **neutral** or **non-past** of the verb. It is used without formal modification of the base with all persons and numbers of the verb except the third person singular, for which a morpheme is added identical to the basic grammatical morpheme used with nouns, i.e., /s/, /z/, /ɪz/ (cf. §§87, 89), according to the quality of the preceding phoneme—the last sound of the base. This ending is spelt morphemically, with *-s*. Thus we form *I, you, we, they, hit, live, grudge; he, she, it, hits, lives, grudges.*

To avoid the cumbrous expression tense-aspect-mood we can refer to this set of forms as **form-set 1**. Its functions in so far as they can be put positively have been well stated by Henry Sweet (1891–1898, §§2223–2231), as being to imply 'that a statement is of general application, and holds good for all time (*the sun rises in the east*), or that an action or phenomenon is habitual, as in *he gets up at six every morning, I always get it at the same shop*, or recurrent, as in *he goes to Germany twice a year, whenever she sees him she begins to laugh*'. In addition, form-set 1 is used for simple futurity in clauses introduced by *if* (conditional clauses) and *when*, as in:

'*If/when she comes, we can talk it over.*'

Palmer (1965) adds uses in commentary (*and he bowls*) and stage directions (*John enters*). Another use, for which the presence of an adverbial of manner or cause is obligatory, is to deflect attention from the issue of an action's duration (*see how they run, Why do you say that?*); duration is a term in one of the aspectual systems of English, and this use of form-set 1 centres upon aspectual rather than tense-contrast. If this seems an odd rag-bag of meanings for a language to group together as the functions of a single formal indicator, the reason can be found in the nature of the system of verb-contrasts in present-day English. Form-set I is the unmarked term in this network of systems; the other terms, being marked, have more positive, more easily specifiable, more related groups of functions. The unmarked term may, in a given use, be in special contrast with the excluded term of a particular system—it may be specifically non-past, non-modal, non-durative or non-perfective; or, more generally, it may indicate the absence of marking in any of these systems. It does what is left over by the other terms. It is like the centre of a circle, itself one and the same in position, but varying relationally, since it is one terminus of radii, each of which has its other terminus at a different point on the circumference. Its formal simplicity makes it the obvious starting-point for a description of verb-systems, but functionally it is the most complex.

Notes

1. Unless it is stated otherwise, all description of verbal forms refers to their use in positive affirmative sentences.

That special verbal patterns are used in other kinds of sentences has already been mentioned (cf. §67).

2. The exception to the pattern of conjugational variants mentioned in §122 is the verb *be*. Its paradigm is unique in three ways—the finite forms are not inflectionally derived from the base, they are not all inflectional derivatives of the same form, and they make distinctions not made in the conjugation of other verbs, separating in form-set 1 not only the third person singular from all the rest, but also the first person singular from the others, and in form-set 2 the singular from the plural (cf. §124 on form-set 2). Its paradigm thus includes five distinct finite forms (*am, is, are, was, were*). But the peculiarities are not only formal, for this verb, though it does function as a lexical verb, is much more freely used as a closed-system item. A number of other verbal forms—*will, can, may*, etc., are without person-variation, but they function only as closed-system items, and will be described in §§130 ff. Apart from these, the only departures from the regular pattern for the formation of the form-set 1 paradigm are that the third singular of *do, have, say* have change of base as well as the addition of the usual morpheme, producing /dʌz/, /hæz/, /sɛz/; the first two have special forms when unstressed, but when they are unstressed they are usually functioning as closed-system items. The unstressed forms are /dəz/; /həz/, /əz/, /z/, /s/. The verb *need* is generally invariable for the third person when it is a closed-system item, but inflected when not, but the existence of the two paradigms naturally leads to confusion (cf. §131).

3. The functions listed in this paragraph belong to all verbs alike. Certain verbs, however, have other functions for form-set 1:

(a) Verbs of (roughly speaking) seeing and hearing use this form-set perfectively (i.e., to imply 'being in a state resulting from having . . .'), as in:

'*We understand you only arrived yesterday.*' '*I hear you've bought a house.*'

This usage belongs chiefly to conversation and letter-writing, and is only common in the first person, though with *see* the second person is perhaps sometimes perfective, in such expressions as:

'*You see I've brought my music with me.*'

(b) Verbs of communicating use form-set 1 with historic force, as in: *Aristotle tells us . . . Macaulay writes . . .*

In general, this usage belongs to written English, sometimes of a rather pretentious or dated kind.

(c) Verbs of coming and going use this form-set with future reference if an appropriate time-indicating word is present in the sentence:

'*I leave for London tomorrow.*' '*She returns to school tonight.*'

(d) All action-verbs have a true instantaneous present use belonging to situations of demonstrating, as in:

'*I cream the butter and sugar and whisk the eggs. . . .*'

Naturally, this is characteristically a spoken usage.

(e) Verbs denoting states of mind or disposition, and performatory verbs (i.e., verbs of such meaning that using them is carrying out the 'action' they denote, such as *promise*) are comparatively rarely used in their complex present forms, and use form-set 1 for a true instantaneous present, as in:

'*I hate you!*' '*She thinks she can manage the work.*' '*We intend to arrive in time for supper.*' '*I forget what the plan was.*' '*I promise to keep your secret.*'

The complex present forms (and the corresponding past forms) are also very rare for *seem, own, contain*.

(f) Verbs of statement have a reinforcing use of form-set 1:

'*I say that you are wrong*'.

4. The second person singular forms *thou* etc., occurring in certain registers have special concord, with -*(e)st* in the non-past and -*(d)st* in the past.

§124. Contrasted with this form-set in respect of one of its components, namely tense, is **form-set 2**, which we may call **past** (without implying that this useful short label gives an exact picture of its functions). The forms here are more varied and complex to describe, lacking the overall regularity of form-set 1, but in one respect they are simpler, since they show no variation for person or number (except in the verb *be*, cf. §123, Note 2). There are two principal ways in which the contrast with form-set 1 may be achieved. An open class of verbs adds a morpheme realised as /ɪd/ after alveolar stops, /d/ after other voiced sounds, and /t/ after other voiceless sounds. Once again, the identity of function between these three forms is recognised traditionally by the use of a common spelling for the morpheme -*(e)d*, sometimes preceded by doubling of the final consonant of the base. Examples are:

end-ed /ɛndɪd/, *rest-ed* /rɛstɪd/; *call-ed* /kɔːld/, *manage-d* /mænɪdʒd/; *wish-ed* /wɪʃt/, *hop-ped* /hɒpt/.

This type of past-formation is often called **regular**, as is the open-class plural formation of nouns.

§125. The other verbs have widely differing kinds of past-formation. As they form a more or less closed class, they can be listed, and most of them are set out below, classified not according to spelling but according to sound. This great range of divergences is controlled without thinking by the adult native speaker of English, and the forms are set out here not for the information they convey but to bring home how 'irregular' English is in this respect.

(a) Certain verbs whose base ends in the voiced sounds /l/ or /n/ add a past suffix /t/ (instead of the predicted /d/), those in common use being *learn-ed* /lɜːnt/, *dwell-ed* /dwɛlt/, *smell-ed* /smɛlt/, *spell-ed* /spɛlt/,

6+

spoil-ed /spɔɪlt/ (note that -*t* spellings are common in these forms). This is a feature of particular verbs, not a consequence of phonological structure—other verbs ending in the same sounds form their past as predicted with /d/, e.g., *fell, despoil, spurn*—and therefore it cannot be incorporated into our morphophonemic rule (sc. rule for the patterning of phonemes in morphemes) of §124. The analogical pull of the 'regular' type of past formation is strong, and for all the verbs in this section the 'regular' suffix in /d/ is also found.

(b) So far the changes for the past have been consonantal. We turn now to a large group having vocalic changes, and therefore sometimes called **vocalic** verbs. These changes are of many different kinds, especially if we group them according to sound thus:

(i) *bind* /baɪnd/: *bound* /baʊnd/ (cf. *find, grind, wind*).

(ii) *drink* /drɪŋk/: *drank* /dræŋk/ (cf. *shrink, sink, stink, ring, sing, spring, begin, swim, (for-)bid, sit, spit*).

(iii) *win* /wɪn/: *won* /wʌn/ (cf. *spin*).

(iv) *ride* /raɪd/: *rode* /rəʊd/ (cf. *stride, smite, write, (a)rise, drive, strive, thrive*; sometimes *abide*).

(v) *bear* /bɛə/: *bore* /bɔə/ (cf. *swear, tear, wear*).

(vi) *tread* /trɛd/: *trod* /trɒd/ (cf. *(for)get*).

(vii) *bleed* /bliːd/: *bled* /blɛd/ (cf. *breed, feed, lead, read, speed*).

(viii) *cling* /klɪŋ/: *clung* /klʌŋ/ (cf. *fling, sting, string, swing, slink, stick, dig*).

(ix) *steal* /stiːl/: *stole* /stəʊl/ (cf., *speak, weave, freeze*).

(x) *hide* /haɪd/: *hid* /hɪd/ (cf. *bite, light*; sometimes *chide*).

(xi) *shake* /ʃeɪk/: *shook* /ʃʊk/ (cf. *forsake, (mis-) (over-) (par-) (under-) take*).

(xii) *break* /breɪk/: *broke* /brəʊk/ (cf. *stave*; sometimes *(a)wake*, see note below).

(xiii) *blow* /bləʊ/: *blew* /bluː/ (cf. *(out-)grow, (over-)throw*; sometimes *crow*).

(xiv) The remaining verbs may be grouped together, not because they are all alike, but because each represents a unique pattern (counting compounds on the same stem as one). They are:

choose /tʃuːz/: *chose* /tʃəʊz/;

(with-) (over-)draw /drɔː/: *drew* /druː/;

(be-) (over-)come /kʌm/: *came* /keɪm/;

eat /iːt/: *ate* /ɛt/;

(be-)fall /fɔːl/: *fell* /fɛl/;
fly /flaɪ/: *flew* /fluː/;
hang /hæŋ/: *hung* /hʌŋ/;

know /nəʊ/: *knew* /njuː/;

run /rʌn/: *ran* /ræn/;
(out-)shine /ʃaɪn/: *shone* /ʃɒn/;
slay /sleɪ/: *slew* /sluː/;

fight /faɪt/: *fought* /fɔːt/;
(for-)give /ɡɪv/: *gave* /ɡeɪv/;
(be-) (with-)hold /həʊld/: *held* /hɛld/;
lie (='be recumbent') /laɪ/: *lay* /leɪ/;
(fore-)see /siː/: *saw* /sɔː/;
(over-)shoot /ʃuːt/: *shot* /ʃɒt/;
strike /straɪk/: *struck* /strʌk/.

Notes

1. There is some measure of confusion between the four similar verbs *wake, awake, waken, awaken*, which largely coincide in function, though not for all speakers. Though these verbs are blended to some extent in all their forms, the confusion is most marked in the past participle, and accordingly the participle forms are included in the following impression of what is the most general British English usage. It is no more than an impression, and it includes some material from other studies of the verb-group:

Base	Past	Past Participle
awake (entered in the *OED.*, but in my experience hardly used as a present)	*awoke*	*awakened* or *awoken*
(a-)waken	*(a-)wakened* *(a-)woke*	*(a-)wakened* *(a-)woken*
wake	*woke* *(a-)wakened*	*woken* (but the phrasal form with *up*, possible throughout the conjugation of this verb, is particularly favoured in the participle); *(a-)wakened.*

It must be added that this account differs considerably from that set out in the entries for these verbs in the *OED.*; though my account is not based on a statistical survey, it does relate to current usage, whereas the *OED.*'s material is now nearly a century old. I can say positively that I have not heard the past participle *awoke* for *awake* given by *OED*. One would expect change to be rapid where there is so much occasion for confusion, and there is some unreality in trying to keep the four verbs apart at all. In a recent survey, R. Kingdon (who does not claim to have made a count) gives the dominant British usage as *wake, woke, woken* usually compounded with *up* (1951, reprinted 1957).

2. Marginal uses, e.g., *cleave* (='cling') /kliːv/: *clave* /kleɪv/, are excluded from the analysis in this section, whose purpose is to bring home the range of patterns in everyday use.

(c) The third major type may be called **mixed**; it is that in which the past is formed by both addition of alveolar suffix and modification of the base itself. Here we can distinguish three main groups, though in phonemic terms the variety of changes is much greater:

(i) has change of vowel only in the base, with addition of the suffix usually in the form /d/ if the base ends in a vowel and /t/ if it ends in a consonant, as in:

say /seɪ/: *said* /sɛd/;
sell /sɛl/: *sold* /səʊld/ (cf. (*fore-*) *tell*);
(*out-*) (*over-*) (*un-*) (*under-*)*do* /duː/: *did* /dɪd/;
shoe /ʃuː/: *shod* /ʃɒd/.

hear /hɪə/: *heard* /hɜːd/;
creep /kriːp/: *crept* /krɛpt/ (cf. *flee, leap, sleep, sweep, weep, deal, feel, kneel, mean, meet* and usually *dream*).

An exception as regards the form of the suffix is:

buy /baɪ/: *bought* /bɔːt/.

(ii) has change of vowel and change or loss of consonant before the addition of the alveolar suffix, usually realised as /t/:

catch /kætʃ/: *caught* /kɔːt/;
beseech /bɪsiːtʃ/: *besought* /bɪsɔːt/;
bring /brɪŋ/: *brought* /brɔːt/;
lose /luːz/: *lost* /lɒst/;
leave /liːv/: *left* /lɛft/ (cf. (*be-*)*reave*, sometimes *cleave* [='sever']).

teach /tiːtʃ/: *taught* /tɔːt/;
seek /siːk/: *sought* /sɔːt/;
think /θɪŋk/: *thought* /θɔːt/;

A unique type of pairing is (*under-*) (*with-*)*stand* /stænd/: *stood* /stʊd/.

Notes

1. Certain paired forms which I discuss under the heading of **modals**, §§130–133, would belong here if one regarded the pairing as one of non-past and past, but I do not so regard it.
2. In the occasional (largely dialectal) past form *durst* /dɜːst/ paired with *dare* /dɛə/ there is addition of consonant to the base before the addition of the suffix. This past is only used with the intransitive verb, and even there is probably less common nowadays than the invariable past *dare* (cf. (e)); the intransitive verb is to be regarded as marginally modal, cf. §131. The transitive verb always has the 'regular' past *dared* /dɛəd/, which can also occur with the intransitive verb.

(iii) has the vowel unchanged, loss of final consonant from the base, and addition of the consonant suffix in the form /d/:

make /meɪk/: *made* /meɪd/;
have /hæv/: *had* /hæd/.

(d) The fourth major type of verb may be called **unvoicing**; it has a base ending in /d/, which is unvoiced to /t/ in the past form, as in:

build /bɪld/: *built* /bɪlt/ (cf. *bend, lend, rend, send, spend*; sometimes *blend, gild, gird*).

Note

Though it is convenient to identify this class by the phoneme ending its base, it is a grammatical and not a phonemic class, and a closed class. Other verbs ending in the same sound, such as *mend*, do not for that reason belong to it, and new formations entering the language do not join it.

(e) The fifth major type of verb uses the base unchanged as its past form, and may therefore be called **invariable**. Here belong *beat, bet, bid* (at auction), *burst, cast, cost, cut, hit, hurt, let, put, quit, rid, set, shed, shut, split, spread, thrust*; sometimes *dare* (intransitive) (cf. (c) ii, Note 2) and *knit*.

Note

With the exception of *dare* (which is peculiar in a number of ways) all these verbs already end in an alveolar sound such as characterises form-set 2 in regular verbs; Palmer argues that for this reason it would be better to interpret form-set 1 rather than form-set 2 as irregular. However, there is no need to assign the irregularity to either form; the essential feature is the displacement of the regular formal contrast between form-sets 1 and 2.

(f) A few verbs use in the past a different base from that found in the non-past; since they supplement their conjugation in this way they are called **suppletives**. There are in current English only two, the verb *be*, past *was/were* (cf. §123, Note 2), and (*for-*) (*under-*)*go*, past *went* (though *forgo* is almost defective in the past).

Notes

1. A few forms, such as *must, ought*, are usually presented as verbs lacking a past tense; they are here regarded as belonging to the closed class of verbal forms analysed in §130 below, and not at all as parts of a paradigm.
2. Other studies of verb-inflection are found in R. Kingdon (1951, reprinted 1957) and B. Bloch (1947), as well as in the standard English grammars and in most introductions to linguistics.
3. Most of the 'irregular' verbs are monosyllables (or compounds on monosyllabic bases), and very common; and a strikingly high proportion of common verbs are 'irregular'. This is only to be expected, as it is the commonest words that are least subject to analogical grammatical influences—that is, to being made like other words of the same class in their patterning. This feature, is, however, much more highly developed among verbs than among nouns.

§126. It will be clear from §125 that the contrast of non-past and past in English verbs is not unequivocally established by regular difference of form. Most verbs do have a form-set 2 in contrast with form-set 1 (even the invariables have the difference that in the past they do not inflect for the third person singular), but the contrast can take so many shapes that we must look to function as the basis of our sense that it is one contrast. More technically, we look for a difference of distribution, in the kind of setting, co-text or context, where each form-set occurs. The functions of form-set 2 are more positively distinctive than those of form-set 1, and in independent clauses are chiefly the denoting of 'actions' thought of as in the past, as in:

'*Who took my book from the table?*' '*I asked you not to come here.*'

In dependent clauses, however, it is used in the sense of the non-past if the verb of the main clause is in the past, as in:

'*I knew you liked oysters.*'

In conditional clauses it has a value of hypotheticalness, tentativeness, as in:

'*If I went, would you come with me?*'

These functions are not unrelated, though they may seem to be because of our ingrained habit of conceiving form-set contrast in temporal terms. The common feature is non-actuality, which may, but need not be, non-actuality for temporal reasons.

Notes

1. The past is in functional contrast not only with the non-past, but also with form-sets yet to be described. Further distinctions will be described when we come to these form-sets.
2. The element of tentativeness reaches independent clause use with the verb *think* in such expressions as: '*I thought he was a teetotaller*' (='*I still do, but I don't want to press the matter beyond the bounds of civility*').

§127. Contrasted with form-sets 1 and 2 in respect, not of tense, but of mood, is the **subjunctive**. It is usual to give a label to the negative term of this opposition, and call it **indicative**. The formal mark of the subjunctive in the non-past is the absence of inflection for the third person singular (or, one might say, the verb-base is used unchanged in all persons for the non-past subjunctive; or again, that the subjunctive has a special form only in the third person singular—save in the verb *be*, where the base is not used in the indicative). In other words, the subjunctive is formally no more than a vestigial survival in modern English, and, as might be expected in the absence of formal distinctions to carry them, its functions are slight. The only obligatory use of the non-past subjunctive is in certain forward-looking formulaic expressions, mostly of wishes and prayers, so the connection with the present is even more tenuous than in the case of the corresponding indicative form-set. By describing these uses as *formulaic* I mean that they exist as wholes, and do not serve as substitution-frames in the ordinary way of linguistic forms. Examples are:

'(God) bless you!'   'God save the Queen!'   'Long live the King!'
'Woe betide . . .'.   'So be it.'
Forward-referring expressions, not wishes or prayers, are:
'Far be it from me . . .'.   'Come what may.'   'If need be . . .'
In other sentence-patterns the non-past subjunctive is optional. In
clauses where the speaker does not commit himself to the actuality of
what is asserted, it can alternate with the indicative, as in:
If it be true . . .'
and in a dependent clause:
'. . . whether it be true or no.'
This alternation is not altogether free, the use of the subjunctive
belonging to more formal English in such sentences. Where this
function occurs in a sentence-pattern requiring inversion of subject and
verb, the same alternation is not possible; instead, the subjunctive
alternates with a complex form:
'Suffice it to say . . .' or *'Let it suffice to say . . .'*
Here, the stylistic difference is less marked, but the subjunctive is
slightly more formal.

§128. If the non-past subjunctive is little used, and only attains full
conjugation in the verb *be*, the past subjunctive is so much more restricted that it can only exist in that verb. Its forms consist of the past
plural used in all persons of the verb, and it is only the verb *be* that
makes a distinction of singular and plural in its past forms, and so is
capable of having a past subjunctive. That category belongs therefore,
not to the form-class *verb*, but to the single verb *be* in present-day
English. However, the uses of *be* as a closed-system item in forming
units of complex conjugation are so extensive that the restriction is less
than it seems (cf. §§130 ff.). At the moment we are concerned with *be*
as a lexical verb in simple conjugation. The unique past subjunctive
form is *were* (even this is only distinctive in the first and third persons
singular), and it has two principal functions—to express, in dependent clauses, either rejected hypothesis or unfulfilled wish, as in:
'If I were you . . .'   'As if he were a fool . . .'   'I wish I were dead!'
Nowhere is the form obligatory, even in these functions; *was* can always
be substituted, especially in conversation. Those who retain the use of
were have the slight advantage that their expression implies early in the
utterance whether or not they reject the hypothesis they put forward,
contrast:
'If he was there I didn't see him' with
'If he were here, we should have seen him by now.'

But one should guard against the view that it is invariably an advantage to be compelled by one's language-system to make the maximum number of distinctions.

In rather dated formal English, a third option is the use of inversion for hypothesis, as in:

Were he to arrive tomorrow he would still be too late.

With this construction the subjunctive is obligatory.

III

§129. We turn now to the second, and much the largest, section of the conjugation of verbs, that involving forms larger than one word, namely complex conjugation. The words involved in such constructions are always of two distinct kinds: there is a member of the open class of verb-forms, always non-finite, and one or more members of the closed system now to be described. The non-finite parts of English verbs are threefold, the infinitive and imperative consisting simply of the base, the present participle, consisting of the base + suffix *ing* /ɪŋ/ (sometimes with sound-modification at the junction between base and suffix), and the past participle. The formation of this is not so regular. It can be set out as follows:

(a) The great majority of verbs, 'regular' and 'irregular', have past participles identical with their past tense forms.

(b) The following verbs with 'regular' past forms make their past participles with suffixed -(*e*)*n* /(ə)n/, after the base, as in:

hew, saw, sew, strew (all of which also have the 'regular' formation);

or after other forms, as in:

swell /swɛl/ (*swollen* /swəʊlən/).

(c) The following verbs with 'irregular' pasts form their participles in various ways:

(i) from the past plus nasal suffix:

bear, bite, break, choose, (for-)get, freeze, hide, lie (= 'be recumbent'), *speak, steal, swear, tear, tread, wear, weave; chide* in so far as it has past *chid*.

(ii) from the base plus nasal suffix:

(be-)fall, be, beat, (for-)bid, blow, (with-) (over-)draw, eat, (for-)give, forsake, grow, know, shake, (fore-)see, show, slay, (over-)throw, (mis-) (over-) (par-) (under-)take.

(iii) with vowel different from that of base or past, plus nasal suffix:

(*a-*)*rise, drive, ride, smite, stride, strive, thrive, write,* all with pattern:

base /aɪ/; past /əʊ/; participle /ɪ/; *do,* with pattern /uː/; /ɪ/; /ʌ/.

We may add here *go,* with suppletive past and participle in /ɒ/.

(iv) with vowel different from base or past, and no suffix:

begin, drink, ring, shrink, sing, sink, spring, stink, swim, all with pattern /ɪ/; /æ/; /ʌ/.

§130. The closed system of verbal forms consists of the following items: *am, is, are, was, were, be, being, been; have, has, had; do, does, did; will, would, shall, should, can, could, may, might, must.*

These fall into four groups, formally and functionally. The first, the group of *be-*forms, is homophonous with the lexical verb *be* (as in *Who are you? God is love*) and like it is conjugationally unique in English; functionally, it is associated with contrast in the systems of voice and aspect (duration). The second, the group of *have-*forms, is homophonous with the lexical verb *have* (as in *I have a headache*); the structure of its conjugation is normal, though the forms constituting the conjugation are not; functionally, it is associated with the system of aspect (perfective). The third, the *do-*group is homophonous with the lexical verb *do* (as in *I can't think what you will do for a living*); the structure of its conjugation is normal, though the forms constituting the conjugation are not; functionally it is associated with clause-contrasts— with the signalling of negation, interrogation or mood-emphasis. The fourth group consists of nine items linked by their common function as signals of modality in the verb; its members cannot be interpreted as belonging to conjugations, normal or abnormal; eight of them can be arranged in four pairs which are in some respects like form-set 1/form-set 2 pairs, but the formal relationships between members of the pairs are unique, and functionally their likeness to form-set contrast is restricted to their use in dependent clauses. The quasi form-set 1 member of each pair (*will, shall, can, may*) lacks the characteristic contrast of a plain form with an *-s* form for third person singular, and there are no non-finites corresponding to them. The ninth item, *must,* is not even paired with something that might be compared with a form-set 2 partner.

A considerable number of items excluded from the list resembles its members in some, but not all, respects; particularly relevant are *get, need, dare, use(d) to, be (about) to, be going to, want to, ought to.* The
6*

full set of criteria for inclusion in the list of closed system items is as follows:

1. The items do not enter into normal conjugations (though their manner of failing to do so is not homogeneous); in addition to peculiarities already noted they tend to have paired strong-weak forms, as *will*, *'ll*, *has*, *'s*, etc.

2. They have unique modes of patterning in the negative and interrogative, and with lexical verbs in the same verb phrase.

(i) They all negate by addition of the negative particle *not*, while lexical verbs introduce a *do*-form as 'carrier' of the negative particle. Compare *I'm not going, I haven't taken it, I shouldn't if I were you*, with *I don't think so, He didn't want to*. The negative particle is colloquially reduced in form to *n't* and attached enclitically to a form (in many cases, a special form) of the closed-system item. Compare /wɪl/ /waʊnt/; /ʃæl/ /ʃɑːnt/; /kæn/ /kɑːnt/; /mʌst/ /mʌsnt/; /duː/ /dəʊnt/. In other cases the enclitic may be added without further change; the negative of *may* varies in form (/meɪənt/ or /meɪnt/—by some speakers it is avoided altogether, or avoided except in the interrogative). /æm/ has a negative with internal change and added enclitic (/ɑːnt/), which is confined to interrogative use. Reduced forms can occur at only one point in the verb phrase; for many negatives, therefore, there are alternative forms according to the placing of stress and of reduction, cf. *he isn't, he's not*. Just which alternatives are available to a speaker depends on the variety of English he speaks.

The *be-* and *have*-forms preserve the characteristic negative patterning even when they function as lexical verbs, but the usage shows influence from lexical verb patterning. The negative imperative of both requires a *do*-carrier (*don't be silly, don't have anything to do with them*); and *have* quite often in British English (as normally in American English) takes *do* in declarative negatives, giving *he doesn't have any food* beside *he hasn't any food* but never **he doesn't have come* beside *he hasn't come*. An alternative solution to the problem that *have* is subject to two sets of analogies is seen in *he hasn't got any food*; here, instead of adding *do* to indicate that *have*, exceptionally, is in this structure a lexical verb, we add *got* as the lexical verb, restoring *has* to its closed system function. Lexical *do* behaves in the way normal for a lexical verb; we say *he doesn't do anything for his living*, not **he doesn't anything for his living*.

(ii) A similar patterning holds in interrogatives. There is simple inversion of clause-element S and closed system items in interrogatives, as in *am I? will you? had they?* In the absence of such an item the appropriate member of the *do*-set is introduced to 'carry' the inversion, as in *does/doesn't he play the piano?* not **plays/playsn't he the piano?* While *be* even as a lexical verb merely inverts (*aren't you coming?*) *have* varies between the two patterns when it is a lexical verb (*have/haven't they any food?* beside *do/don't they have any food?*); as in negation, the situation is sometimes avoided by using *have got* as the lexical verb. *Do*, as in negation, conforms to the lexical pattern when it is a lexical verb (*do you do anything for your living?*).

(iii) With the closed-system items the contrast between mood-emphasis and lexical emphasis is made by difference of stress-placement, while in lexical verbs a do-form functions as 'carrier' of mood emphasis (*he* **will** *come, I* **am** *looking*, but *he did promise, you do look nice*).

Notice that the three criteria under 2 hold together because they all relate to mood in the clause. We have already seen that there can be contrast between word-emphasis and clause-emphasis; that the same distinction holds for negation can be seen in the case of *must* (*he doesn't have to come* as contrasted with *he mustn't come*).

3. The sequence-rules for closed-system items differ from those for lexical verbs.

(i) They are directly followed by *to*-less infinitives, as in *I do remember, he'll come*, as against *I am trying to remember, he ought to come*; or by other non-finite parts of lexical verbs, as in *he was injured, I've heard that record*.

(ii) They have to be repeated in clause-sequences where for lexical verbs substitution of a *do*-form (which, on the analogy of *pro-noun* could in this function be called a *pro-verb*) is required, as in *I am ready and so is Mary, they can swim and so can John*, as against *I like skating and so do they, he rides well and so do you*. Since the term *proverb* would be ambiguous it is perhaps better to adopt J. R. Firth's term **code** for this kind of patterning. Cf. also §§96, 150, 154, 156.

These formal criteria correspond to a certain likeness of role within the verb phrase, the nature of which will emerge in the course of this chapter.

Note

There are important statements of the multiple criteria for the closed-system items in Palmer (1965) and Svartvik (1966); I am indebted to both, but I have only been able to include a selection of the material they adduce. The full complexity of the multiple classifications involved should be read up in these two works.

§131. Of the forms which more or less resemble those on our closed list, *need* and *dare* are most difficult and most interesting. They pattern to some extent in both the closed system and the lexical verb ways, and even in mixtures of the two. It has recently been shown that for *need*, in negative as well as positive forms, the lexical verb pattern is strongly preferred (*he needs to win, he doesn't need to win*, as against *?he need win* [only common in sequential structures, e.g. *I don't think he need win*], and *he needn't win*). The same is true for *dare* (*he dares to go, he doesn't dare to go* being more common than *he dare(s) go* [more usual in sequence than in isolation] and *he daren't go*). In both verbs one kind of blend is found (*he doesn't need go* and *he doesn't dare go*) but not the reverse kind of blend (**he needn't to go, *he daren't to go*). In the interrogative we have *need he go?* beside *does he need to go?* (less often the blend *does he need go?*). Perhaps unease about this divided usage fosters a preference for *have to* (/hæftʊ/). In the past negative and interrogative are of lexical type. For *dare* we have interrogative *dare he go?* beside *does he dare to go?*; less often, *does he dare go?* Divided usage in the preterite of *dare* is of very high complexity. Almost certainly, difference of preferred use will also be found from person to person in the verb. For investigations of some of these problems, see Quirk and Duckworth in Jensen (1961), Quirk and Svartvik (1966).

§132. The *get*-forms parallel those in the closed system in the nature of their function in the verb phrase, and in their capacity to be directly followed by the non-finite part of a lexical verb (*I got hurt in the crash*); in other respects (normal paradigm, negative-interrogative-emphatic patterning) they are like lexical verbs (*he didn't get hurt, did he?*).

Use(d) to is also marginal, and shows divided usage. It is current only as a past form, and so shares the 'disturbed conjugation' characteristic of the closed-system items. In its sequence patterning it is like lexical verbs (with the condition that *to* might be treated as enclitic to it rather than part of a following infinitive; cf. the assimilation /juːstʊ/). Functionally it is parallel to the modals (*he can, could, may, might, will, would, used to, come*). These divergent affinities have given rise to patterns of negation and interrogation on both models (*used he to come?*; *he usedn't to come*; against *did he use(d) to come?*; *he didn't use(d) to come*).

In both these verbs the distribution has been affected by prescriptive teaching, but in different ways. Teachers have often advised against *get* in any circumstances (as lexical verb or semi closed-system item), even asserting (on what conceivable authority?) that the word does not exist in the English language. With *use(d) to* prescription has taken the form of supporting the *do*-less forms against the forms with *do*. It is my impression (I have not made a survey) that in this case the open-class pattern (with *do*) is, as with *need* and *dare*, most usual, at least in colloquial use and in the speech of the young. Colloquial speech is the principal domain of both verbs.

Ought (to), like *must* and *use(d) to*, lacks non-past/past contrast. It has a compulsory *to* component, which speakers may feel to belong to it rather than to a following infinitive. However, it shares the closed-system type of negative/interrogative patterning (*ought he to? he oughtn't to*). Its affinities with lexical verbs are sufficient to have given rise to the use of *did he ought (to)? he did ought (to)* among some speakers, though these forms are doubtfully standard. Omission of *to* is common with these forms, which shows how the *to* is felt as part of *ought to* when it is not lexical, but as part of the following infinitive when it is.

Ought (to) thus straddles the area between the closed system already identified and another special class, called by Palmer (following Twaddell, 1960) **catenatives**. These are verbs that, without belonging to the list in §130, form a chain-like sequence with a following infinitive, such as *want to, keep + -ing. Have to, be (about) to* also show divided usage between the patterning of catenatives and of closed system items.

§133. It is convenient to have a term less cumbrous than closed-system item for referring to the second kind of verb-like element. A traditional name for them is *auxiliary (verb)*, but this is not really very illuminating. Their function may be summed up as that of carrying the grammatical meaning of the verb-phrase, while the other component carries the lexical meaning; what they do is show what the lexical item is up to in a given sentence. A name given them by the late Professor J. R. Firth suggests this function much more clearly. It is the term **operator**, borrowed from mathematics, that is, a symbol indicating that an operation (multiplication, subtraction, etc.) is to be formed upon a component, an indicator of the processes due. The series of numbers 1 3 5 does not present any total mathematical meaning to us until its members are linked by operators—say, $(1+3) \times 5$; the total value of this we should know, namely twenty. Similarly, the items *it ... give* without linguistic operators convey no clear meaning, but when they are added, the expression is clear:

'*It would give them all pleasure if you accepted.*'

It is clear, however, that though there are overall likenesses, so that we need a term for the closed-system items as a whole, yet they do fall into two distinct groups. The first group—the first fourteen items on the list in §130—form something akin to ordinary conjugations, but the remainder, the last nine items, do not; no non-finite forms correspond to them, and though some of them link to some extent formally in pairs, they do not do so on any of the known principles of past tense formation, and the functional relationship between the paired items is not at all that of non-past and past in lexical verbs; they are all, moreover, invariable for all persons. They are finite in a functional sense, having subjects, but not formally. Functionally, the first group is an 'envelope' class, concerned with indicating clause-type, voice, tense and aspect; the second group has a different and narrower function, which we may summarise as that of indicating mood. Of course, mood is not kept altogether distinct from other categories, especially tense, in English, but the division of function is clear enough for us to label group 2, the non-conjugational items, as **modals**, and the rest as **non-modal operators.** For display of the systems of contrast the *get*-forms are best included with the non-modal operators, though formally, as we have seen, they are somewhat distinct. The two sub-classes have quite different distributions in the verb-phrase. Together these make up an extremely complex system, which we can analyse most clearly if we tackle it bit by bit, starting with the rules for order and the permitted combinations of elements.

§**134.** The permitted components and arrangements of the finite verb-phrase can best be shown diagrammatically. In the following diagram, constructed by Colin Strang, all permitted ways of proceeding from finite operator form to non-finite lexical verb, either directly or via non-finite operators, are shown by connecting lines from left to right; brackets indicate a choice in the manner of proceeding:

Fig. 6

Finite operator form	Non-finite operator form(s)	Non-finite part of lexical verb		
		Base	Past Part.	Pres. Part.
get/gets/got			●	
modal	get			
do/does/did		●		
has/have/had			●	
	got			
modal	have been		●	●
am/is/are/was/were	being/getting		●	
modal	be		●	●

Note that a finite verb-phrase must contain one, and only one, item from column one; one and only one from column three (hence, where two blobs are found terminating lines in sub-sections of column three, they indicate exclusive alternatives); it may contain none, one, two or three from column two, and if there is more than one, the items will occur in the order indicated.

Notes

1. This diagram does not cover the structure of the non-finite verb-phrase, which is not purely verbal. However, all infinitives can be read off from the diagram by putting the particle *to* in modal position and adding use of the base alone; participial phrases cannot be incorporated without confusing the picture—they also require the extra element *having* in column one. Non-finite phrases are described in §§144 ff., and are not so complicated as to need diagrammatic presentation.

2. The passive forms included in this diagram, namely all forms ending in a past participle preceded by any form of *get* or *be*, do not exist for all verbs. They are found in transitive, not intransitive or linking verbs, cf. §§69.

§135. If we remember that in the diagram of §134 the term *modal* stands for about nine different items, it will be apparent that the number of possible constructions covered by this summary runs into hundreds, and clearly the distinctions we can make by exploiting the system are extremely fine. These complicated distinctions, which in speech we make without thinking, are best presented analytically in terms of a small number of binary oppositions of meaning. These oppositions have a characteristic structure of the marked-unmarked term type— always in their functions, and sometimes in their forms. For this reason they can most simply be labelled in terms of a positive characteristic contrasted with its absence (the unmarked term); I have adopted this practice, though where traditional names are available for the negative term I have given them in brackets. The first five of these contrasts operate throughout the range of the conjugation, and are free independent variables. Others have different distributions—they may present one out of several options, or an additional contrast available only in certain ranges of the conjugation.

The contrasts of independent variables are:

1. **non-interrogative (affirmative) ∼ interrogative ;**
2. **non-negative (positive) ∼ negative ;**
3. **non-passive (active) ∼ passive ;**
4. **non-durative ∼ durative ;**
5. **non-perfective ∼ perfective.**

The first two are already familiar. Like them, the third is clausal, but unlike them it operates only if the internal structure of the clause is of certain kinds. It is commonly described in terms of a distinction between S as actor and S as undergoer of the 'action' of the verb at P. Thus, the basic structure of the kind of clause in which the system operates is, for the active:

$S(NP_1) + P(VT) + C(NP_2)$ [+Adverb of Manner] (*John hit Sam [viciously]*);

for the passive:

$S(NP_2) + P(VT, be + past participle)$ [+C/NP_1 as agent] [+Adverb of Manner] (*Sam was [viciously] hit [by Sam]*)

(with probable transposition of the adverb, as shown). As independent variables, these three contrasts yield thirty-two different forms (2^5).

Before we can list these forms, we must examine the two aspectual terms we have introduced, **durative** and **perfective**. The **durative**, as positive term in a contrast, draws attention, where necessary, to the fact that an 'action' is thought of as having (having had or to have) duration or continuingness (hence, there is relatively little use for the durative of verbs whose meaning requires duration, such as *feel*, *think*, cf. §123, Note 3[e]). The **perfective** adds a positive implication of 'being in a state resulting from having . . .'; it indicates that the 'action' is thought of as having consequences in or being temporally continuous with a 'now' or 'then' (past or future). As with other terms to do with verbs, it must be remembered that these are technical labels for a dominant kind of meaning the aspect has; no term, and no paraphrase, can do exactly the job of discrimination that the grammatical contrast itself performs. In this analysis I disregard the variables of person and number already considered under simple conjugation (cf. §123), taking to represent each item the third person singular (masculine). The choice of one person and one lexical verb for the examples throughout may lead to the generating of some unlikely or grotesque forms; but there is no grammatical oddity about these forms, as can readily be seen by changing the person or the verb in any doubtful case. The subject-form has to be included as the relative position of subject and finite forms is a variable significant part of the structure of the phrase. The symbolisation of the analysis depends on including the number, from 1 to 5, of the contrasts as listed above, whenever the positive term of the contrast is a component in a given phrase. Thus, *he is eating* is non-interrogative, non-negative, non-passive, non-perfective, but is durative, and will be symbolised by 4. All forms including the component passive (symbolised 3) are missing from the conjugation of intransitive verbs. A general statement about the forms of passives has been made at §134, Note 2;

duratives consist of operator and present participle; perfectives of operator and past participle.

§136. 0 = *he eats*
    1 = *does he eat?*
    2 = *he doesn't eat*
    3 = *he is eaten*
    4 = *he is eating*
    5 = *he has eaten*
    1,2 = *doesn't he eat?*
    1,3 = *is he eaten?*
    1,4 = *is he eating?*
    1,5 = *has he eaten?*
    2,3 = *he isn't eaten*
    2,4 = *he isn't eating*
    2,5 = *he hasn't eaten*
    3,4 = *he is being eaten*
    3,5 = *he has been eaten*
    4,5 = *he has been eating*
    1,2,3 = *isn't he eaten?*
    1,2,4 = *isn't he eating?*
    1,2,5 = *hasn't he eaten?*
    1,3,4 = *is he being eaten?*
    1,3,5 = *has he been eaten?*
    1,4,5 = *has he been eating?*
    2,3,4 = *he isn't being eaten*
    2,3,5 = *he hasn't been eaten*
    2,4,5 = *he hasn't been eating*
    3,4,5 = *he has been being eaten*
    1,2,3,4 = *isn't he being eaten?*
    1,2,3,5 = *hasn't he been eaten?*
    1,2,4,5 = *hasn't he been eating?*
    1,3,4,5 = *has he been being eaten?*
    2,3,4,5 = *he hasn't been being eaten*
    1,2,3,4,5 = *hasn't he been being eaten?*

§137. Further, over the whole range of phrase-types listed in §136 we may add contrastive meanings of either **tense** or **mood**, but not both together. Tense-contrast is two-way (cf. §124), **non-past** or **past**. The mechanism for expressing pastness in simple conjugation has already been described; in complex conjugation it consists of selecting finite operators *had* in place of *has/have*, *was* in place of *am/is*, *were* in place of *are*. The modal system offers much more than a two-way choice in detail, but is still overall a binary opposition, **non-modal** or

modal. In some ways, modality and tense are so intertwined in English that it would be convenient to combine them as a single variable, but formally this would be difficult, partly because tense-variation is formally mixed, its exponents belonging both to simple and to complex conjugation. The two mutually exclusive components we are now considering should not be regarded as presenting a three-way choice, but a pair of binary choices: *non-past* ~ *past, non-modal* ~ *modal.* We may symbolise them by the figure 6, specifying if necessary *6p* for *past* and *6m* for *modal.* Since 6p can co-occur with all the phrase-structures listed so far, it alone brings our total to 64.

§138. The phrases including the component 6p are:

6p = *he ate*
1,6p = *did he eat?*
2,6p = *he didn't eat*
3,6p = *he was eaten*
4,6p = *he was eating*
5,6p = *he had eaten*
1,2,6p = *didn't he eat?*
1,3,6p = *was he eaten?*
1,4,6p = *was he eating?*
1,5,6p = *had he eaten?*
2,3,6p = *he wasn't eaten*
2,4,6p = *he wasn't eating*
2,5,6p = *he hadn't eaten*
3,4,6p = *he was being eaten*
3,5,6p = *he had been eaten*
4,5,6p = *he had been eating*
1,2,3,6p = *wasn't he eaten?*
1,2,4,6p = *wasn't he eating?*
1,2,5,6p = *hadn't he eaten?*
1,3,4,6p = *was he being eaten?*
1,3,5,6p = *had he been eaten?*
1,4,5,6p = *had he been eating?*
2,3,4,6p = *he wasn't being eaten*
2,3,5,6p = *he hadn't been eaten*
2,4,5,6p = *he hadn't been eating*
3,4,5,6p = *he had been being eaten*
1,2,3,4,6p = *wasn't he being eaten?*
1,2,3,5,6p = *hadn't he been eaten?*
1,2,4,5,6p = *hadn't he been eating?*
1,3,4,5,6p = *had he been being eaten?*
2,3,4,5,6p = *he hadn't been being eaten*
1,2,3,4,5,6p = *hadn't he been being eaten?*

Note

The relationship between active and passive is by no means simple or one-to-one; see the very important study by Svartvik (1966) and his forthcoming paper *A new generation of passives* (Proceedings of the Tenth International Congress of Linguists). On the functions of the other systems of contrast see Palmer (1965).

§**139.** The next variable, **modalisation**, is more complicated, since within its positive term a number of options are available. Nine of these are current throughout the range of phrase-types, adding another 288 constructions, and others have a partial range. Some constructions are marginally possible, so that no final figure for the number of phrase-types can be given, but we can say it is substantially over 350 so far. The following are the nine main modals, with suggested labels and symbols. Once again, readers are warned not to take the labels too narrowly; the functions of some of the modals will be considered in §143.

will (negative *won't*), mood of **determination (d)**;
shall (negative *shan't*), mood of **resolution (r)**;
may (negative usually *may not* rather than *mayn't*), **permissive (pe)**;
might, **concessive (cc)**;
can (negative *can't*), **potential (po)**;
must (the formal negative here, *mustn't*, is not in the ordinary negative
    contrast with this positive; instead there is suppletion from a phrasal
    verb, *have to*, negative *doesn't* [etc.] *have to*), **compulsive (cp)**;
would, **conditional (cd)**;
should, **determinative-conditional (d-c)**;
could, **potential-conditional (p-c)**.

In addition, *need* and intransitive *dare* usually conform to operator (modal) patterning when they are in interrogative, negative or interrogative-negative non-past phrases, though for the most part they do not in positive affirmative phrases, and they never do in past ones (cf. §130).

§**140.** Taking *will* as an example of modalisation, we construct the following thirty-two phrases:

6m (d)=*he will eat*
1,6m=*will he eat?*
2,6m=*he won't eat*
3,6m=*he will be eaten*
4,6m=*he will be eating*
5,6m=*he will have eaten*
1,2,6m=*won't he eat?*

1,3,6m = *will he be eaten?*
1,4,6m = *will he be eating?*
1,5,6m = *will he have eaten?*
2,3,6m = *he won't be eaten*
2,4,6m = *he won't be eating*
2,5,6m = *he won't have eaten*
3,4,6m = *he will be being eaten*
3,5,6m = *he will have been eaten*
4,5,6m = *he will have been eating*
1,2,3,6m = *won't he be eaten?*
1,2,4,6m = *won't he be eating?*
1,2,5,6m = *won't he have eaten?*
1,3,4,6m = *will he be being eaten?*
1,3,5,6m = *will he have been eaten?*
1,4,5,6m = *will he have been eating?*
2,3,4,6m = *he won't be being eaten*
2,3,5,6m = *he won't have been eaten*
2,4,5,6m = *he won't have been eating*
3,4,5,6m = *he will have been being eaten*
1,2,3,4,6m = *won't he be being eaten?*
1,2,3,5,6m = *won't he have been eaten?*
1,2,4,5,6m = *won't he have been eating?*
1,3,4,5,6m = *will he have been being eaten?*
2,3,4,5,6m = *he won't have been being eaten*
1,2,3,4,5,6m = *won't he have been being eaten?*

§141. The next binary opposition is that of **non-emphatic** and **emphatic**. Of course, any part of any utterance may be emphatic or not, and as long as the formal difference consists simply of stress variation, with its phonological consequences, it can be covered by one general rule for the language as a whole. But in one part of the range of verb-phrases it is conveyed in another way, by a special set of lexical elements, and must therefore be included in our list of verb-phrase forms. The widespread presence of operators in the verb-phrase means that generally emphasis can be placed either upon them, or upon the lexical verb, according to whether the grammatical or the lexical import of the verb-phrase is to be given prominence. In phrases where an operator would not otherwise be present, one may be introduced as **emphasis-carrier** in order that this distinction may still be made. The forms used as emphasis-carriers are *do/does/did*. The two phrase-types fitting the case are o and 6p; symbolising the new variable as **E**, we get the following constructions:

E = *he does eat*
6pE = *he did eat*

§142. Another distinction is made in only a limited part of the conjugation. There is an extra contrast of aspect in the passive (3) forms,
marking off a **non-mutative** from a **mutative** type; we may symbolise the new contrasting term as **M.** In a sense, any passive construction implies that a process has taken place, that there has been a
change or mutation from one state to another. But although this
implication is inescapable, the ordinary English passive does not explicitly direct attention to it. There is, however, an extra set of forms,
particularly in informal or spoken English, which does explicitly direct
attention to the change of condition involved, and which, accordingly,
I have labelled **mutatives.** The operators used are *get/gets/getting/got*
(in contrast with *am/is/are/was/were/being/been*). The forms are:

3M = *he gets eaten*
1,3M = *does he get eaten?*
2,3M = *he doesn't get eaten*
3,4M = *he is getting eaten*
3,5M = *he has got eaten*
1,2,3M = *doesn't he get eaten*
1,3,4M = *is he getting eaten?*
1,3,5M = *has he got eaten?*
2,3,4M = *he isn't getting eaten*
2,3,5M = *he hasn't got eaten*
3,4,5M = *he has been getting eaten*
1,2,3,4M = *isn't he getting eaten?*
1,2,3,5M = *hasn't he got eaten?*
1,3,4,5M = *has he been getting eaten?*
2,3,4,5M = *he hasn't been getting eaten*
1,2,3,4,5M = *hasn't he been getting eaten?*

In this list it will be noticed that the mutative forms do not behave
exactly like operators, for they do not form interrogatives by simple
inversion, or negatives by simple addition of particle (cf. 1,3M; 2,3M;
1,2,3M, with *does[n't]*). Bearing this in mind, and referring to the
diagram in §134, we can easily work out the sixteen forms for mutative
past, and sixteen sets of variables for mutative modals. These bring
our types of finite verb-phrase up to more than 550.

§143. The functions of the modals can to some extent be plotted from
the relevant entries in the *OED*, and they have now been surveyed very
fully by Palmer (1965). The following are miscellaneous remarks on
points of special complexity or liability to confusion:

(1) It may seem merely perverse to avoid reference to a future tense
in English. Pure futurity is probably rather rare as a grammatical

category (cf. C. C. Fries, 1925, p. 1022 N. 49 and 1927, pp. 87–95), and there are historical reasons why we should not expect to find it realised in English. Nevertheless, it is clearly true that a dominant element in several of the modals and near-modals listed above is that of futurity. I have already stressed (§122) that in English we do not have pure tenses, pure moods or pure aspects; two or three of these kinds of meaning are always inseparably present in any given verbal form. Certainly it is true that the modals *shall* and *will* have futurity as a dominant element, and this is implied by the (otherwise somewhat arbitrary) choice of names for them, moods of resolution and determination, for you cannot make resolutions or determinations about the past or even the present. But on formal grounds these operators go with modals rather than with tense-operators. Even more important is the consideration that it is only by seeing them in contrast with each other, two forms, either of which can occur in a given grammatical frame, that we can give a proper account of them. For the contrast between them is something that has nothing to do with tense—both are future-referring, with exactly the same kind of time-reference. The contrast lies in the implied attitude to, or ground of expectation of, the future 'action', and that is a contrast of mood (cf. §122 [c]).

(2) Thus, the labels for *shall*, *will* focus on modal rather than tense contrast. I hope the element of arbitrariness in the choice will serve as a reminder that such labels can be at best mnemonic aids; they cannot possibly express the whole range, and nothing but the range, of a modal's functions.

The question how these two forms are distributed is an ancient bone of contention, and until 1925 grammarians were more willing to lay down rules than to enquire what the distribution actually was. In that year, however, the results of a careful enquiry were published by C. C. Fries (loc. cit.). He found that writers differed greatly in what they said was the usage, or ought to be the usage, and that it was difficult to relate any of the conventional doctrines to his findings, which were:

(a) in independent declarative (non-interrogative) sentences:
- 1st per. c70% *will*, c30% *shall*
- 2nd per. c78% *will*, c22% *shall*
- 3rd per. c90% *will*, c10% *shall*

(b) in direct questions:
- 1st per. c5% *will*, c95% *shall*
- 2nd per. c97% *will*, c3% *shall*
- 3rd per. c83% *will*, c17% *shall*

(c) in dependent clauses:
- 1st per. c26% *will*, c74% *shall*
- 2nd per. c96% *will*, c4% *shall*
- 3rd per. c89% *will*, c11% *shall*

These figures are derived from dramatic material published in the years 1902–1918; a survey of the previous 350 years showed that the one respect in which usage had fairly recently undergone striking change was that of the increase of *will* forms for second person in independent declarative sentences. The value of the figures is that they clearly show what nonsense it is to speak of *will* in first person as the equivalent of *shall* in second and third: the kind of yarn most schoolchildren have heard. It is only for direct questions that the figures give clear support for this view. The weakness of the figures is that on so changeable a topic they give us information half a century out of date, and that they do not examine the distribution of the *shall* and *will* forms to discover what are the differences in function once it is established that the differences are not differences of mere conjugation. In fact these differences are too subtle and various to be analysed here; there are important treatments of the question in both Henry Sweet (1891–1898, §§2196–2202), G. O. Curme (1913, pp. 515–539), and the *OED.* entries for the two words, but these were written a whole lifetime ago, and will bring home not only the intricacy of the problem, but the extent of changes in the intervening years. Palmer (1965) is recent, but does not use survey-methods or show the full extent of internal (dialect) borrowing. As could be expected in a century of increased social and geographical mobility, change has been extremely diffused; for instance, I am aware of changes in my own usage in recent years as a result of contact in adult life with northern and Irish speakers, and I have no doubt many readers could say as much. Therefore, only a survey on a scale not yet envisaged could lead to sound generalisations about present-day usages and trends.

One more point should be made on this vexatious subject. The commonest form for these words is that with reduced stress. There is a reduced form *sh'll* /ʃl/ which is unambiguous, but much commoner *'ll* /l/ is not. No doubt historically, and from the viewpoint of theoretical phonology it corresponds to stressed *will* /wɪl/, and this is how grammarians have generally interpreted it (cf. Fries, 1925, p. 989, N. 26), but there is strong grammatical pressure on speakers to relate it rather to *shall*. A very common sentence-pattern in spoken English is that in which a **tag-question** corresponds to the affirmative form of the main clause—'*You would, would you?*' Since there is a range of usage in which affirmative *will* largely corresponds to interrogative *shall* (1st per.), there are many sentences in which affirmative *'ll* is 'tagged' with *shall*—'*I'll do it right away, shall I?*'; this inevitably creates a sense of analogy—*'ll* is to *shall* as *'ld* is to *would*—equating unstressed *'ll* with stressed *shall* and *will*.

In addition to the problems of differentiating between *shall* and *will* in what may be regarded as general grammatical functions, we must note that there are special idiomatic uses, e.g., '*Will I do as your partner?*'

(3) *would* and *should* have extremely divergent uses for which readers should consult the *OED.* under *will* and *shall*, and specialised studies, e.g. Frank Behre (1955).

(4) similarly, though *may* is labelled *permissive* from one of its uses, it has many others, especially implying ability, capacity and possibility (in the sense that it can gloss 'perhaps will'). For a full survey students are referred to the *OED.*

(5) so with *might*, whose uses are listed by *OED.* under *May*, v.[1] It is rash to attempt brief statements on such a subject, but tempting to say that *might* could be summed up as like *may* with the confidence taken out; '*Might I go?*' is a more tentative form of enquiry than '*May I go?*', and '*I might go*' a less committed prediction than '*I may go*'. A striking development of recent years is the occasional use of *may have* (as well as *might have*) as equivalent of *could have*, when it is known that the envisaged outcome did not occur. An example from the *Sunday Sun*, 12 October, 1961, communicated to me by J. C. Maxwell, reads, 'Had a claim been made when the accident occurred, you may well have recovered substantial damages' (p. 3, column 2). The relationship between them (as between *will/would*, *shall/should*) is certainly not, as *OED.* implies, anything to do with tense in present-day English.

(6) the relationship between *can* and *could* (cf. *OED.* under *can* for details of functions) is rather similar. There is still a tense relationship here:

'*I can't stand on my head now, but I could when I was your age*'

but there are pressures favouring a suppletive periphrasis for the past form:

'*I used to be able to.*'

So the dominant one is again a modal relationship, *could* being rather like *can* with the confidence taken out and replaced by doubt or reservation.

IV

§144. The non-finite verb-forms are of four kinds, **infinitives, gerunds, participles, imperatives.** These kinds are identified functionally, and each includes both simple and complex forms.

(A) Infinitives. (i) The plain infinitive has already been described (§129) as consisting of the base or dictionary form of the verb. There is a negative form consisting of the particle *not* followed by the base. It is used as the lexical-verb component of a verb-phrase after operators (including the operator-like imperative element *let*, cf. §149); after the rather operator-like idioms *had ('d) rather/sooner/better, can't but, do(no) more than, do anything(nothing) but*, and sometimes after *do anything(nothing) so [adj.] as*; in the idioms *let fall, let slip, make believe, make do* (here, negation of the second component is not possible); after verb + object when the verb is *feel, hear, have, let, make, see, watch*, and after passive constructions with *let*; also in free variation with the *to*-infinitive after *bid, help, have known*, and as any member but the first of a series of infinitives; occasionally after *listen to* + indirect object in the active voice.

For full examples, see G. Scheurweghs (1959, §§382–387), a work on which section IV of this chapter is heavily dependent.

§145. (A) (ii). The second infinitive is constructed from the particle *to* (/tu:/, /tʊ/, before vowels and /tʊ/, /tə/, before consonants) followed by the base of the verb. This may be regarded as the normal infinitive, in the sense that it is the form used in infinitive position unless there is positive reason for using the plain infinitive (cf. §144) or a passive, perfective or durative infinitive. Infinitive functions are very numerous, and can only be summarised here, as follows:

The infinitive may be subject, object, complement or further nominal or adjectival part of the predicate of a finite verb (*To err is human; I should hate to make a mistake; they hoped to come; it would be a pity to miss them; he is to blame*); and as a complement of longer verbal phrases (e.g., *make up one's mind; swear an oath; have the heart; think/see/ consider fit; know better than; have no alternative but*); it may be the complement to certain adjectives, roughly classifiable as psychological adjectives and adjectives of prediction (e.g., *afraid, ambitious, anxious, apt, privileged, ready, sorry; certain, sure, likely, possible*, and their opposites) it may be the complement or other adjunct of predicate adjectives, or of nouns, pronouns or adjectives in various syntactic relations to it (*it was pleasant to hear; his decision to return; somebody to help him; money to burn; no way to talk to them*); it may be an adverbial adjunct (*who are we to judge?*), especially after *enough, sufficient, sufficiently* + adj., *so* + adj. + *as, such* (+ noun) + *as, as though, as if, so as, in order*, and participles (*hoping to discover, sent to find out*); it may serve in quasi-imperative function as an absolute free adjunct (*the owner to provide unrestricted access; not to worry*); and absolutely, not as an adjunct (*to put it another way*); it may be part of a construction of object and infinitive (*knowing it to be a forgery*); or of passive transforms of such constructions (*the temperature was believed to approach absolute zero*).

For further notes on distribution, cf. §147 Note.

The negation of this infinitive is formed with the particle *not*, usually preceding the whole construction, but also directly before the lexical verb component.

Note

A much more detailed analysis, with abundant examples, can be found in Scheurweghs (1959), §§330–387, which covers all forms of *to*-infinitives.

§146. (A) (iii). Other infinitives, which may have forms with or without *to*, are formed as follows:

(a) present passive, (*to*) *be*+past participle;
(b) perfective, (*to*) *have*+past participle;
(c) perfective passive, (*to*) *have been*+past participle;
(d) present durative, (*to*) *be*+present participle;
(e) present durative passive, (*to*) *be being*+past participle;
(f) perfective durative, (*to*) *have been*+present participle;
(g) perfective durative passive, (*to*) *have been being*+past participle;
(h) mutative passive, (*to*) *get*+past participle;
(i) perfective mutative passive, (*to*) *have got*+past participle;
(j) present durative mutative passive, (*to*) *be getting*+past participle;
(k) perfective durative mutative passive, (*to*) *have been getting*+past participle.

The distribution of forms with and without *to* is like that described for the infinitives in §§144–145. The infinitives can be fitted into the diagram given in §134, cf. Note 1 to that paragraph. They can all, of course, be symbolised according to the code used in §§135 ff., the figures being preceded by **I** for *infinitive*. Intransitive verbs are deficient in all passive infinitives.

Note that English has no future infinitive, though certain operator-like formations can be used in the infinitive for future reference—*be about to, be going to*; the 'normal' infinitive is much less a present than a non-past form, and is much used in forward reference (cf. §§144–145). Negatives for all these constructions are formed with *not*, usually before the whole construction, but also directly preceding the lexical verb component.

Note

On the placing of adverbs in relation to infinitive constructions, see the general remarks in Chapter X, especially §§154 ff. It need, I hope, hardly be said at this date that there is no more reason for preserving unbroken the unity of the *to*-infinitive than there is for refusing to put adverbs anywhere else in the course of verb-phrases. Fussing about split infinitives is one of the more tiresome pastimes invented by nineteenth-century prescriptive grammarians. The question is, in any case, one of usage, not principle, and though much remains to be explored in this matter, one thing that is clear is that in speech the split infinitive is common even among speakers who on principle reject it with horror. The subject has been examined in an unpublished thesis by Winifred Smith, 'A Survey of Writings since 1700 on the Integrity of the Infinitival Phrase in Modern English', which may be consulted (by the author's prior permission) in the library of the University of Durham.

§147. (B) Gerunds. The gerund is formed (generally speaking) from the verb-base with suffix *-ing* /ɪŋ/. Its functions may be summarised as follows:

(i) noun-like, as subject, complement (object or otherwise, absolute or modified by a predicative adjunct) of another verb; following prepositions, and entering into constructions expressing the genitive (*of-*)relation; alone or accompanied by the adjuncts appropriate to nouns (cf. §§106 ff.), and itself serving as a noun-adjunct. Examples are: *seeing is believing; he hates hunting; she found dusting an unmitigated nuisance; the trouble of listening to what is said; the writing of papers; single-minded hankering* [note the linking-*r*] *after luxury; retiring age.*

(ii) verb-like, accompanied by the normal adjuncts of a verb, as in *answering correctly, composing music.*

(iii) dual (having verb-adjuncts but the syntactical functions normal for nouns), as in *resolutely keeping your nose to the grindstone is not enough in this work.*

A passive gerund is formed with *being* followed by past participle, and a mutative with *getting*+past participle; a perfective consists of *having been* (mutative *having got*)+past participle. Their functions parallel those of the 'normal' gerund, but they are not very common. All gerunds are negated by the addition of *not* before the total structure for the positive form.

Note

Both infinitives and gerunds are grammatical forms referable to verb-conjugation, but functioning sometimes like nouns, sometimes like verbs, sometimes with the characteristics of both. As might be expected, the analysis above shows a considerable range of territory common to infinitives and gerunds, but also some that is distinctive for each. We may discriminate cases in which the differences are too slight to formulate (*his chief occupation is sitting and staring/to sit and stare*); those in which both infinitive and gerund are possible, but with substantial differences of meaning (*Just stop thinking what you're doing!/Just stop to think what you're doing!*); those in which an infinitive is possible, but not a gerund (*he decided to go and look for himself*); and those in which a gerund is possible but not an infinitive (*I believe in going straight to the point*). Two principles of distinction must be observed here, the lexical or idiomatic, and the grammatical. By the first, certain lexical items invariably or preferentially 'select' either the infinitive or the gerund to follow them— e.g., with infinitive, *ache, afford, arrange, attempt, contrive, date, decide, deserve, determine, endeavour, expect, fail, hesitate, hope, long, omit, plan, prepare, presume, pretend, proceed, promise, profess, propose, purport, reckon, refuse, resolve, seem, seek, strive, write*; and with gerund, *avoid, complete, delay, enjoy, finish, postpone, prevent, risk*. Though some common threads of meaning may be detected in each group, it is not on the basis of such common meanings that the groups are established, for near-synonymous verbs may pattern differently (*enjoy/like*). Where selection has not been exercised on the lexical principle, it may be exercised grammatically; for instance, the frames *I like . . .* and *I should like . . . if I had time* may both be completed by either *to read* or *reading*, but *I should like . . .* only by *to read*. Other types of grammatical selection have been presented in the separate analysis of functions for the two sets of forms. In those positions where a choice is possible, where two forms are in contrast, a rough generalisation can be made about the nature of the contrast—no more than approximate, because the language is not well equipped to express in paraphrase distinctions which are grammatical in it, but perhaps of some use as a mnemonic if it is used with proper caution. It is that the gerund expresses the abstract notion of the 'action' of the verb, the infinitive presents that notion not abstractly, but as an semantic element of purpose or result is present, but it is not used where such an element would be inappropriate.

It must be emphasised that comparisons between non-finite parts of verbs and other parts of speech concern their sentence-function only, not their morphological grouping; though infinitives and gerunds behave like nouns in the sentence, they do not inflect like them, and though participles behave in varying degree like adjectives (see next paragraph) none of them are subject to comparison, and the past participle has a special secondary modifier(cf. §157) *much*.

§148. (C) **Participles.** English has two participles, commonly called **present** and **past**, whose formation has already been described (cf. §129), as have their many uses in the formation of complex conjugational forms (§§ 130ff.).   Each participle alone is used with quasi-adjectival force; in addition, there is a trio of perfective participles: active, formed from *having*+past participle; passive, formed from *having been*+past participle; and mutative passive, formed from *having got*+past participle; also what we may by analogy call a durative, formed from *being*+past participle. The functions of these forms can be divided into two main types, those in which there is a blend of the verbal and the adjectival producing a form-class different from either (*having led a sheltered life, he was ignorant of such things*) and those in which the adjectival type of patterning predominates, and appropriate modifying words may be used (*he was very interested, minutely exacting*, but not **he was very eaten*) (a third type, represented by patterning of the kind *he was eating intently*, has been presented as a complex, *was* *eating* being one form in the conjugation of the verb, §138). From the point of view of sentence-patterning, we need to distinguish, therefore, between participles and participial adjectives; there is no difference in patterning between participial and other adjectives (except as mentioned in the Note to §147); but the term is in practice useful, especially in describing unexpanded expressions which leave us uncertain whether we are dealing with adjectives or participles (e.g., *he was calculating*—expandable to *he was very calculating* [participial adjective] or *he was busy calculating* [participle or gerund]). The formulation of our doubt in placing such ambivalent expressions brings home clearly the difference of class-meaning that emerges from the characteristic functioning of verbs and adjectives—the former for changing phenomena (participle, *he was busy calculating* [at the time]) the latter for lasting attributes (participial adjective, *he was very calculating* [by nature]). Though in the present we distinguish the two functions only and always in terms of sentence-patterning, in the past there is occasionally internal difference to mark the distinction, cf. the word-pairs *rotted* (participle)/*rotten* (occasionally also *rotted*) (participial adjective); *shrunk/shrunken; drunk/drunken*. These 'special' adjectival forms are not quite assimilated as members of the adjective class—for instance, *shaven* and *drunken* can both be freely used attributively, but not predicatively (except for *shaven* as part of the compound *clean-shaven*).

Though in isolation gerunds and present participles are indistinguishable, in actual utterances they can often be distinguished by the role they play in the sentence, the kind of words they pattern with, and when used attributively, the kind of superfixes they carry. Thus, *dancing feet* (*dancing* = participial adjective) is different in stress, rhythm and intonation from *dancing shoes* (*dancing* = gerund) (cf. §117 Note 1). There remain (as we saw in the example of *busy calculating*) many sentence-patterns in which none of the criteria of distinction are present; in such patterns, no meaning can be assigned to a distinction between participle and gerund, and the form is best labelled non-committally the *-ing-form*.

Participles are negated by the addition of *not* before the construction.

Note

The uses of participles are described by Scheurweghs, 1959, §§256–293, but on a system of analysis very different from that used here.

§149. (D) **Imperatives.** The only true imperative in English is the base of the verb used in address to one or more persons, ordering or instructing them to carry out the 'action' of the verb. It may stand alone, or be accompanied by the normal adjuncts of a verb:

'*Eat!*' '*About turn!*' '*Behave yourself!*' '*You do what you're told!*'

But it is customary and convenient to include under this heading other kinds of hortatory verbal form, constructed with operators. The first, *do* (emphatic)+base, is often addressed to second person; it is a 'coloured', emphatic form, encouraging if the intonation pattern is a drop between level tones, exasperated if there is tone-movement on the last syllable. The second is constructed, in the other persons, with *let*+non-subject form of the personal pronoun+base, and though formally it makes a paradigm, its functions differ according to person, between almost purely hortatory in the first person plural ('*Let's go now!*') and various shades of the permissive and optative in other persons ('*Let me do it for you!*' '*Let him work it out for himself!*' '*Let them come if they want to!*'). It will be clear that these forms do not make up a paradigm in the same way functionally as the forms described in §§130 ff.; formally, too, it would be difficult to fit *let* into a neat scheme of operator-description. In patterning it is marginal as an operator in that it can be followed by the plain infinitive, but negates by the use of *don't* and is followed by an object intervening between it and the lexical verb. The true imperative, like other non-operator forms, also makes its negative by the use of *don't*. There is no interrogative since imperative and interrogative verb-forms mark clause-types which are in systemic contrast with one another.

V

§150. The next point to be made about the verb is in no sense conjugational, but rather on the borders of grammar and lexis. The verb is in English one of the kinds of word in which one member of the class can serve as a generic substitute for any other (cf. §§96, 154, and for a similar structural pattern in terms of sentence-structure rather than form-class, §156). The series *do/does/did/doing/done*, with appropriate operators, can substitute for any full verb already specified in the context; it is thus lexically empty, but serves to carry the grammatical meaning for the verb in its new occurrence, as in:

'*I thought you liked sausages?*'
'*Yes, I did, but I don't now that I've had them three days running.*'

There is thus a limited analogy between this use of the *do*-series and its use as carrier of the negative particle or of interrogative order or of grammatical emphasis (cf. §§68 and 141).

With verb-phrases involving operators, there is no need for this device of substitution, since the operator(s) alone can be the vehicle of grammatical meaning; in such cases, use of the *do*-series is optional, as in:

'*I thought you would have got there by nine?*'
'*Yes, I would have (done), but the traffic delayed me.*'

As in the operator-function of the *do*-series, so here, the existence of an alternative to the full verb-phrase means that in cases where contrastive stress is required, it may, by the selection between the options, be placed on either the distinctive grammatical meaning or the distinctive lexical meaning. In answer to '*I thought you liked sausages*', the expression already quoted is grammatically contrastive, implying '*but I don't now*'; a reply of '*Yes, I do, but that doesn't mean I want to spend all my days eating them*' is lexically contrastive, implying '*but within reason only*'.

VI

§151. We turn now to another plane of analysis, in order to distinguish four different kinds of verb. So far we have considered verbs which, in their base forms, are one-word items. But just as we treat of complex forms in conjugation, so we are compelled by lexical and other evidence to recognise the existence of units, functioning and conjugated as verbs, consisting of two or three words—which may not even always follow one another in unbroken sequence. The lexical consideration is that such combinations may have lexical meaning quite different from that of the components strung together as distinct lexical units. Thus, if we know the meaning of the separate items and the grammatical patterns according to which the elements are combined, we know the meaning of the remark:

'*I came across the fields this evening.*'

But, knowing only these things, we do not know the meaning of:

'*I came across an old friend this evening.*'

The words *come across*, in this use, form an idiom, a unit which has to be learnt as a whole, and cannot be understood by deduction from the meanings of its parts. Once we recognise the existence of more-than-one-word verbs, other considerations show us that we must distinguish three principal types amongst them. One is called the **prepositional verb**, since it consists of an item that on its own functions as a verb, plus an item that on its own functions as a preposition (cf. §160); the second is called a **phrasal verb**, since it consists of an item that can be a verb plus a particle that can be either preposition or adverb (reasons for distinguishing these types will be given below; for adverbs cf.

§§153 ff.); and the third, combining the characteristics of the other two, is called **prepositional-phrasal.**

The three types may be distinguished in terms of the following criteria in addition to the criterion of 'idiomaticness' described above, which differentiates all three from sequences of verb + particle:

(1) the prepositional verb is transitive, and if active must be followed by its object. Examples, with *take to, come across*, are:

'*I took to him at once.*' '*We came across him again only recently.*'

The corresponding collocation of verb + particle may be transitive or intransitive, and if there is an object, it must be interpolated between the verb and the particle:

'*I took it to him*' or '*I took the case to him.*'

In passive constructions, the prepositional verb has the particle in final position, but the verb + particle has it followed by its object:

'*It isn't a thing to be laughed at.*' '*It isn't a thing to be taken to the police.*'

(2) the phrasal verb may be transitive or intransitive. There are four special characteristics:

(a) position of object. A pronominal object must be interpolated between verb-component and particle, a nominal one may have either that of post-particle position, thus:

'*He turned the light (it) off*' or '*He turned off the light*'

(contrast, '*He turned off the road (it)*' but not *'*He turned the road off*').

(b) stress. The particle is normally fully stressed, which it would not generally be as a separate item, thus:

'*He can't be taken in at any price*'

(contrast '*It can't be taken in large doses*'; this is a contrast only for preposition-like components).

(c) intonation. The intonation of the particle is dynamic, though the direction of movement varies according to context; if the particle is a separate item or part of a prepositional verb it is normally, especially if prepositional, spoken on level tone. Thus:

'*He can't be taken in*' (falling tone, 2, with tonic on *in*), but
'*He can't be laughed at*' (tonic on *laughed*).

(d) adverbs (cf. §153). Adverbs cannot be interpolated between the components of a phrasal verb as they can in a sequence of verb + preposition/adverb. Thus:

'*He turned off the road suddenly*'
'*He turned off the light suddenly*'
'*He turned suddenly off the road*'

are all acceptable, while *'*He turned suddenly off the light*' is not.

(3) the prepositional-phrasal verb has two particles in addition to the verb-component, the group being uninterrupted by objects or adverbs, as in:

'*I can't put up with it any longer.*'

Note that the pronoun object in such idioms has a fixed position not otherwise permitted to it.

It is impossible to determine the exact range of these three types of construction, both because they are not sharply delineated, but shade off indefinitely into ordinary verb+particle sequences, and because new formations, and new values for old ones, are constantly coming into existence. Similarly, it is impossible to draw a line between accepted and merely fringe or even nonce usage. These points were made in a study published by A. G. Kennedy in 1920. The author rarely tries to label forms as slang, colloquial or accepted, but the indications and omissions we do find in his work are often strange to British English speakers only forty years later, and give a hint of the rapidity of change in this aspect of the language. But some general statements are possible. Kennedy was able to find over 900 combinations (Preface), the vast majority formed by monosyllabic verbs (p. 29), amongst which twenty were the most productive—*back, blow, break, bring, call, come, fall, get, give, go, hold, lay, let, make, put, run, set, take, turn, work*, entering into 155 combinations with at least 600 fairly distinct uses (p. 35). He analysed formations involving 16 particles, *about, across, (a)round, at, by, down, for, in, off, on, out, over, through, to, up, with* (p. 9), amongst which the most productive by an enormous margin was *up* (nearly 250 combinations, pp. 23–25); some of them have not survived, and some are not British English, but on the other hand the list is not exhaustive for its time and language, covering only 'the most common combinations' (p. 25). Lastly, certain verbs are rarely used without a particle (e.g., *clutter up, peter out*—about three dozen in all, p. 29), and some have intransitive uses only in such combinations (*calm down, keep in, light up*, etc., loc. cit.). In using Kennedy's figures one must remember not only that he presents them very tentatively, but also that they represent the whole spectrum of what he calls 'combinations', from verb+particle as separate items through all the gradations up to the prepositional-phrasal verb.

Note

The separation of prepositional and phrasal verbs from verb+particle

7+

sequences is now a commonplace. The distinction of the three types of verbs is due to T. F. Mitchell (1958, especially pp. 103–106). To this article the examples and criteria of distinction listed above are due. Mitchell sets up a system of particles for the phrasal verb including *up, down, in, out, off, on, to,*—a closed system that could be catalogued exhaustively. Productive verbs of the pattern are *bring, come, get, go, keep, run, put, take, turn, set, send, fall, stand, look,* among others forming an open class, which could not, of course, be catalogued. The productive particles for prepositional verbs are those listed by Kennedy.

Mitchell's criteria for the phrasal verb include no mention of rhythm. Clearly the examples with *taken in* differ as much in rhythm as in stress and intonation, and I should prefer to speak of a complex of related differences (a superfix) part stress, part rhythm, part intonation; but so little is agreed about the analysis or notation of rhythmical patterns in English that this aspect of structure cannot yet be given its proper place in description.

EXERCISES

Write out each of the verb-phrases in the following piece of dialogue, describing the structure and, for finite verbs, giving a number identification by the code explained in §§135 ff.:

'But what've you been doing all this time?'
'It isn't what I've been doing so much as what's been being done to me.'
'Well, if things weren't going well for you, why couldn't you have come to see me about it?'
'You don't have to be told everything about me, even if you do think you're the only one who can keep my life in order.'

CHAPTER X

Form-Classes (III)

§152. The classes considered in this chapter are those not primarily or exclusively functioning in either the noun- or the verb-phrase. They are rather a mixed bag, but that at least they have in common, and there are other family resemblances, though there is no criterion applicable to all. They are more often closed systems than open classes and they tend to be invariables. There are two main kinds, those fully incorporated into the structure of clauses and those not so incorporated. We shall begin with those that are incorporated, and among them again we find two main kinds, which can be roughly labelled as adjunct-words and relationship words; we shall begin with the adjunct-words, taking first those that are adjuncts to the verb. Such forms, patently, could be discussed at least as properly in Chapter IX as here; but there are practical and structural reasons for putting them in this chapter. The practical one is that Chapter IX is already somewhat distended; the structural one, that there is a continuous spectrum of classes from those functioning as adjuncts to verbs to a host of other kinds of adjuncts—the verb-adjuncts are at one end of the spectrum and should be seen in relation to it as a whole. But in effect, we are beginning with material marginal between this chapter and the last.

It is especially in the form-classes treated in this chapter that the inadequacy of the word as basis for determining form-classes is felt. A number of the items treated are of more than word-length—not only in the minor sense of word(W) but also in the important sense that in speech their component parts may function as distinct words (without change of stress and intonation). Yet in the senses we are examining, they function as wholes, as idioms, and since they function as terms in closed systems they must be placed in the form-classes constituted by those closed systems.

§153. The clearest criterion for taking a word to be a verb-adjunct is that it should be a form (other than a noun-like one) capable of filling the third (and only) post-verbal position in the structure S P (realised by verb of type VI) X (where X is stressed). The class so defined has,

as we shall see, a certain coherence; it is contrasted with the class
occurring in similar position after verbs of type *be, become* (cf. §§115,
120), and with unstressed elements in the same position (cf. §§151,
160) though mostly such elements require that the sentence should not
end at the third position.   But although the class has a certain coherence, it is by no means uniform.   Some of the members are variables, most are not; some of the members are confined to this position
and function, most are not; if more than one adjunct functions with
a single head they fall into positional sub-classes; and the various
differences do not much coincide, so that it is impossible to make a
really neat presentation.   We may follow tradition in applying to the
class of verb-adjuncts as a whole the term **adverb**.   When we come to
make distinctions within the general class of adverbs it will be useful to
think in terms of a spectrum of functions rather than a spectrum of
form-classes, and that is a situation we shall be meeting throughout this
chapter.
    Using our test-frame to establish adverbs, we distinguish first a
sub-class of what we may call pure adverbs, that is, words especially
distinctive of the class because they do not have any other function but
as adverbs.   Such are *here, now, there, often, seldom, perhaps, still, once,
twice, always,* in such a frame as '*I came/am coming . . .*'; these words
are not confined to this position, but to what may roughly be called
adverbial functions.   Also fitting here, but less distinctive since they
also function non-adverbially, are words like *yesterday, downstairs,
home, last, first,* and the ordinal numerals; and words like *up, through,
along, down,* which also function as prepositions (cf. §160).   There are
also words in this position which also function as adjectives, such as
cheap, hard, well; but these bring us up against another consideration.
For the adverbs considered hitherto have all been **invariables**.   But
there is a smallish class of **variables** and its membership is similar to
(not identical with) that of the class of dual function (adjective and
adverb) words.   The variation is for **comparison**, and the terms are, as
with adjectives, **positive, comparative, superlative**; the distribution
is similar to that of the three terms in adjectives—there are situations
where any of the terms may be used, and only referential considerations
will tell us which belongs in a given frame, and there are *than*-con-
structions which require a comparative, and *of-all*-constructions which
require a superlative.   Examples are:

It sells cheapest/washes whitest of all detergents'
'*He flew lower than the regulations permit*'.

The forms in general are as for the comparable adjectives; the suppletives are similar too, except that the adverbial positive term in the series
worse, worst is usually *badly*/bædlɪ/.   As well as these two-function

forms, *often* and *soon* have comparison in the usual forms; *often* can also have the analytic form of quasi-comparison (cf. §115 Note 1) with particles *more, most,* and so can *seldom,* but generally speaking the other 'central' adverbs (pure and otherwise) cannot (not **more yesterday,* **most there,* etc.).

But mention of *badly* a few lines back has brought us to another topic. There is a sub-class of adverbs that can be described in terms of its morphological structure, as consisting of an adjective base (normally of the central, placed adjective kind) followed by suffix *-ly* /-lɪ/; the ordinal numerals can also form adverbs in this way. Not all adjectives give rise to adverbs of this form; those terminating in *-ly* do not at all (*goodly, homely, lowly*) or do reluctantly (*lovely, lively*); nor do adjectives of size, and colour-adjectives only marginally; adjectives in *-ic* (except *public*) form adverbs in *-ally* /-(ə)lɪ/ instead of *-ly*; and some adverbs are identical with adjectives, as we have already mentioned (but some of these may also form *-ly* adverbs too—cf. *hardly,* though that is only used in a kind of adverb-functioning we have not yet examined, cf. §155). Generally, the *-ly* adverbs are different in patterning as well as internal structure in being subject to comparison—normally, the quasi-comparison with preceding particles *more* and *most,* but for a few adverbs suppletive inflectional forms from the adjective may be used. Thus, the three terms for *slow* may be illustrated:

John ran slowly

John ran more slowly   *John ran slower*

John ran most slowly   *John ran slowest.*

Without having done a frequency survey, I believe that in the comparative the analytical form is preferred, in the superlative, the inflectional. Adverbs which function only in the way that *hardly* does are not subject to any form of comparison. Because of the link in class-meaning between adverbs which compare and those which pattern with the adjuncts *more, most,* these adjuncts have been brought into the discussion at this stage. But in general terms they are like other adjuncts-of-adjuncts that will be described systematically in §157.

Lastly, on this classification, we come to a sub-class like the first we described, but morphologically different, and the most limited of all in patterning. These are derivatives, formed from (a) prefix *a-* /ə/+a closed class of noun bases (*adrift, astir, abroad,* etc.); (b) suffix *-wards* /-wəːdz/ after a closed class of bases (*forwards, homewards,* etc.; the form with *-ward* is sometimes used, but in British English is mostly adjectival); (c) one of the determiners *some-, any-, every-, no-* with a closed class of bases (*somehow, anyway, everywhere, nowhere*); (d) (well established in American English, and after a long period of eclipse now returning to British English) noun base+suffix *-wise*, as in *publicity-wise, campaign-wise*, forms which function chiefly in the kind of adverbial use described in §156. These do not compare, and do not pattern with *more, most*.

In the present dimension, we have established four sub-classes: the first consisting of the most central adverbs, pure or functioning in other ways; the second of central variables; the third of de-adjectival adverbs, and the fourth of other derivatives; but since these divisions are partly linked with others, the distinctions are not too clear-cut.

Notes

1. The test-frame we have taken is a minimum one; if a complement is present it usually stands between verb-phrase and adverb.
2. One very important verb-adjunct, more closely integrated into the structure of the verb-phrase than those examined in this chapter, is *not*, cf. §130.
3. The very complicated subject of the adverb has been treated by all the major grammarians of English, from many of whom I have tried to learn. In this respect I draw particularly on the work of W. N. Francis (1958), pp. 281–290, and H. E. Palmer (1928), §§351–389 (especially for my §150). Jespersen (1909–1949), Vol. II, Ch. 1, 13–15, 22, and Sweet (1891–1898), §§336–377 are also of great importance.
4. Since key features in the identification of adverbs are position and function it is useful to have a term which shows the relationship between adverbs and larger structures which share adverbial position and function. There is, for instance, something important in common between the occupants of column III in the following examples:

I	II	III
She	came	*yesterday*
She	came	*on the hour*
She	rode	*beautifully*
She	rode	*on a white horse*
She	stood	*there*
She	stood	*at the corner*

The larger structures can be called **adverbials**. This term indicates their function in a larger structure, but leaves us free to describe their internal structure as we think best (in the examples cited, they are prepositional phrases).

§154. The classification of adverbs given in §153 cuts right across another. Adverbs, like adjectives, may occur in clusters with a single head, and then the ordering of them is not a matter of individual discretion, but follows fixed conventions. Hence arise three positional sub-classes, which we may number 1 (nearest the head), 2 and 3. These sub-classes are another of the kinds of word to have a generic substitute (cf. §96) approximately corresponding to the range of words in them; in position 3 adverbs having as generic substitute *thus* or *so* (also called, from their type of lexical meaning, adverbs of manner) tend to occur, in position 2 those having as generic substitute *then* (adverbs of time) tend to occur, in position 1 those having as generic substitute *there* (adverbs of place) tend to occur. Typical patterns are:

Subject	Verb	*Adjuncts*		
		there-group	*then-group*	*thus/so-group*
		⌈ outside	to-day	easily
I	may go ⟨ past	early	regularly
		⌊ indoors	sometimes	foolishly

The generic substitutes do not cover every case (for instance, *then* cannot substitute for *now*, which is positionally like it, nor *there* for *here*) and in that way the traditional names are superior; but in using them we must remember that the classes are defined formally and not from their kind of meaning-content.

As soon as we try to construct examples of the three positions we find a difficulty; a few sentences read naturally with the three occupied, but generally it seems more natural to dislodge the manner-adverb and advance it to a position before the verb:

'*I easily went outside to-day*';
'*I regularly went past early*';
'*I foolishly went indoors sometimes.*'

This is not to say that the three classes are artificial, for 1 precedes 2 and 2 precedes 3; only that they do not so commonly occur together in a cluster. But there are exceptions—for instance, it may be a different one of the three that is advanced ('*She sometimes stays resolutely indoors*'), especially if contrasted types of adverb-function are involved, cf. §155; and there are some adverbs that do not fit the scheme at all (e.g., *instead, perhaps, again*). It should hardly need mentioning at this stage that the adverb-conventions may be overridden if adverb-like forms are functioning in phrasal verbs (cf. §151). There is, too, still much to be discovered about the matter. At any rate, we can say that some sort of positional classification is built into our use of many adverbs. More than one word from a given group may occur in a single cluster; the items must then all occur in the same sentence-position and will be separated by *and*, or, if they are more than two, by pauses until the last two, which will often, not invariably, be separated by *and*, e.g.:

'*She looked up and down quickly and suspiciously*';
'*She looked up and down, quickly, furtively (and) suspiciously.*'

In such patterns, each adverb has a fresh intonation contour.

Note

The positional classification given above does not agree with that given for American English by Francis (1958), p. 288; his observations do not hold for my own speech, and I must assume there is an Anglo-American difference of usage here. But the positional groupings as so far analysed are in any case not exhaustive, cf. *He reeled drunkenly upstairs to-day.* Jacobson (1964) is an important study which shows the complexity of the conventions for adverb placement in English.

§155. We examine now the functioning of adverbs in positions other than that we have adopted in our test-frame. Here again there is much ignorance, and no doubt the few generalisations we seem able to make will need revision as knowledge advances. What does seem clear is that adverbs, being adjuncts, have the function of modifying, and that their position depends in many cases on the nature of the modification. There are cases where the placing in one of two positions appears to be merely a matter of stylistic preference, as we have seen in §154; but we are now concerned with those where choice between positions is significant. In such cases, H. E. Palmer distinguishes between the functions of modifying as **epithet** and modifying as **complement.** When an adverb functions as an epithet its value may be roughly described as adding intensity, but nothing more specific, to the utterance as a whole; it occurs early in the sentence, before the verb, or even before the subject. Some forms have only this function, and so are not central adverbs in our sense; but many have it along with what we have called the central adverb function; others again never have it. Those confined to it include *just, hardly* (e.g., '*I just wanted to borrow a cupful of flour*'; '*I hardly knocked it at all*'). Examples of the two functions for those that can have both are:

'*I naturally wanted him to answer*'; '*I wanted him to answer naturally*'; '*She stupidly mistook the time*'; '*She mistook the time stupidly*' (and cf. pre-verb *foolishly* in the example in §153).

The second of each pair of examples illustrates the complement use, in effect, the use we have been concerned with in previous paragraphs. By contrast with the now-distinguished epithet use, we can see that it carries fuller lexical meaning and is given greater prominence in the utterance; positionally it is post-verbal unless the pressure of fellow-adverbs pushes it forward (cf. §154). We have agreed not to class forms as central adverbs unless they have this function, but we must note here some that are confined to this function, e.g., *daily, out, intentionally, after, below, differently*; but not all, even of these, are confined to post-verbal position.

Notes

1. A full catalogue of adverbs classified according to manner of modifica-

tion and other criteria is given in Palmer (1928) §§387–388; he does, however, include under adverbs words I have placed elsewhere (e.g., as interrogatives, §103).
2. Like an epithet in function, but exceptionally limited in collocational range and pre- or post-verbal in position, is *needs*, e.g., '*She needs must/must needs go and let the cat out of the bag*'.

§156. The next complication about adverbs is that not only do they modify in the two different ways we have noted, but many of them also modify quite different kinds of linguistic structure from those we have encountered so far as heads. In the first place, they modify whole sentences, examples being *naturally, actually*, in such sentences as '*Naturally, they hoped to travel together*' and '*Actually, it's the very last thing I wanted to do*' (contrast the epithet use in '*They naturally hoped to travel together*'; complement, '*They wanted to live naturally*'). Sentence-modifying adverbs usually stand at the beginning or the end of sentences, bearing a separate intonation contour; cf. sentence-modifying *naturally* in '*They wanted to live, naturally*'. The class of central adverbs functioning in this way is fairly small, but in this function they are indistinguishable from a rather larger class having this function without the central adverbial one; such words may be called **sentence-modifiers**, and include *perhaps, probably, certainly, however*, occurring (in this function) either at the beginning or the end of sentences, usually, not necessarily, with a separate intonation contour. These again share a function, that of substituting for a sentence, with another small group, *yes, no*, often called **sentence-substitutes** since this is their primary function; along with them we may mention the **clause-substitute** *so* (as in '*Did he promise to come? Yes, I thought so*'). In this way we have followed through yet another spectrum having the adverb at one terminal, but quite other form-classes at the other.

Now we must return to our base, to consider what other forms can be modified by adverbs. Some, especially central adverbs without other functions but these, modify nouns (cf. §118), preceding or following their heads, and tending towards being adjectives; they retain more of their adverbial character if they follow the noun; cf. *the back door, the way back; the down line, the journey down; the upstairs flat, the flat upstairs*. In this class too there are marginal cases, forms which are adjuncts to nouns but not to verbs—or perhaps are epithets but not complements. Functioning in relation to nouns, they follow their head, but in other functions they precede; examples are *especially, particularly*, cf.

'*John,* $\left\{\begin{array}{l}\textit{especially,} \\ \textit{particularly,}\end{array}\right.$ *hated the elaborate rituals*' (i.e., hated them more than others did)

'*John* $\left\{\begin{array}{l}\textit{particularly} \\ \textit{especially}\end{array}\right.$ *hated the elaborate rituals*' (i.e., more than he hated other things)

7*

Others again have fixed position before the structure they modify, such as *quite, rather*, as in *quite/rather a lot of people, I quite/rather like oysters*. Following a composite noun-head *alike* is partly like an adjective, partly like an adverb ('*Young and old alike suffered from his extortions*'); with some predicatives it seems pointless to maintain the distinction between adjective and adverb (cf. *asleep* in '*He was asleep*', '*He fell asleep*'; *here* in '*He is here*', '*Come here!*'). The important thing is to have a clear notion of the central functions of each form-class involved so that we know which principles are called upon in any placing of borderline forms; how we actually classify or even whether we do classify, is secondary to this.

Also operating in relation to whole sentences are the **civility-formulas**, *kindly* and *please*, most commonly at the outset of sentences, but found also elsewhere; *please* especially favours that position, and declines in civility when it leaves it (though there are supporting differences of superfix too); *kindly* favours post finite-verb position, and also loses in civility (such civility as it has) if displaced. Though their inherent functions are similar, they differ in patterning, since *please* cannot be modified, and *kindly* patterns with the modifier *very* (cf. §157).

We have distinguished four principal positions for adverbs and adverb-like words. Our test-position was post-verbal, and to it we may now add sentence-initiating (usually pre-subject), pre-verbal and sentence-closing (which in an expanded sentence may be different from post-verbal). We have seen that some adverbs favour a certain position or positions, others range more freely. What remains is to say that for most forms these positions are not compulsory; there are inherent placings which may be altered for special effect. Displacement, especially forward-displacement, usually adds to the prominence of an adverb, cf. '*He might well apologise*' and '*Well he might apologise*'.

Notes

1. Other borderline forms are 'apparent' adjectives in adverb position in idioms, e.g., *clean, natural*, in *come clean, come natural*. Form-class analysis is of limited application to idioms.
2. Predicatively *quite, rather*, in secondary modification (cf. §157) function only in positive constructions (*very* corresponds in negative ones), cf. '*I can manage quite/rather well*'; '*I can't manage very well.*'
3. Somewhat adverb-like are forms above the level of the word used in adjective-modification, e.g., *lovely and, nice and*; somewhat similar in relation to verbs is *try and* (marginal between operator and adverb).

§157. There remains another spectrum of modifying functions in the adverb, which I shall call **regressive modification**. So far we have considered the modification of words which are heads and the modification of larger structures; but adverbs, and a range of words linked to them by family resemblances, also modify adjuncts and even adjuncts of adjuncts. Since different forms can fulfil the different functions, it is worth distinguishing **secondary, tertiary**, etc., modification, but for the phenomenon as a whole the term regressive modification is useful. Examples of adverbs in our central sense which also modify secondarily are *unexpectedly, definitely, faintly*. Contrast:

'*She arrived unexpectedly*' (complement, primary): '*She was unexpectedly beautiful*' (modifier of adjective, secondary): '*. . . and danced unexpectedly well*' (modifier of adverb, secondary);
'*I can't tell you definitely*' (complement, primary): '*You are definitely disqualified*' (modifier of adjective-like form, secondary);
'*The voice echoed faintly through the caves*' (primary): '*I felt faintly uneasy about it*' (secondary).

There are forms fulfilling this function without the central one of adverbs; *extremely* is a marginal case, since it is used in such patterns as '*I liked her extremely*' but is not common as a central adverb, and is very common as a secondary modifier; so are *awfully, terribly*. The form which only has regressive modifying functions is *very*; *more, most, too, nearly, rather, much, really, so, such, just*, etc., belong to this closed system, but also function in other ways. For sequences in which the full extent of the possible regression in modification is realised cf. *very much too much, very much more nearly*, to be completed by an adjective-like or adverb-like form. *Much, any*, function secondarily only with comparatives and crop up again in tertiary modification. From the kind of function they have in relation to their heads, regressive modifiers are sometimes called *intensifiers*. This is a good name in so far as they are a separate form-class, but it obscures their functional continuity with central adverbs. One of them, *enough*, though it ordinarily functions after the verb ('*Hasn't she done enough?*') or adjective-like before a noun ('*enough harm*'), has post-position in secondary modification, following an adjective or adverb it modifies ('*not good enough*', '*not quickly enough*'). Otherwise secondary modifiers precede their heads. A more limited secondary modifier is *right*, collocating with certain adverbs and also with certain prepositions, as in '*Come right in!*', '*He came right in(to) the house*', '*She went right there*'; and with prepositional phrases '*right up to the door*'. Certain tertiaries can best be described in terms of correlative pairs, *far* + comparative (inflectional or analytic) + *still/yet/than*; (*very*) *much* + comparative (inflectional or analytic) + *than*; *even* + comparative (inflectional or analytic) + *than*. Examples are:

'*You could do it far more neatly still if you practised regularly*';
'*Susanna was always very much more elegant than Jane*' (or '*even more charming than . . .*').

Expressions above the length of the word that can conveniently be classified here are *a lot, a little (bit), a (good) bit*; in a sense, post-positional *of all* in superlative constructions could be included too. A correlative pair functioning with positive forms is

as $\left\{ \begin{array}{l} \text{positive adjective} \\ \text{positive adverb} \end{array} \right\}$ *as* $\left\{ \begin{array}{l} \textit{possible} \\ \textit{I}, \text{ etc., (possibly) } \textit{can/could} \end{array} \right.$

Another limited-collocation secondary is *about* as **numeral modifier**, as in '*I'm expecting about eleven people to coffee*', '*Come at about eight*'.

The forms *once, twice* (*thrice* for those who use it), which are central adverbs with group 2 position ('*I have been there twice already*'), also have subject-function and so are a little noun-like ('*Once is enough . . .*'); they are secondaries in participial compounds (i.e., morphemically, but not at the rank of the word) as in *twice-brewed* (cf. also *half* in *half-baked*).

One modifying function is performed uniquely by *even*, which otherwise functions as central adjective ('*on even dates*'), namely the intensification of a following term which may be head of a noun- or verb-phrase, adverbial phrase or whole clause; cf. '*Even John didn't know*'; '*He even signed for it*'; '*I haven't heard even now*'; '*They didn't turn up even on that occasion*'; '*Even if you were free to help me I couldn't manage*'. It also patterns with the clause-substitute *so* (§156), as in: '*Even so they should be here by now.*'

§158. Although we have been considering our central type of adverb as a point of reference, and tracing related kinds of forms as they diverged from it as radii might from a centre, in reality the position is more complicated. For there is a great deal of overlapping and criss-crossing quite independently of the centrifugal lines we have followed. A form that does not modify a verb may modify both sentences and adjectives, cf. *perhaps* in '*Perhaps they will be in time to ask you themselves*' and in '*His insistence on consultation, perhaps irritating* (or *irritating perhaps*) *at the time . . .*' And some words have all these different modifying functions, cf. *partly, practically*, and the following sentences with *only*, taken from the *OED.*'s quotations:

'*I have been only twice*'; '*that belongs only to the judges*'; '*attachments of which only a mother or a nurse is thought capable*'; '*only one*'; '*only he*'; '*only this*'; '*only beneath*'; '*that which is right only because it is established*'; '*I have not laboured for myself only*'; '*with two buckets only*'; '*what belongs to Nature only, Nature only can complete*'; '*in one only of the casements*'; '*not benevolence only*'.

Reading through these examples, we may be reminded of the situation Randolph Quirk discovered in his analysis of the relative pronoun (cf. §102), that constructions used in literature and even accepted in a substitution-test are not necessarily what speakers spontaneously pro-duce; all the patterns quoted above have, evidently, been used, but not all are equally favoured, especially in speech. On the other hand, a pattern that is greatly favoured in speech is the epithet use of *only*, in which it is placed before the verb, as in '*I only asked the question from politeness*'; the editors of *OED*. consider this acceptable in speech though it 'is now avoided by perspicuous writers'; yet the example they quote is from so distinguished a contemporary (of their own) as Jowett, and could not possibly give rise to misunderstanding. Since that time there has been increasing condemnation of the use even in speech—an utterly pointless bit of pedantry, since no objection is raised to epithet-use in general.

Distinct uses of *only* from those so far listed are exemplified in:

'*Only think how long it is . . .*'; '*If only they could obtain the help of such a force . . .*'; '*If you will only wait . . .*'; '*If I could only give you one half of the stories . . .*'

In its sentence-modifying function *only* is akin to a conjunction (and is often so classified); cf. '*Only will there be room for us all?*', and the opening of §161 Note.

Note

This is perhaps the aptest place for the classification of swear-words. Standing alone, they are like adverbial sentence-words (cf. §156) or like interjections (cf. §163); their superfixes favour rather the second inter-pretation. However, when they occur within syntactic structures they function like pre-posed adverbs, as adjuncts to nouns, adjectives, verbs, and as secondary modifiers.

§159. From our survey of the adverb it has emerged that there is a central type, with marginal types so divergent that at one point or another they impinge on the borders of the noun, pronoun, relative, interrogative, adjective, preposition, conjunction, interjection and sentence-substitute; on everything, in fact, except the verb (cf. below Note 2). The reader is bound to ask whether there is any sense in isolating a class which is so little distinguishable from the rest. A positive answer should already have emerged: the central function is distinct, but it is linked to all the marginal functions by the fact that at each stage there are words having membership in adjacent sub-classes, and further by the fact that no one scheme of sub-dividing adverbs ties in with any other. No presentation is likely to be altogether clear, straight-forward, comprehensive and free from repetition; but the most promising way of dealing with the related phenomena seems to be to take them as a whole and classify them in various ways—like cutting a cake first horizontally and then vertically. The cake gives us a real starting-point and helps us to envisage the relationship of its segments; how we proceed to dismember it is up to us—but we shall not find out much about it unless we cut it up somehow.

Notes

1. On the need to analyse form-classes in terms not merely of a single criterion, but of the total distribution of a word, cf. Roberts (1955).
2. A verb-like use can be found in such patterns as *Up, Jenkins!*; *Down, Towser!* where the first form in each case is imperative-like; an alternative analysis would be to regard any form appearing in such a pattern as evidence of the existence of a verb. In other words, we have met yet another pattern in which our form-class boundaries are meaningless; it cannot be insignificant that this happens so often in adverb-territory.

§160. There is a specially close relationship between adverbs and the closed system of clausally-incorporated words of relationship, **prepositions**, since many forms belong to both classes. Prepositions, happily, present a much simpler subject for analysis than adverbs. Their membership is clearly defined, they have one distinct syntactical function and one typical position. They indicate relationship between one noun-like item and another, the nature of the relationship being defined by the function of the preposition in the total system of English. It is important to realise that each relationship is so defined, and is not merely a reflection of something pre-existent in the non-linguistic world; consider what was said about *of* and the genitive relationship in §90, and think of languages with prepositions but lacking them for what seem to us obviously existing relations—*up*, for instance, in Latin. The second noun-like term in the relationship has something like object-function, in the sense that it follows the relating term (as an object usually follows its verb); where the second term is a word variable for subject and non-subject case, it is the non-subject case that follows the preposition. The catalogue of English prepositions includes morphemically simple and complex items, and items larger than the word, as follows:

about, above, across, after, against, along, amidst, among(st), around, as, at, before, behind, below, beneath, beside, between, beyond, by, concerning, considering, despite, down, during, except, following, for, from, in, into, like, near, of, off, on, opposite, out, over, per, regarding, round, save, since, than, through, throughout, till, to, towards, under, underneath, unlike, until, up, upon, with, within, without; across from, along with, alongside of, apart from, away from, because of, down from, due to, except for, inside of, instead of, off of, onto, out of, outside of, over to, together with, up to, up with; in spite of, on account of, by means of, in addition to, with regard to, in front of, on top of, on behalf of.

The items larger than the word cannot be exhaustively listed; they shade off indefinitely into two-word sequences.

There are three main kinds of use:

(1) preceding the noun-like expression which is the object or second term of the relationship, as in '*Sheila ran round the field twice*', '*Jim felt on top of the world*', '*Mary's taller than me*';

(2) with its own head or object forming a phrase (called a **prepositional phrase**), the whole of which may modify a preceding noun-like head, as in, *Men at work, House for Sale*;

(3) collocating with preceding verbs, not only in patterns covered by (1) and (2), but also in others which require us to take the sequence *verb+preposition* (or *verb+adverb+preposition*) as an idiom and not to make separate analysis of the words composing it, as in *I give it up*, cf. §151.

Although their distinctive features have in the past established the tradition that prepositions should be treated as distinct from adverbs, they are really at one end of a continuum which has the central adverbs at the other; nearly all the one-word prepositions can also be adverbs, and in that case all we are distinguishing is that the same forms used without object are adverbs, with object are prepositions—no more than the distinction we make between transitive and intransitive verbs. There is as much to be said for as against the division. But we should look more closely at the forms which are not identical with adverbs. *Than* is peculiar because it functions in comparative constructions only, and must have the second term of the comparison expressed; on the other hand it functions also in comparative correlatives that have come under discussion amongst the adverbs (§157). The others are terms like *concerning, considering, regarding, because of, due to, except for, in addition to, with regard to, on behalf of,* and perhaps one or two others that are distinct anyway among the prepositions. For in general, prepositions which are also adverbs have a specific linguistic form as their 'subject'; those that are not may not. So we have '*Considering the opposition he's up against, I think he's done very well*', where *considering* has an object-like term expressed in the utterance, but not a subject-like one. In any case the prepositional relationship is closer and more specific with the object-like term than the subject-like term ('*Jack and Jill went up the hill*'—the second term is *hill*, but is the first term *Jack and Jill* or *Jack and Jill went* or just *went*? We know it is somewhere there, for we know who did what in relation to the hill, but we cannot be more specific); so the total 'generalisation' of the subject-like term is hardly a reason for not counting these forms as prepositions.

Note

Than patterns not only as a preposition but also as a conjunction (*'taller than me'*; *'taller than I [am]'*).   Before a 'human'-gender relative it is always prepositional (*'than whom no-one could be kinder . . .'*), which makes all the more inexplicable the popular pedantry of opposing its use as preposition where its second term is within the clause.

§**161.** Less consistently incorporated into the structure of clauses are the next forms, traditionally called **conjunctions,** joining words. They fall into two clearly distinct types, which we shall treat separately, **co-ordinators** and **subordinators.**   Co-ordinators are link-words between equivalent structures—members of the same form-class, or phrases, or clauses, or even sentences. The point could be put even more positively—they function as signs that the structures they link are functioning as equals (Fries, 1952, p. 95, calls them signals of levelling). This again is a closed class, the members being *and, or, not, but, rather/ sooner than, as well as,* in such constructions as:

'She left at one and I had to cope single-handed'; 'Don't upset yourself or I shall feel guilty'; 'I wanted rolls, not a loaf'; 'I didn't want to go but I thought I should'; 'I'd give them away rather (sooner) than let them waste'; 'You work faster than I do'.

A trifle marginal in our kind of English is *nor,* which is also exceptional in that it is followed by inversion of verb and subject, as in:

'. . . nor have I ever said I would.'

In addition, an important group of co-ordinators consists of words functioning in linked pairs, one before each of the co-ordinated structures; such linked pairs are called correlatives, and the relevant ones are, *both–and, either–or, not(only)–but(also),* and marginally *neither–nor* (with inversion after *nor* if a clause follows), in such constructions as:

'I wanted both to go to the meeting and to hear the lecture'; 'Either you or I should be there'; 'It's neither one thing nor (in speech also or) the other'; 'Do come along—not necessarily now, but later when you're free'; 'It's not only tiring but terribly unrewarding.'

The placing of these correlatives is merely an extension of the principle normally applying to co-ordinators, that they are placed between the items they link, directly preceding the second one.

  The class of co-ordinators is exceptionally well defined; in view of the fact that the only difference of immediate patterning between prepositions and co-ordinators between noun-like expressions is in the form of the first and third person pronoun, it is not surprising that the two classes in a sense form a continuum, mingling at the point represented by *than* (cf. Note to §160).

A special function of linking-words is the joining of clauses to make them into a single sentence. All members of the class of co-ordinators function in this way, as we have already indicated, but our second class of conjunctions, the subordinators, function only in this way. The central members of this closed class are *because, therefore, although, for, nevertheless, if, whether,* together with a number of other forms that also function as adverbs, prepositions or both (*after, before, since, so, when, whenever*). A few illustrative sentences are:

'*I'm going because I want to*'; '*After I've gone you can do what you like*'; '*If you don't try you can't hope to improve*'.

These items are more closely linked, and are semantically linked, with one of the two clauses, and this one must immediately follow them; the other may go before or after this complex. Though these forms always function to show relationship between clauses or sentences, we must distinguish two kinds of relationship conveyed by them. The one we have taken as normal is truly **conjunctive**, but it is different from the co-ordinating function because it makes both related clauses quite different in function from what they would be standing alone. A co-ordinator between clauses can be cut out with only stylistic difference, the related clauses then standing juxtaposed as separate sentences ('*I arrived at ten* [*.*/*and*] *I knew you couldn't be there so early*'); the presence of a subordinator alters both related clauses ('*I knew you couldn't be there if I arrived as early as ten*'). Of the many possible ways of classifying clauses in their functional relation to the sentence as a whole, we have already suggested that in English it is most useful to distinguish between independent (α) and independent (β) (cf. §67). Where a clause-linking subordinator (such as *if* in the last example) is present, one or more clauses in a sentence may be dependent. Remember that the functional system of dependence is independent of the structural system of mood.

The second function of subordinators is rather **disjunctive**, implying contrast, dissociation, between the related items, and this difference is signified in speech by a different superfix (pause at the end of the first clause, acceleration over the subordinator and opening words of the second clause—the order of clauses being fixed in this function) and in writing often by making a sentence(W)-break before the subordinator, as in:

'*She promised to come.* . . . *But I don't rely on it.* . . . *Although you never know.*'

Similar in this function only is *however*, which otherwise functions as an adverb; also *at least, at any rate*.

Note

Whether–or are like correlative co-ordinators, only when they link clauses the second item is usually a clause-substitute rather than a full clause, as in '*I shall go whether he comes or not*'. *Than,* because it is tied to comparative constructions, is marginal between co-ordinators and subordinators. On *like,* cf. §115, Note 4.

§162. Loosely attached at the opening of clausal structures are the forms we may call **utterance-initiators.** They are of two kinds, those chiefly used to introduce utterances beginning a new conversation or topic (**situation utterances**) and those used only with responses to other utterances (**response utterances**). *Oh, now,* have both functions; *I say, listen, look (here)* are common with situation utterances, *why* more usual in American than British English; *well* much the commonest in response utterances. Situation utterance-initiators may be followed by a pause and a fresh intonation contour, or be unstressed and lead in without pause to the main syntactical structure they introduce; response utterance-initiators usually lead in uninterruptedly and are regularly unstressed. A sequence with examples is:

'*I say, are you going to the dance to-night?*'
'*Well, I don't know whether I can spare the time.*'
'*Oh, nonsense, you'll work all the better to-morrow.*'

In some speakers these forms are almost indispensable as markers of the initiation of an utterance; in the speech of such people these forms represent a real structural difference between utterance and sentence.

§163 Right outside clause structure are the words and other forms traditionally known as **interjections**, which are defined from the fact that they cannot enter into syntactical relations. Some correspond with forms used in other functions, such as *Damn! Good Lord!*; others are unrelated to other forms in the language, and indeed may not even be related to its ordinary sound-system, cf. the forms conventionally written *Ouch! Ugh! Tst! Psst!* They are often more directly expressive than other linguistic forms, and indeed seem so natural that speakers of one language are often surprised to find that other languages have different conventions from their own in this matter. Only the doggedly unreflecting suppose that *sheep* is the obvious thing to call a sheep ('*Rightly is they called pigs because of their disgusting habits*'), but many English people assume that it is natural to say *Ow!* when you are hurt (cf. §6 in this connection). In various respects—the lack of syntactical relations, absence of a morphological paradigm, departure from the normal sound-system, and abnormally direct expressive character—the interjection stands at the fringe of language. It is language, because it is governed by the conventions of a speech-community, but it is nearer than anything else in language to non-linguistic vocal sound.

Exercises

A

Read the following passage; list the adverbs, prepositions, conjunctions and utterance-initiators in it, describing where necessary of what kind they are. Make a note of borderline or difficult expressions, and explain on what principles, if at all, they can be classified:

"I have, in addition to my often expressed desire for a universal state, another craving, up till now unexpressed (that is publicly). I would, if I were able to, suppress all out-of-date discrepancies of *tongue*, as well as of skin and pocket. I desire to speak Volapuc, to put it shortly. I cannot help it, it is if you like a crank, but I should like to speak, and write, some Volapuc, not English—at all events some tongue that would enable me to converse with everybody of whatever shade of skin or opinion without an interpreter—above all that no shadow of an excuse should subsist for a Great Chemical Magnate to come hissing in my ear: "Listen! That low fellow" (magnates always speak in such lofty terms, partly for fun) "says *ja*—I heard him! Here is a phial of deadly gas. Just throw it at him, will you? He won't say *ja* any more, once he's had a sniff of that?" '
(Wyndham Lewis, *Paleface*, 1929, p. 68.)

CHAPTER XI

Grammar: Further Dimensions

§164. We have already met a number of the basic terms necessary for linguistic description at the formal level—*unit, scale, rank, system, structure, class, delicacy* and *exponence*—and we have glanced at their use in the description of English. The treatment has necessarily been sketchy, since the subject is so vast and so complex. But even at its own level it has avoided questions that must sooner or later be faced. If we had to characterise the deficiencies in a single sentence that sentence might run something like this:

Speakers are generally more or less conscious that the way their utterances work depends not only on what is there in the utterance (the relationship of part to part and part to whole)—or even what might be called implicit in the utterance (a certain form has a certain meaning partly because it is recognised as not merely an item but also a member of a class); speakers and listeners also draw on material that is *not* there—that is 'understood', or potential, relevant though absent; as yet the book has taken too little account of these factors.

Recent linguistic theory has been greatly preoccupied with them, with identifying and classifying them, discovering how they can best be fitted into description, and showing how what is there calls upon what is not for its interpretation. Differing answers are given, sometimes with great vehemence, and it would not be right to conclude without venturing into this area.

§165. A sense of the need to go beyond what is there can arise in various ways out of our everyday experience of language. Two sentences may look alike in their surface structure and yet feel as if they belong to different kinds. Often quoted in this connection are:

John is eager to please; John is easy to please.

Or structures which are superficially different may be in some other, perhaps, we feel, more important, way, the same:

Do you need to go? Need you go?
I'll look up the reference; I'll look the reference up.

Indeed, the point hardly needs demonstrating that in our normal use of language, as speakers and listeners, we do draw on an understanding of organisation underlying the surface, and not always in one-to-one relationship with it.

The beginnings of modern linguistics were shaped by a desire to get away from subjective and non-linguistic criteria for language analysis, abandoning intuitions and inaccessible ideas in favour of sole reliance on the evidence of what is there in the data, the material produced as evidence of the language under analysis. What was there was postulated to be structured, and the linguist's job was to analyse and describe that structure; hence the name, *structural linguistics*. The data used could only, on these premises, be a corpus of utterances actually used by one or more speakers of the language. One outcome of a quarter of a century's work on these lines was the widespread recognition that the task structural linguistics had set itself was in principle incapable of achievement; and this is not, as it might at first seem, a different thing from saying that the conception of language as exhausted by corpus-data, and of the structure of language as exhausted by what appeared on the surface in the data, was invalid. It is inadequate because it leaves out essential components of the activities we engage in when we use language. To say this is not to say that the work was wasted; it produced many insights, if not enough, and in a sense one of the insights was precisely the understanding that surface structure was not enough—an understanding truly tested only by the attempt to do without anything else. Now that that stage has been reached its implications must be examined.

§166. The first implication is one which has been more or less assumed in this book, namely that the most central characteristic and revealing kind of linguistic unit is the sentence. It is in sentences that we use language (even in earliest language acquisition, when sentences commonly consist of one word), deploying a finite number of elements in an infinity of structures; the open-endedness of lexical resources, in so far as it exists, does so by a kind of backwash from the patterns of sentence-formation (see Chapter XII). Thus, it is primarily in sentences that our linguistic creativity is displayed (though derivatively, secondarily, such creativity is reflected in word-formation). In sentences the inadequacy of a building-block model for linguistic constructions is most plainly demonstrated. If the main focus of interest amongst linguists is on sentences, linguistics must embrace, some would say it consists of, study of the mechanisms that produce this body of potential material, study of rules rather than of data; its primary concern is with what speakers can do, their linguistic competence, rather than with what on a limited number of occasions a limited number of speakers have done, their linguistic performance. On this view linguistics will say that the evidence of a corpus, however large, is insufficient, even irrelevant, because a corpus is by definition finite, and the body of potential sentences in a language infinite. Some scholars, bearing in mind the proved difficulty of ascertaining competence, believe that corpus-study must be retained, but adapted in such a way as to get round its limitations; that view will be adopted here.

§167. Starting with sentences, observers have long been struck by the difference between two kinds; the distinction has been formulated in different ways at different times. We shall put it like this. There are sentences like *This is the house that Jack built* which imply more elemental, more basic, assertions not actually stated in them—*This is a/the house; Jack built a/the house* (with the proviso that at least one of the optional forms must be realised as *the*). There are also more basic structures, such as those into which the first example was analysed, which are not capable of further analysis without losing their character as sentences. In this fashion (which may remind us of atomic theory in chemistry) a first distinction may be made between the basic or **kernel** sentences, and the others that can be made from them, the **transformations.** Notice that the term *transformation* here conforms to its mathematical sense in that it is used for an operation (and the product of such an operation) which alters shape while retaining structural relations intact. Those who postulate that the essential feature of language is sentence-generation hold a **generative** theory of language; if they further postulate that finite elements in finite numbers of patterns are deployed in a potentially infinite number of sentences by processes of **transformation** (which may be recursive) their theory is **transformational-generative (TG).** This is, like so many in linguistics, a subject on which generalisation is dangerous, because a diversity of scholars have regarded themselves, or been regarded, as transformationalists, and the most eminent TG thinkers are still evolving and modifying parts of their theory. It should be added that some accept the dual starting-point described here without being committed to the belief that current TG analysis follows from it.

Note

In the paragraphs that follow some terms will be introduced which are not used elsewhere in the book, and familiar ones will be given new senses. Terminology which is not to be used extensively in this book is introduced with rather little explanation; for explicit definition readers should turn to the works cited in, and at the end of, this chapter.

§168. The kernel sentences of English are, for the most part, those we distinguished at §67. A variable affecting the entire kernel sentence is the selection from the mood-system; a factor (called a **morpheme,**

though the sense differs from that adopted at §64) assigns the clause to one of the system-terms, *Declarative* or *Affirmative, Interrogative, Imperative*; most would now say also to some terms of the voice-system, *active, passive.* Apart from such generalised morphemes, the structure of the kernel is essentially bi-partite, consisting of a *Noun Phrase* (*NP*) in subject-function and a *Verb Phrase* (*VP*) in predicate function; even in kernel sentences these elements may have considerable subdivision (for instance, the VP may split into Verb plus a further NP; thus, though there is some correspondence between some TG uses of NP and the use of nominal groups in this book, that likeness is deceptive. Transformations work on the kernel sentences by addition, transposition and deletion; they are not just a matter of adding; indeed the bipartite structure may lose either its NP or its VP in surface structure.

While it is sentence-generation that is seen as central to the functioning of language, the rules of syntax do not account for the whole of language. A semantic component is needed, consisting of a dictionary, listing the values of lexical items, and a set of rules determining which meaning or meanings are compatible in a given syntactic string; and since the items in the syntactic string are abstractions, a further set of morphophonemic or phonological rules is needed to realise the abstractions as speech-forms.

§169. To show a little more clearly what is meant by this highly abstract and general statement, I give a brief statement of the main kernel and a few transformational rules for English syntax, summarised and adapted from the popular textbook, Roberts (1964). The strength of the theory emerges even from so inadequate a presentation as this: its rules are of so high a level of generality that description can be extremely brief. As far as seems desirable, I give a formulaic statement of the rules in the left-hand column and a discursive explanation on the right.

S → Mood + Voice + NP + VP	(i.e., the basic functional unit of this [or any] language, S [sentence] is to be realised, or re-written, as a two-part structure, NP + VP, whose forms and relations are determined by a specific selection from [what is here called] the mood-system, affirmative, imperative, etc., and of the voice-system, active/passive
Mood → Aff., Int. Imp.	(i.e., select one term of the mood-system whose rules are here assumed)
Voice → Active, Passive	(i.e., select one term of the voice-system whose rules are here assumed)

$$NP \rightarrow \left\{ \begin{array}{l} \text{proper noun} \\ \text{indefinite pronoun} \\ \text{Det.} + N \end{array} \right\}$$

(i.e., re-write NP as one of the three specifications given, the rules for which follow)

proper noun → *John, Mr. Smith, Newcastle*

(i.e., re-write proper noun as any one of an indefinitely large list of items of the kind given)

indefinite pronoun → *some-, any-, no-one, body, thing*

(i.e., re-write indefinite pronoun as any one of the six items [closed system] specified)

Det. → (pre-article) + Art. + (Demon) + (Number)

(i.e., re-write Det. as Art. [a compulsory component], which may, as the brackets show, be preceded by a pre-article, and may be followed by either Demonstrative or Number or both)

pre-article → *several of, many of*

$$\text{Art.} \rightarrow \left\{ \begin{array}{l} \text{Def.} \\ \text{Nondef.} \end{array} \right\}$$

Def. → *the*

(i.e., it is normally re-written as *the*, though in personal pronouns def. is already present, and does not need separate realisation)

$$\text{Nondef.} \rightarrow \left\{ \begin{array}{l} a \\ some \\ \phi \end{array} \right\}$$

(i.e., select [in the singular] *a*, [in the plural some [e.g. *some books*] or zero [*books*])

$$\text{Demon.} \rightarrow \left\{ \begin{array}{l} D_1 \\ D_2 \end{array} \right\}$$

(i.e., if the element is present select D_1 which together with Def. yields *this/these*, or D_2, which together with Def. yields *that/those*)

$$\text{Number} \rightarrow \left\{ \begin{array}{l} \text{card.} \\ \text{ord.} \end{array} \right\}$$

(i.e., if the element is present, select either cardinal or ordinal)

card. → *one, two, three, . . .*
ord. → *first, second, third, . . .*

$$N \rightarrow \left\{ \begin{array}{l} \text{pers. pron.} \\ \text{common noun} \end{array} \right\}$$

pers. pron. → *I, you, he, she, it, we, they*

(i.e., select one from a closed system of items, already containing the element Def.)

$$\text{common noun} \rightarrow \left\{ \begin{array}{l} \text{count} \\ \text{noncount} \end{array} \right\}$$

(i.e., select one of two possible types of common noun, countables and non-countables)

$$\text{count} \rightarrow \begin{Bmatrix} \text{animate} \\ \text{inanimate} \end{Bmatrix}$$

(i.e., countable nouns may be of these two types, and the difference is syntactically important, as we see from the acceptability of *The boy admires the decision*, as against the deviance of **The decision admires the boy*)

animate → *boy, cat, horse*, . . .
inanimate → *table, tree, decision*, . . .
noncount → *porridge, furniture, sarcasm*, . . .

Though this is only a summary, the striking omission is one that would survive in full presentation, namely that no reference is made to the role of adjectives in the NP; indeed, adjectives are assigned to transformational structure, in such a way that, for example, *the good men* is derived from *the men are good* by a transformational rule; attributive adjectives are not seen as part of kernel structure. This point is discussed in §172.

§170. The second constituent component, VP, has, in outline, the following kernel structure.

$$\text{VP} \rightarrow \text{Aux.} + \begin{Bmatrix} \begin{Bmatrix} be+ \text{ substantive} \\ \text{Adv-p} \end{Bmatrix} \\ \text{verbal} \end{Bmatrix}$$

(i.e., there must be a component Aux., yet to be specified, and in addition something else—a selection of either an appropriate form of *be*, which itself will require a further component, or a verbal, which can stand alone, and has yet to be specified)

Aux. → tense + (M) + (aspect)

(i.e., Aux[iliary] has a compulsory tense component, with the optional addition of M[ood] or aspect or both)

$$\text{tense} \rightarrow \begin{Bmatrix} \text{present} \\ \text{past} \end{Bmatrix}$$

(i.e., tense involves choice of one of two terms, realised for each verb by rules that belong to morphophonemics)

M → *can, may, shall, will, must*

(i.e., the optional element M is realised by one of these five items; the series *could, might, should, would* is introduced by pastness in tense-selection) aspect → *(have+*part.*)* + *(be+ ing)*

(i.e., the optional element aspect requires selection of an appropriate part of *have* followed by a past participle, or an appropriate part of *be* followed by an *-ing* participle, or both; the two choices correspond to our perfective and durative)

subst. → $\begin{Bmatrix} \text{NP} \\ \text{(Int.+) Adj.} \end{Bmatrix}$

(i.e., *be* needs to be followed by one of a class of items amongst which the distinction between NP and Adj. is [in this position] irrelevant [if the choice is Adj. there may, but need not, be a preceding Intensifier]; or by Adv-p)

Int. → *very, rather, . . .*
Adj. → *good, sad, beautiful, . . .*

(i.e., predicative, though not attributive, adjectives, belong to the kernel)

Adv-p → *there, downstairs, in the house, . . .*

verbal →

$$\begin{Bmatrix} \begin{bmatrix} \text{VI} \\ \text{VT+NP} \\ \text{V}_b\text{+substantive} \\ \text{V}_s\text{+Adj} \end{bmatrix} + \text{(Adv-m)} \\ \text{V}_h\text{+NP} \end{Bmatrix}$$

(i.e., verbal must be realised as one of five classes of items, to be specified below; after any of the first four an adverb of manner must be possible, though it is not obligatory; it cannot follow the last; the second to fifth have obligatory following components, of kinds now familiar)

$$\text{VI} \to \begin{Bmatrix} \text{Vi}_1 \\ \text{Vi}_2\text{+Prt} \\ \text{Vi}_3\text{+Comp} \end{Bmatrix}$$

(i.e., VI [intransitive] must be one of three types, one self-sufficient, one requiring a particle, one requiring a complement)

Vi_1 → *occurred, laugh, wait, . . .*
Vi_2 → *glance, look, come, . . .*
Prt → *down, up, in, away, . . .*
Comp → *on the sofa, in the corner, . . .*
Vi_3 → *stand, lie, stay, . . .*

$$\text{VT} \to \begin{Bmatrix} \text{Vt}_1 \\ \text{Vt}_2\text{+Prt} \\ \begin{Bmatrix} \text{Vt}_3 \\ \text{Vt}_{to} \\ \text{Vt}_{ing} \end{Bmatrix} + \text{Comp} \end{Bmatrix}$$

(i.e., VT [transitive], which requires a following NP and must be capable of taking a following Adv-m, must belong to one of five sub-classes, specified below)

Vt_1 → *see, find, terrify, . . .*

$Vt_2 \rightarrow$ *put, look, throw,* ...   (i.e., verbals of types Vt_3, to, ing,
$Vt_3 \rightarrow$ *consider, elect, give,* ...   require completion by a complement,
$Vt_{to} \rightarrow$ *persuade, expect, try,* ...   as in *elect X chairman, persuade X to*
$Vt_{ing} \rightarrow$ *enjoy, avoid, imagine,*...   *come, imagine X singing;* note that the
structures realising Comp. here are
different from those given before)

$V_b \rightarrow$ *become, remain,* ...
$V_s \rightarrow$ *seem, look, taste,* ...
$V_h \rightarrow$ *have, cost, weigh,* ...

§171. These kernel rules map out the basic elements of sentences in their basic patterns and relationships. Transformational rules operate on the product of the kernel rules, preserving relationships and meanings. They are usually divided into single-base transformations, which re-arrange single kernel structures, and double-base transformations, which relate two kernel structures into a composite unit. Single-base transformations do such things as re-order stems and affixes so that, for example, tense affixes come in the correct surface-structure pattern ($-s+be$ becomes *is*, for instance); they introduce *do* in clause-types requiring it; convert personal pronouns from *I, he,* etc. to *me, him,* etc. in appropriate environments; make *wh*-interrogatives (non-polar interrogatives) and *there*-subject structures.

We have already seen that a double-base transformation is taken to account for attributive adjective structures. They are likewise taken to account for possessives (genitives), so that such a structure as *John's house* ... is derived from an underlying *John has a house*. They account for complement-sentences by the insertion of, e.g., *Mary was beautiful* into the matrix *John considered+Comp.+Mary* to produce *John considered Mary beautiful*. Relatives, and indeed all sentences of more than one clause are accounted for by their means; details can be found in Roberts (1964), O'Neil (1965), Thomas (1966), as well as in the primary sources cited at the end of the Chapter.

§172. Though this book has not been written in TG terms, the basic ideas of the theory must be referred to at this late stage since we now need to draw upon concepts and terms from it. It must be made quite clear that this borrowing of terms does not constitute an adaptation or watering down or partial borrowing of the theory. What is presented as a coherent body of doctrine cannot be partially borrowed; fragmentation turns it into something quite different. Nevertheless, when parts of a theory have afforded valuable insights those parts can best be discussed in familiar terms, rather than re-named. That is the procedure to be followed here.   With this caveat we may look at some further dimensions of linguistic organisation.

Having conceded that deep structure in some sense controls surface structure, so that different structures may be 'really the same' and same structures 'really different', we need to set alongside this conclusion independent evidence that surface structure, through analogies in multiple dimensions, exercises a pull that can draw a pattern away from the orbit of its underlying structure.   This may sound unduly metaphorical, and unduly diachronic.   Yet this process of drawing away, which in one sense takes place through time, in another sense takes place simultaneously in the form of a range of concurrent variants within a speech-community.   Divided usage (even within a single speaker) is a necessary condition of linguistic change as we know it.   This state of affairs, and study oriented towards it, can be referred to as 'dynamic synchrony' (Jakobson, 1961).   The orientation of this book is governed by a belief that we must look at English not only to see how deep structure shapes surface structure, but also to see how one surface structure shapes another surface structure, thus revolutionising the relationship between surface and deep structure.   The words in which such a statement must be formulated still sound diachronic; but examples will show that the subject belongs to a study of a given *état de langue*.   I should like to begin with two examples in which dominance of surface structure analogy has, I believe, been established in English; and then to consider patterns of distribution which show the conflict of the two directions of pull actually in operation.

§173.   The first example is prenominal or attributive adjectives.   These are defined in TG in terms of embedded relative structures with predicative adjectives (since predicatives belong in kernel sentences), with deletion of certain items.   For example (Thomas, 1966, p. 91): the sentence *Invisible God created the visible world* is derived from *God (God+is+Adj. [invisible]) created the world (the world+is+Adj. [visible])*.   (Cf. also Roberts, 1964, pp. 232 ff., O'Neil, 1965, 73 ff.)   This is a revealing way of grouping and accounting for the many items that are alike in attributive and predicative function.   But it excludes from the definition *Adj.* items whose value differs in the two functions (*a man who is inside/outside*; *an inside/outside man*).   Nor does it account for items whose function is not descriptive, but might be called validating, such as *potential* in *he's a potential champion*, which can properly be said when neither *he is potential* nor *he is a champion* can.   An important class of items not covered by it is that called by Marchand (1966), **transpositional adjectives**; an example is *criminal* in *criminal law, criminal lawyer*, plainly not derived from *the law is criminal, the lawyer is criminal*, though the ambiguity of the surface structure is often exploited in jokes. Less serious are the problems arising from idiomatic usages, such as *a cool thousand*, though it seems natural to wish to take this as having adjectival modification, even if the adjective is lexically specialised in meaning.

At the very least we might say that an alternative way of looking at prenominal modification in English is to say that between the very highly structured (systemic) determiner position and the head position there is an intermediate position, structured, but less highly so, whose characteristic kinds of filler show a good deal of overlap with those of the non-substantival predicative after *be*, V_b, V_s. Further, that by now the position is institutionalised among speakers, and that by virtue of various analogies they have accustomed themselves to filling it in various ways. The position itself is, in a sense, independent, a force to be reckoned with, a mould which can be filled in several ways. The correspondence of forms in predicative and attributive use is not one-to-one, though it is close enough to be exploited in jests, or to tend towards the establishment of new usages (e.g., *the well man*, drawing on the two principles that *sick* and *well* contrast, and that a contrary has the same position-filling capacity as its partner, together with the predicative/attributive analogy *the man is well* [which does produce a relative, but which is not established in the deleted, transposed pattern yielding (TG) Adj., *the man who is well → the well man*]).

§174. Next we may look at possessives or, as this book labels them, genitives. Here, what is isolated, in transformational generative grammar as elsewhere, is a class or set of forms alike in construction and position; in fact a surface-structure pattern; as so often, there is extensive, but not one-to-one correspondence between surface and deep structure. Often there is a possessive structure, *X has a Y*, underlying a pattern of the *X's Y* type—*John's house, my typewriter*; often there is not—*John's defeat, boys' school, day's work, Shakespeare's plays*. No single non-possessive relationship is so common as the possessive, but this is not to say that the possessive is the norm. We do not know what is the norm; but we do know that one factor that makes the possessive seem dominant is the diversity of non-possessives. This is a good reason for avoiding a 'transparent' label that suggests greater uniformity than we have evidence for. Any monolithic explanation of the observed evidence leaves out some untidy bits. The preference for the term *possessive* reflects a theoretical disposition to see an underlying verb of possession as in some sense essential to *N—'s* structures; it is not adopted here because that interpretation does not seem to have been established. Indeed, Thomas (1966) expresses dissatisfaction with all published (TG) accounts of the genitive (pp. 199); he takes the view that further analysis is needed. This may be so; on the other hand, it may be the case that this is an area in which unity exists only on the surface.

It is because of such reservations that a case can be made that while TG has brought many insights into the structure of English, the time is not yet ripe for adopting the theory outright in a teaching work. If one is not committed to working in that way or leaving a problem untouched, the choice is then open as to how far one starts from surface, and how far from deep, structure, in several parts of the grammar. So eclectic an approach draws on intuition, is subjective, and patchy; it does not, however, conceal the difference between the evidence and the author's seeing of a pattern in it.

§175. With such considerations in mind we may examine some recent work on English. Quirk (1965) distinguishes three sets of features in language: (a) **manifested features**, i.e., what is observable in the text; (b) **potential features**, i.e., capacity for substitution, expansion, not observed from the text but traceable by comparison; and (c) **transformational features**. The first are overt, the second and third covert; the first and second are constituent features, the third process features. Comparing the italicised nominal groups in:

'They disapproved of *his running after Mary* and even *his liking for Mary*'

he identifies the manifested feature (*a*) in various terms, e.g. *deictic* (= *det*) + *head* + *postmodifier*. The potential features (*b*) 'will include the fact that *him* can replace *his* in the first nominal group within certain (stylistic) limits that permit no such replacement in the second; that *running* (but not *liking*) may be preceded by an adverb such as *eagerly*; that neither N(ing) can be made plural.' The transformational features (*c*) relate 'to the degree of similarity with which the two sequences are related to other structures in the language by regular "process" or transformation. Thus, both nominal groups have a comparably statable correspondence to a finite-verb clause, such that the possessive pronoun corresponds to the subject and the N(ing) to the verb; but in the first case the preposition remains while in the second it does not: *he runs after Mary*, but not **he likes for Mary*'.

This paper arose out of the work of the *Survey of English Usage*, which is a corpus-based study. It puts forward a mode of description which is economical in the sense that it draws on all available evidence, rejecting or wasting nothing usable. By the same token it can be seen to overcome the limitations of corpus-study. It draws on evidence from outside the corpus, if necessary, for the elucidation of covert features in texts belonging to the corpus. It is thus based on, but not confined to, corpus evidence. Use of the covert features in this way is by no means a simple matter, since it is first necessary to establish what they are; sophisticated techniques for this have been developed and are reported in Quirk and Svartvik (1966), though further work is still in progress. Meanwhile, there is a sufficiency of clear-cut cases for a framework of description to be developed.

In brief, by plotting the three types of variables we can build up a picture of the degree of identity between forms. We can then give a precise account of the degrees of identity (and difference) between, say, such sequences as:

(1) *She watched the man;*
(2) *She listened to the man;*
(3) *She stood near the man.*

Quirk diagrams this:

α	β^1	γ^1
		γ^2
	β^2	γ^3

'It is perhaps easiest to supply some of the characteristics which formed the parameters leading to the lowest degree of identity (γ) that needs to be distinguished here; γ^1 acknowledges the unique absence of a preposition; γ^2 acknowledges the inadmissibility of the shortened form *She listened to* beside the admissibility of both *She watched* and *She stood near*; γ^3 further acknowledges the difference between *to* and *near* which allows the latter to be preceded by *very*. The point on the scale of delicacy at which the identification labelled β^1 becomes relevant reflects the readiness of the passive transformation in *The man was watched* and *The man was listened to* but not in *The man was stood near*. The basis for the maximum degree of identity, labelled α, is perhaps less obvious, but it is important to recognise in English clause structure an abstraction SVX, embracing SVC and SVA, where 'X' can be informally read as "post-verbal piece". It is not perhaps sufficiently realised that model intransitive clauses of the type *Birds sing* are significantly rare, and that only about one in thirty of the clauses occurring in spoken or written text have this minimal SV form. We need in fact to recognise the broad but apparently basic degree of identity that is manifested not only as α in the three sentences above but also in others such as *He arrived late, The dress suited the girl, The man was seen by a porter,* and *The man was seen in the road.'*

§176. Another type of display uses a matrix with cells marked + for presence of a feature and − for its absence. Where a line between plus and minus forms a diagonal we have an instance of **gradience** (Bolinger, 1961), that is, of a graded variation in likeness and difference. Quirk illustrates this from the privileges of occurrence of certain finite verbs. The seven selected features, variables, or parameters, are:

1 He X^1 and X^2 come every day
2 He X to come every day
3 Did he X to come every day?
4 He would X to come every day
5 He X that
6 He X us to come every day
7 He X that we should come every day.

Testing seven finites for these features, we can arrange the following display:

	1	2	3	4	5	6	7
intends	+	+	+	+	+	+	+
wants	+	+	+	+	+	+	−
seems	+	+	+	+	?+	−	−
has	+	+	+	+	−	−	−
used	+	+	?+	−	−	−	−
is	+	+	−	−	−	−	−
may	+	−	−	−	−	−	−

Notice that the matrix excludes the irrelevant—there is no point in in cluding items that are all −; notice, too, that question-marks appear along the diagonal, indicating that usage is divided just where, because of conflicting analogical pulls, you would expect it to be. You may well find that your own queries, even your +'s and −'s, will fall in different places from those shown; but most of the evidence of divided usage will cluster along the diagonal. Finally, notice that while the divided usage confirms our expectation that we have an example of gradience, the analytical display is created by the linguist to bring this out (since the variables are so numerous the sorting is of course done by means of a computer). If the linguist had ordered his finites or his features in a different sequence the incidence of +'s and −'s could have appeared wholly unpatterned. Sometimes so orderly an arrangement is not possible—either because there is no gradience, or because the gradience is multi-dimensional and cannot be represented on paper. A kind of gradience of great importance in linguistic organisation is the series of overlapping resemblances, patterning in this kind of way:

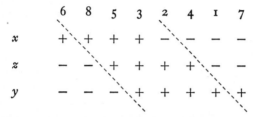

To it Quirk gives the name **serial relationship**. This, with some neighbouring material, he plots for forms clustering around such structures as 'S+*BE*+ said to be +C':

	1	2	3	4	5	6	7	8
pretend	+	+	+	?	−	−	−	−
feel	?	+	+	+	+	?	−	−
say	+	+	+	−	+	−	−	−
know	−	+	+	+	+	−	−	−
find	−	+	+	?	+	+	?	+
think	+	+	+	+	+	+	+	+
declare	−	+	+	+	+	+	+	+
regard	−	−	?	?	?	+	?	?
like	−	−	+	+	−	+?	−	−
persuade	−	−	−	+	+	−	−	−
make	−	−	−	−	+	+	+	+
call	−	−	−	−	−	+	+	+
elect	−	−	−	−	−	−	−	+

For this matrix, the key to the parameters is:

1. They V so. (e.g. *They think so*)
2. They V that he is Adj. (e.g. *They think that he is nice*)
3. It is Ved that he is Adj. (e.g. *It is thought that he is nice*)
4. They V him to be Adj. (e.g. *They think him to be nice*)
5. He is Ved to be Adj. (e.g. *He is thought to be nice*)
6. They V him Adj. (e.g. *They think him nice*)

8+

7. He is Ved Adj. (e.g. *He is thought nice*)
8. They V him N (where N and *him* are co-referential). (e.g. *They think him president*)

It is in relationships of this kind that the existence of derivation on two axes, not merely one, becomes apparent; that is, that analogous surface structures, as well as underlying structures, can be seen as 'the source' of the sequence actually used, and of divided and doubtful uses.   Quirk writes:

'In the theory of serial relationship, we go beyond noting the gradient between structures with *say, find, think*, etc., and make the claim that vertical agreement in the matrix is actually generative by reason of the total configuration of gradience.   That is to say, given that it should be found convenient to set up a general rule in the language deriving passives from actives, it is reasonable of course to take horizontal agreement in respect of parameters 4 and 5 as equivalent to deriving the property of 5 from the property of 4.   But while property 4 may be a usual, it is not a necessary condition for property 5.   The subclass represented by *like* (other members are *want, love, need*) shows that the mere existence of the active does not entail the existence of the passive transform (**He is liked/wanted/loved/needed to be careful*).   More interestingly, as we see from the description of *say* and *make* in the matrix (cf. also *find*), the existence of the passive does not entail the existence of the corresponding active (**They say/ make/ ?find him to be careful*).   In these instances, the configuration of gradience suggests the possibility of 'vertical' derivation; because *say* has a common distribution with *feel* and *know* in such expressions as *They feel/say/know that he is careful, It is felt/said/known that he is careful* (parameters 2 and 3), and because *feel* and *know* have a further property in such expressions as *He is felt/known to be careful* (parameter 5, 'regularly' accountable through the postulated relation with parameter 4), there is developed directly from this the possibility of using the *say*-subclass in this structure without necessitating the prior—or indeed subsequent—acquisition of property 4.   It is no doubt relevant to this postulation (and relevant also to estimating the value of observation-based description) both that we find instances of the structure type *He is Ved to be Adj* occurring considerably more frequently in the corpus than instances of the type *They V him to be Adj*, and also that there are roughly twice as many verbs for which we would register a plus in column 5 as there are verbs positive to parameter 4.'

The value of the theory in focusing on likely domains of divided usage is illustrated from the position of *regard* in the matrix; its properties are very unsettled at the moment; it remains a particle-associated verb (*regard as*) but its relationships tend to attract it into the orbit of verbs like *think*, which is not particle-associated.

§**177.** Taking account of the complex and infinitely variable network of relationships in which every item and structure is caught up, we could hardly expect the production of sentences to depend on processes of a single kind; instead, Quirk postulates a complex interplay involving both transformation and a 'sentence-frame manufacturing device' (a term he borrows from Miller, 1962). This interplay may be envisaged in terms of a metaphor of *diverging paths*, illustrated thus:

The sentences *The man gave the boy a book* and *The girl showed the inspector a ticket* are similar, four-part structures, which we may symbolise abcd, a'b'c'd'; they are congruent in the structure frame. The corresponding passives: *A book was given the boy by the man*; *A ticket was shown the inspector by the girl* (dbca, d'b'c'a') are doubly related—on a horizontal axis by transformation, and on a vertical one paradigmatically. But we find other structures in which the relationship holds on only one axis (*The dinner cost the man a pound*, but not **A pound was cost the man by the dinner*, α β γ δ but not **δ β γ α*; conversely, *The facts were presented us by the Public Relations Officer* but not **The Public Relations Officer presented us the facts*, 1234, but not **4321*). In a diagram showing the divergent paths this appears:

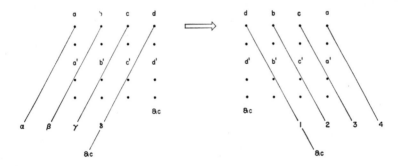

The economy and diversity of coverage in this approach seem to afford the most promising framework for further understanding of the structure of English.

Note

For a further application of this mode of analysis see Quirk and Mulholland *Complex Prepositions and Related Sequences* in Zandvoort (1964.)

EXERCISES

1. Evaluate a TG analysis of the following: the English clause-system; the English NP; the English VP.
2. Design one or more matrices showing serial relationship amongst operators and similar forms in the English verb phrase.

FURTHER READING

As usual, many important works have been referred to in the text. A very large number of other Bibliography entries are also relevant. It is difficult to classify, since a work may be mainly concerned with general principles of grammar, but exemplify so fully from English that it virtually constitutes a grammar of English; or may work from a very wide base to a highly restricted final focus, which alone is reflected in the title. Very roughly, suggestions for further reading can be grouped under three heads:

1. General reviews of method, relevant to English grammar, in the works of Chomsky and his associates (e.g., Katz, Fodor, Postal, Lees, Klima), Halliday and his associates (e.g., Huddleston, Hudson), Quirk and his associates, Carvell and Svartvik, Lamb;
2. General studies of English grammar, on various scales and from various points of view, see the work of Sweet, Jespersen, Curme, Kruisinga and Erades, Zandvoort, Sledd, Hill, Francis, Gleason, Quirk;
3. Studies of specific parts of English grammar, Fillmore, Halliday, Quirk, Lees, Klima, Olsson, Rosenbaum, Strang, Zimmer.

The major anthologies in the Bibliography include work under all three heads.

CHAPTER XII

Lexis

§178. While grammar is the domain of systems, lexis is the domain of vast lists of formal items about which rather little generalisation can be made. It is a level of linguistic organisation that immediately attracts interest, but it has so far been capable of rather little systematic investigation, and in consequence has, during the present century, been increasingly abandoned by scholarly investigators. Now again new techniques of investigations are reversing that trend; there is little to report as yet, but the subject cannot be passed over in silence.

§179. The traditional form for descriptive lexical studies is one of recording rather than analysing, in the dictionary and the thesaurus. The nature of lexical material is such that it is easier, perhaps even more appropriate, to list it, even to arrange it, than to generalise about it. Lexis characteristically consists of large masses of rapidly changing, highly diverse, material; it grows fast, obviously, dramatically (as we shall see below): it develops like a population explosion, while grammar develops almost imperceptibly, like a mature oak-tree. Nevertheless the two areas are not wholly unlike; indeed lexical growth is most prolific in the field of word-formation, which is very closely related to grammar.

Since listing is an obvious way of avoiding silence on lexis, and since dictionaries, at any rate, are compilations almost everyone uses even if they never see any other linguistic book, the status of dictionaries deserves our attention. They are not, clearly, all of one kind. Our concern is only with unilingual dictionaries. Even these are not all alike, but they commonly agree on listing alphabetically words and similar items (the principles of this similarity may be obscure and unexplained). Next, the items are commonly glossed; though since they are themselves not homogeneous the mode of glossing also has to be diverse. Three modes, at least, should be recognised:

(1) paraphrases
(2) renderings in a learned language or technical terminology ('the wren, *troglodytes troglodytes*')
(3) explanations of function in larger structures.

Notice that (1) and (2) complement each other for items that we should regard as genuinely lexical; hard words are explained by easy ones, and easy words by hard ones. (3) operates in a different dimension, serving for items we regard as chiefly grammatical and therefore un-paraphrasable, like *the*.

Thirdly, the gloss is often preceded by a form-class assignment: this is often of a conventional kind, with unexamined premises, even in work of high scholarly achievement; in other words, it aims to be self-explanatory to the amateur whose only linguistic interest is expressed by 'looking it up in the dictionary'. Also, there is likely to be an indi-cation of pronunciation, also usually addressed to the amateur; this component tends to reinforce the half-formed idea some people already have that the normal mode of access to new lexical items is through the written form and to the unit in isolation. This is not a fault in dic-tionaries; they are arranged for use chiefly when new items are met in this way. Yet it is a consequence of the availability of dictionaries, and the absence of other kinds of lexical record, to reinforce and give false prominence to a mistaken idea.

Finally, there is likely to be an etymology. Only in the fullest dictionaries are the etymologies in usable form, and then it is usually a form that cannot be interpreted without linguistic training. Only, unfortunately, as the etymology usually comes at the end, and every-thing before it has been pre-digested for the linguistic layman, the in-clusion of etymological hints tends to suggest to the layman that these too are self-interpreting. Much confusion results.

Much less common, because it is so costly, is a tradition long estab-lished in scholarly dictionaries, a tradition of supporting the explana-tions given by inclusion of examples quoted in context. Readers of this kind of dictionary are in any case a select company; the great dictionaries cannot act directly to correct misunderstandings about how words mean. What is sad is that of those who do use them, only a fraction really understand the relationship between the 'definitions' or 'meanings' and the exemplification. Perhaps the dictionaries are some-what at fault in the poverty of their explanations on this point; certainly their arrangement fosters the impression that 'the rule' comes first, and what follow are examples mediating its force to the reader.

Finally, items are arranged in an order not governed by linguistic considerations but of service solely to the person who only knows about a lexical item the alphabetical order of its letters. This is a useful function, but the provision of it, in the absence of other kinds of lexical study, again tends to create a false authoritarian approach, as if the neophyte were enquiring of the master.

§180. The last paragraph cannot fail to sound harsh and tendentious. I hasten to add that I am a confirmed dictionary-browser and revere the great English lexicographers.   My point is that, in a sense, dictionaries are works that ask to be misunderstood, and get just what they ask for.   In consequence they have a powerful, and sometimes damaging, influence on public opinion about language.   To understand English lexis we must understand the origins of, and wriggle out from under, this influence.

Format and presentation leave even the great dictionaries open to misunderstanding, to creating the impression that they are the true repositories of lexical knowledge, the source of authority, to which the ignorant speaker, the man-in-the-street who 'doesn't know his own language' can turn for enlightenment.   Furthermore, from schooldays onwards, most speakers who use dictionaries do turn to them for enlightenment; even worse, the facts of economic life being what they are, 'the dictionary' most people turn to, is usually a derivative of some larger, more original work.   Ultimately in the chain of abridged, shorter, concise, pocket, handy dictionaries, there is a full dictionary which has actually been made by a named scholar or team.   But commonly the layman's eye view is not of a work by somebody, and having just as much or little authority as that person, but of an anonymous version, the 'the dictionary', bearing, at best, a publisher's name, but very often no evidence of how the publisher obtained the text.   The correlation between absence of author and numinousness of authority is very high; 'the dictionary' comes to be more than formally parallel to 'the bible', and the publisher is almost a channel of grace.   Both the rules of the game of *Scrabble* and the way these rules are habitually applied by players indicate the strength of the view that the lexical resources of English are authoritatively determined by 'the dictionary'; if usage is different, too bad for usage.

A moment's reflection on how dictionaries (fountain-head dictionaries, that are actually *by* somebody) come into existence, will show that this reverent attitude to dictionary authority is mere superstition.   A dictionary can only generalise about what a sufficient number of speakers do (or, if it is historical, used to do); it cannot have any other source of evidence or authority.   The dictionary derives its authority from us, not we from it; though as it speaks for more of us than any single individual, we are right to show it a decent respect.   The point is well put by Angus McIntosh in *Patterns and Ranges* (McIntosh and Halliday, 1966, pp. 194–195):

'The meanings a given word has (however we may define meaning) are in some direct way associated with our experience of that word in a variety of contexts, our association of that word with other words which have, in our experience, a somewhat similar range, and our association of the word with other words of similar shape, often but

not always etymologically related.   Such similarly shaped words may
well play diverse grammatical roles, so they will not necessarily have
at all the same range; the association, by thus straddling grammar,
may therefore lead us to draw conclusions about a word with one
such range from another with another range.

   'The experience and associative habits of no two people are exactly the same, though we tend to have a good deal in common with
others in all this for the obvious reason that we necessarily share
much of our linguistic experience with them.   Even so there are notable discrepancies, as we may gather from the chastening experience
of looking at a large dictionary, which tells us something of the combined lexical habits of many people.   In doing so, it lists sometimes
words of which I have had no previous experience, sometimes words
which turn out to be capable of meaning things I did not know they
could, i.e., which can stand in certain collocational relationships of
which I was hitherto unaware.   We should also note that the dictionary does not accept anything that falls below a certain generality
of experience; it does not cover those private (e.g. family) words or
collocations which are only shared within a small circle.   And of
course it cannot provide us, by paraphrase or definition or in any
other way, with anything like all the numerous delicately discrimi-
nated shades of meaning which a word may have in (say) ten thousand
different instances.   All it can do is to list (and perhaps connect)
different meanings in rough classes, each class representing what I
call a use, i.e. a group of instances classed together because the
meaning therein seems to require or justify a definition or paraphrase
different from that of some other class.'

§181. A corollary of the false model of lexical authority is a false model
of the nature of lexical meaning.   If there is an authority 'out there'
issuing dictionaries, it will be seen as dealing in set terms, with things
that definitely are, or are not, the meanings of particular items.   If,
on the other hand, *we* are the authority, we must look at how we formed
our conceptions of the meanings of words—especially, at the beginning,
the meanings of those common, basic items in terms of which we want
'hard words' paraphrased.   We formed them, of course, not by paraphrase (how could we begin?), but by inference from context and co-
text (including ostensive definition but by no means only in this way).
We are chiefly made aware of this process in mature life by comic
episodes related about children's 'mistakes'.   Most people have a fund
of stories of this kind; I personally believed for a time that *hysterics* was
a shop in Oxford Street (an aunt had described 'going into hysterics'
on a shopping expedition that had already taken her to Selfridge's and
Bourne and Hollingsworth's).   We need to look more closely at what

children are doing when they make these mistakes. The child is isolating a new and unfamiliar item in a context of more familiar items and
patterns, and inferring from known relationships and analogies the
likely value of the new counter in the linguistic game. The method is
valid; it is the normal way of extending linguistic control. What is
'wrong' is that the basis of the inference is too narrow. When the
basis is much too limited, as in my own case with *hysterics*, the inferred
meaning is sooner or later seen to clash with the inferences (and consequent usage) of people with a wider range of linguistic and contextual
experience. The clash may be spotted by the child and silently corrected before it has emerged as a funny usage; or it may only be
detected when the child says something that strikes adults as odd.
Notice three things about the process. Although dramatically deviant
inferences are chiefly characteristic of childhood, the process of mutual
adjustment between speakers goes on throughout life, mainly on a small
scale and at a subliminal level. The cases of perceptible clash draw
attention to themselves, but only because they are so rare; normally
lexical control is extended imperceptibly and 'rightly'. Finally, the
process of isolation, inference, use and adjustment is the only ultimate
source of our knowledge of lexical items and their meanings; there is
nothing else 'out there' from which we can learn about words.

What is of particular importance is that our lexical understanding is
idiosyncratic not just passively (because the total word-experience and
association-patterns of each of us are unique) but also actively, because,
individually, we have made our own inferences, and linked them together in our own synthesis of total lexical patterning. There are
many senses in which speakers are creative even in their everyday uses
of language; we consider elsewhere creativeness in word- and sentence-
formation. But at the heart of linguistic creativeness, and all too often
overlooked, is the process in every speaker by which he is commonly
said to 'learn' the words of his language. It should now be clear that
'learn' is used in a rather special, though familiar, sense. He is re-
creating—and more than that, creating afresh, in childhood, and
throughout his speaking life.

§182. We can see more clearly in the light of this analysis how a
dictionary can be of use to us. It serves as a short-cut to the experience, inferences and syntheses of an immense range of speakers—in-
calculably more than we could ever have direct access to; we might say
that its resources are unrivalled in psychedelic power. This being so,
speakers of English are privileged in having, in the *Oxford English
Dictionary*, what is widely held to be the greatest dictionary ever
written for any language. For students of English it must be, however
physically burdensome, a constant companion. It can be corrected in

8*

countless particulars—at times, correcting it has been a popular academic parlour-game; yet in all it is a staggering achievement, inexhaustibly rewarding to study. Do not insult it by using it with no more discrimination than is required for the role of a dictionary in a game of Scrabble. Study its prefatory material, its aims and methods. The more linguistic (and other) learning you bring to your use of it, the more you will get out of it.

Being well informed about it, you will realise that it cannot be up-to-date, mirroring the present state of English lexical resources. In so far as it aims to provide such a reflection for any period, that period is long past. Note when the material was collected, when the main volumes were published, when the Supplement appeared. Most people have little knowledge of the rate of lexical change (a subject we shall consider later), but almost everybody realises that there is change. No thinking person could suppose that a dictionary prepared in his grandparents' or even parents' youth, could adequately reflect current usage. Yet for an undergraduate now the gap may be as much as three generations since the main collections were made for the *OED*. I find I am not the only parent to have been asked 'Mummy, what's a gramophone?' But only when my daughter (b. 1957) asked did I realise that the word, once familiar, had entirely dropped out of my own current vocabulary.

Though recent developments are not recorded in the main *Dictionary*, however, the publishers continue to sponsor recording of English vocabulary. Mr. R. W. Burchfield is preparing a Second Supplement; in the meantime newly recorded items can be found in current editions of the *Shorter Oxford Dictionary* and the *Concise Oxford Dictionary of Current English*; news and queries also appear in the monthly journal *The Periodical*—students may be able to take a small part in this major record of English vocabulary if they watch the columns of this journal.

Meanwhile, American English has the benefit of a recently-revised major dictionary (Webster, 1961). A very much smaller enterprise of recording British English deserves mention here because it is an original compilation, because it cuts out much material kept in other dictionaries for purely traditional reasons, and because it tries to include the most important new words and to discard the archaic. It can be criticised, but it is a remarkable, almost single-handed, achievement on the part of its editor, G. N. Garmonsway. This is the *Penguin English Dictionary (1965)*.

Notes

1. For a discursive treatment of some recent developments in English vocabulary, see Barber (1964), Chapter IV.

2. A thesaurus arranges lexical items on a (hitherto) intuitively-determined basis of semantic likeness and association; it is thus more nearly linguistic in principle of arrangement than a dictionary. There is a good modern edition of Roget's *Thesaurus* (1962). Some lexicologists have been interested in making a formal study on similar lines; see Matoré, *La Méthode en Lexicologie,* Paris, (1953) and further references given there.

§183. Notice that though usage is subjective in that we have no direct access to the inferences of other speakers, it is a socialising rather than an individuating force, since our own inferences, though private, are about other people's supposed inferences, and our applications, by and large, are meant to conform with what we believe other people's to be. There are certain areas of usage, however, where the process of mutual adjustment between speakers is carried on in a somewhat more explicit way.

Up to a point this might be maintained of all technical usages, though, as we have seen in studying language, technical and general uses of the same lexical items can co-exist, often with a minimum of friction. In one domain lexical usage affecting not merely certain specialists, but virtually all members of the speech-community, has been entrusted by society to special custodians, responsible for determining or maintaining agreed values for certain words (which thereby become *terms*). These custodians, who formulate and legislate for the society, do so by virtue of their position in society, not by virtue of any special understanding of language. Frequently in the past they have shown startling ignorance of how language functions; nowadays less so. They are entrusted with the task of decreeing that usages shall follow certain rules or pronouncing that certain rules have established themselves and must be conformed to. Individuals flout their pronouncements at their peril—not their linguistic peril (the danger of being misunderstood) but their social peril (the danger of formal punishment according to law). For example *big* and *large* have a considerable overlap in contextual and collocational meaning; they also diverge in ways we feel, in general, to be under our control as speakers. But in describing for sale hen's eggs weighing two ounces we may freely use the designation *big*; if we call them *large* we have violated a standard laid down by society's delegates for the definition of large eggs. In this instance, usage in a restricted domain has been prescribed in advance in such a way as to circumscribe the freedom of application, and so of change, for a particular item.

This kind of restraint may also operate retrospectively, when a court pronounces on whether some thing or process comes under the head of

a legal provision.   During the last few months these examples have been
reported in the press:

(a) *The Times*, 16, xi. 66, headline: '"FAMILY" AND "HOUSEHOLD" ARE
   DIFFERENT'.   Section 15 defined such houses as those which were
   let in lodgings or which were occupied by more than one family.

   Counsel for the landlord contended that the premises were not
   let to members of more than one family.   "Family" must be
   construed in its broad general meaning. . . .

   Counsel for the borough council, however, submitted that the
   County Court Judge had wrongly construed the statutory words in
   not enquiring whether there were in fact two families.   Although
   the Allens were tied by blood relationship they constituted two
   households and therefore came within the ambit of the Act. . . .

   His LORDSHIP said that . . . it was merely a family arrangement.
   These were all members of one family and the council therefore
   had no right to serve the notice.

   LORD JUSTICE DAVIES, concurring, said that . . . it would be
   straining the language of the section too far if the argument of
   counsel for the local authority were accepted, to say that the word
   "family" meant "household" would be a wrong and an impossible
   conclusion.

   LORD JUSTICE EDMUND DAVIES, concurring, said that . . . since
   the word "household" was used later in the section it was incon-
   ceivable "household" and "family" could mean the same thing.'

(b) *The Times*, 25, xi. 66, headline: 'STALLHOLDER MUST NOT SELL
   ASPIRIN' (Section 129S) of the Pharmacy and Medicines Act, 1941,
   provides a defence to the charge of selling in contravention of
   section 12 (1) on proof, *inter alia*, that the sale was effected "at a
   shop".   The justices dismissed the information on the grounds
   that the stall was "a shop" within the meaning of the Act of 1941,
   being that of the Shops Act, 1921, which, by section 19 (1) defines
   "shop" to include "any premises where any retail trade or business
   is carried on . . ." . . .

   The LORD CHIEF JUSTICE said that the respondent had a tenancy
   agreement with Wigan Corporation, paying a weekly rent of £12,
   and the stall, within the general area of the market, consisted of a
   tubular steel framework with a permanent canvas awning, was
   equipped with electric light and an electric sign, and mail addressed
   to the respondent had been delivered to the stall from the Post
   Office.   When the Wigan Fair was held twice yearly the stall was
   carried bodily away but, apart from that, was always in the market
   area in the same place, defined by a painted white line on the
   ground, and the respondent had a staff of five conducting a retail

business in medicines and detergents from 9 a.m. to 5 p.m. every day of the week except Sunday and Monday.

His LORDSHIP, approaching the case apart from any authority, would clearly have concluded that the stall could not properly come within the expression "shop" [but there are authorities, which are quoted at some length, including Viscount Caldecote:] '"I think that this definition must be read as including in addition to that which is a 'shop' in the natural meaning of that word a permanent place, with limits which can be defined precisely, on which or on part of which there is some sort of structure, where a regular retail trade can be carried on."' [Nevertheless, his Lordship concluded that:] 'It was sufficient for this case to say that everything which could generally be called a "stall" and would have been covered by the definition in the Shop Hours Act, 1892, was now a "'place other than a shop".'

Those who have the patience may turn up similar discussions on such topics as *Cremation not a process within Income Tax Act* (*The Times*, 8.3.67), the meaning of *paid* (*The Times*, 14.6.67), and whether a mobile crane is a machine (*The Times*, 21.6.67).

§184. We are left with the question whether any approach to lexical study is possible, or desirable, apart from dictionary-like compilations and records of change. The answer seems to be that it is desirable, and that recent developments in computers make it possible.

We need first to agree on the basic unit that operates at the lexical level. Difficulties in defining *word* have already been noted, and we have settled for *word* as a unit on the grammatical rank-scale. We cannot assume that the same unit operates in lexis. When we consider the kinds of linguistic meaning that are not accounted for in grammar (i.e., that must by definition be accounted for in lexis) it is evident that in many cases the unit is co-extensive with the word, as we use the term. On the other hand, many cases are not, such as *put up with, make up for*. It seems best, therefore, to use a distinct term, **lexical item**, recognising that it will in many instances be co-extensive with the grammatical unit, *word*. There does not seem to be any compelling reason to set up a scale for lexis, and until one is found we shall operate with this single term. Like *rank* and *scale*, the grammatical categories of *structure* and *system* seem simply irrelevant to lexical analysis; indeed, lexis is defined as an area of organisation in which systems do not operate (this is what distinguishes it from grammar); without these three categories, *structure* is not a relevant category, and must be abandoned in favour of linear co-occurrence. The two axes of relationship, paradigmatic and syntagmatic, are still the basis of classification, but do not involve the kinds of organisation implied by structure and system. For co-occurring in syntax we may use the term **collocate**; an item collocates with another in its environment, the two together forming a **collocation**. To the paradigmatic class of items with the same privilege of occurrence we may give the name *set*. On the difference between grammatical and lexical items and assignment to classes M. A. K. Halliday has written illuminatingly (*Lexis as a Linguistic Level*, in Bazell, etc., 1966, pp. 150–1):

'The sentence *he put forward a strong argument for it* is acceptable in English; *strong* is a member of that set of items which can be juxtaposed with *argument*, a set which also includes *powerful*. *Strong* does not always stand in this same relation to *powerful*: *he drives a strong car* is, at least relatively, unacceptable, as is *this tea's too powerful*. To put it another way, *a strong car* and *powerful tea* will either be rejected as ungrammatical (or unlexical) or shown to be in some sort of marked contrast with a *powerful car* and *strong tea*; in either case the paradigmatic relation of *strong* to *powerful* is not a constant but depends on the syntagmatic relation into which each enters, here with *argument, car* or *tea*.

'Grammatically, unless these are regarded as different structures, which seems unlikely, they will be accounted for in a way which, whatever the particular form of statement the model employs, will amount to saying that, first, *strong* and *powerful* are members of a class that enters into a certain structural relation with a class of which *argument* is a member; second, *powerful* (but not *strong*) is a member of a class entering into this relation with a class of which *car* is a member; and third, *strong* (but not *powerful*) is a member of a class entering into this relation with a class of which *tea* is a member. It would be hoped that such classes would reappear elsewhere in the grammar defined on other criteria. *Argument, car* and *tea*, will, for example, already have been distinguished on other grounds on the lines of 'abstract', 'concrete inanimate' and 'mass' but these groupings are not applicable here, since we can have *a strong table* and *powerful whisky*, while *a strong device* is at least questionable.

'The same *patterns* do reappear; *he argued strongly, I don't deny the strength of his argument, his argument was strengthened by other factors. Strongly* and *strength* are parallelled by *powerfully* and *power, strengthened* by *made more powerful*. The same restrictions have to be stated, to account for *the power* (but not *the strength*) *of his car* and *the strength* (but not *the power*) *of her tea*. But these involve different structures. . . . *Strong* and *powerful*, on the other hand, have been assigned to the same class, so that we should expect to find *a powerful car* paralleled by *a strong car*. The classes set up to account for the patterns under discussion either will cut across the primary dimension of grammatical classification or will need to be restated for each primary class.'

It is for such reasons that Halliday regards the case for recognition of a distinct level of lexical organisation in language as proved.

A full-scale investigation of lexical material, which for the first time will take us beyond the noting of instances that are intuitively striking, is now under way. For a first report, see John Sinclair, *Beginning the Study of Lexis*, also in Bazell, etc. (1966).

§185. Meanwhile, certain aspects of lexical organisation remain about which something can at present be said. The nature of collocational patterning has been surveyed by Angus McIntosh in *Patterns and Ranges* (McIntosh and Halliday, 1966). He distinguishes, in terms of their acceptability, three kinds of sentences:

1. sentences which we accept without hesitation, e.g. *Jane has just come in*;
2. sentences which are not ungrammatical, but which we boggle at because we cannot readily imagine an occasion for their use, e.g., *The flaming waste-paper basket snored violently*; further thought will suggest that, for instance, in a fairy-tale they could find a place;
3. sentences which, though made of English words, are clearly unacceptable, which could not have a use in any conceivable environment, e.g., *Twenty because tomorrow the had a it*. These do not conform to any admitted pattern.

We can also distinguish among lexical formations:

1. forms which are obviously acceptable, i.e., actual, words, such as *basket*;
2. words which are not actually in use, but which do conform to accepted patterns, and might at any time come into use, such as *histle, plint*;
3. totally ineligible forms, i.e., forms which do not fit either of these classes; it does not make sense to give examples since it is not clear what distinctively English components could go to their making; perhaps they are not strictly lexical, but the possibility of forms not fitting 1 or 2 must be mentioned.

Yet there is a difference in the criteria we use in assessing the two cases (a difference already reflected in the terms we have had to use in setting them out). We say that certain forms are words in English because we know from experience that they have the kind of role we attribute to words; but in evaluating sentences we do not call on experience in this simple sense, that is, we do not ask ourselves whether we have previously encountered the structure in the role of sentence; we appeal to criteria rather than collected cases.

Having established this difference between words and sentences, McIntosh turns to a problematic case of a different order:

The molten postage feather scored a weather.

We cannot object to this on grounds of pattern since another exponent of the same pattern is perfectly acceptable:

The aged chemistry professor caused a sensation.

Nor can we say that, like the flaming waste-paper basket sentence, it merely awaits a use; for now we are dealing with a structure to which we cannot attach enough meaning to imagine what that use would be. The grammatical meaning of the SPC structure comes through, but the collocation of lexical items within the places of the clause-elements (*molten postage feather/scored a weather*) is opaque. He comments:

> 'This is a way of saying that words have only a certain tolerance of compatibility, only a certain *potential of collocability*, quite apart from any considerations of pattern in the grammatical sense.' (pp. 186–7).

The essential question is whether we judge the eligibility of collocations as we judge that of words (by experience of the particular case) or as we judge that of sentences (by applying criteria of pattern).   McIntosh concludes that we do use criteria of pattern, and that the patterns are different in kind from grammatical ones:

> 'In taking different attitudes towards these two sequences [*the molten postage feather* and *the aged chemistry professor*] we rely, I suggest, not only on the test of familiarity, but on criteria of pattern.   But the underlying patterns which are relevant here are of quite a different order from the grammatical patterning of which I have spoken hitherto.   Hereafter I shall therefore distinguish this new kind by speaking of *range*, using "pattern" only in relation to grammar. There is for instance a range, however laborious it may be to define or describe, which is represented by the fairly strictly limited inventory of nouns which may without any question be qualified by the word *molten*.   The set of alternative available possibilities which this inventory consists of is just as much a part of the form of the language as is a grammatical system, and a full account of this set goes a long way towards constituting the meaning of molten.   Now this meaning itself rests (though it will of course depend on other collocational relationships as well) to a considerable extent on a certain similarity of meaning of all the nouns in question; this, in turn, is merely another way of saying that there are marked similarities between the

collocational habits of each and all of these. Therefore if (ignoring *postage* for the moment) an attempt is made to collocate *molten* with a noun of a quite different "family" (that is, one with a very different set of collocational habits) such as *feather*, the only experience we can fall back on to deal with it is experience of that aspect of linguistic form which in one way or another has to do with the phenomenon of range.'

§186. There is widespread awareness of the fact that vocabulary changes—changes perceptibly during an individual's lifetime. The awareness is accompanied by certain beliefs which are false; that generally speaking when a change occurs it is noticed, and that the number of changes is quite small. In a New Year's Eve television programme at the close of 1965 Robert Robinson, surveying the year's events, referred to 'the year's meagre crop of new words'. Even more recently, *The Observer* carried the following:

'MICHAEL YOUNG . . . is one of those rare people who have given a word to the Language. Whenever the word "meritocrat" is used— and it is in constant use—he should receive a royalty' (16th July, 1967).

These observations clearly imply the conviction that lexical innovation can sufficiently be recorded by the amateur, and (or perhaps because) it is a fairly rare thing. In fact, it is not at all a simple matter to know whether a word is new or not, or even to work out how one would know. Does one say: 'It's new to me, so it must be new'? Clearly not; though there are many deep-rooted popular illusions about language, they do not take the form, at least in my experience, of a speaker, however paranoid, supposing that there are no English words he does not know. As we have seen, the tendency is to show in this matter too much self-distrust. Does one take a consensus of one's friends? Even this will seem to almost everyone to represent a far too limited spectrum. Does one go to the dictionary? Again, as we have seen, there is no exhaustive dictionary that is up-to-date. Presumably one puts together information from as many divergent sources as possible, says that is the best one can do, and recognises that the evidence is far from complete.

Such caution is a far cry from popular assertiveness about what is new in language (especially, but not exclusively, in lexis). While the circumstances of first use of the words *meritocracy, meritocrat*, are such that *The Observer's* account may well be right, many bold claims are made about innovations which are demonstrably wrong; during the past year a complaint was published of a list of neologisms which included *fall* (*sensu autumn*)—a meaning so old in English that the Pilgrim Fathers took it with them to America. Students of English should be on guard against such claims, not only because in a particular instance they may be clearly erroneous, but because they are trying to do what in principle can only rarely be done.

Would we, then, be on safe ground in saying that we can never be sure a lexical item is new, but we can be sure if it is not? Hardly. For if an item has been produced by a speaker in the belief that it is new, it is of no relevance to that use to point out that someone else 'invented' the same word some time ago. If an item has not been experienced before by its user there is certainly a sense in which it is new; the only sense in which it is not new belongs to the history rather than the structure of the language.

§187. It may seem strange to speak of lexical innovation as having any place at all in linguistic structure, as opposed to linguistic history. Innovation may seem to be always a process through time, even if we narrow the time-span so closely as to refer only to our own life-time, or less. Language cannot be understood if it is thought of as something which has structure in one dimension and history, intersecting, in another. Saussure used the analogy of a tree, whose growth, through time, accounted for the ring pattern which appears in a transverse section (1916, p. 125). In so far as this indicates dependence it is illuminating. But it is not a complete analogy. It does not also make history depend on structure—that is to say, it does not show that there is that about the pattern found on transverse section that makes change a necessary, not an accidental property of language, somehow requiring additional explanation. At several points as we disentangle the structure of English we find conditions that would necessarily give rise to historical change—conditions of which we may say that potential for innovation is necessarily present in the structure. Nowhere is the evidence clearer than in the matter of lexical development. For the new words that catch commentators' eyes are the thinnest of cream on the surface. In one sense, lexical innovation is going on all the time on a literally immeasurably large scale. Though it can take many forms, the kind that accounts for the layman's and the linguist's views is a kind that is wholly unobtrusive—commentators do not notice it is going on, and users do not notice they are doing it. This is word formation, which, in its combination of creativeness with unobtrusiveness, involves something like the inventive freedom of sentence-making. Perhaps it should be seen in terms of realisation of potential rather than innovation. Word-formation and other modes of innovation account for such abundance of new lexical material that in checking a single issue of, say, *The Sunday Times*, for forms not accounted for in the major English dictionaries, you will normally compile a list of at least one hundred items. The issue should be chosen 'blind' (for instance, by fixing in advance on the issue for a given date); the dictionary search should cover both the direct entry and coverage by word-formation rules; and the list should exclude the vocabulary of advertisement, which is often ecccentric (though students will also be interested that bizarre innovations are successfully interpreted).

§188. The role of word-formation (WF), and its special position in the structure of the language, require our attention.   Formation is a process word and an object word; it refers to the making of certain composite structures, and also to the structures themselves.   The structures, once formed, obviously belong to synchronic description, and they need separate mention because they often reflect in lexical form relations that are otherwise expressed syntactically.   But the process of formation is something that happens through time; at any given time, one might argue, a structure has been formed, and belongs to synchronic description, or it has not, and does not so belong.   However, two features of WF, as the term is commonly understood, make it necessary to consider formation-as-process in synchronic study.   One is the rate and profusion of production by formative methods; the other (or perhaps they are really the same) is that, of many composites, it is impossible to say whether they are established or new.   We know, in a sense, by heart, such composites as *blackbird, blackboard*; we are perfectly well aware that we have met them before.   But in a normal day's talk or reading we will encounter and use hundreds of forms about which we cannot be sure whether they are learned or new (generated); they are in this respect like sentences rather than words.   They represent the area in which history and structure mingle most inextricably.   The properties in which it resembles syntax bind WF as process, like WF as structure, into the complex whole which is a given *état de langue*.

The subject has been explored with great learning and subtlety in Marchand (1960); it is not well adapted to summary treatment, but some hint of the riches of this field of study can be indicated in brief. Marchand defines WF as:

'that branch of the science of language which studies the patterns on which a language forms new lexical units' (p. 2).

It deals with composites which can be analysed both as to their formal components and as to their semantic constituents ('A composite rests on a relationship between morphemes through which it is motivated' *ib.*).   Such a definition includes items like *renew, reform, research*, but excludes items like *recoil, release, receive, conceive, deceive*, since in the second group there is no morpheme *re-*, etc. or *-ceive*, etc. to which the parts of the whole word can be referred *both formally and semantically*.

Typically, motivation arises from use of established morphemes in established patterns; it is evident in English *blackbird*, and absent from French *merle*. Though common, this is by no means the only form motivation can take. Marchand distinguishes two main types of motivated composites, and of these two types the first is most relevant to synchronic analysis. This type comprises composites which are grammatical syntagmas, i.e., patterns (characteristically, but not necessarily, sequences) of morphemes in relationships analogous to those of discursive syntax. There are five sub-types, the first three of them covering the material commonly thought of as belonging to WF.

(a) **Compounding**: 'The compound is . . . made up of a determining and a determined part. In the system of languages to which English belongs the determinant generally precedes the determinatum' [thus, in *rainbow* the second element *-bow* tells us what class of items is in question and the first, *rain-*, specifies or determines what kind of bow we are to understand]. 'The types which do not conform to this principle are either syntactical compounds (e.g. *father-in-law*) or loan-compounds (e.g. *Macdonald, Fitzgerald*) with the "inner form" of a non-English language.' (Marchand, p. 11). WF of this kind is particularly productive and multifarious in English and will require further notice at §188ff.

(b) **Prefixation**: 'We call prefixes such particles as can be prefixed to full words but are themselves not words with an independent existence' (Marchand, p. 85). There are some sixty of them in English, such as *ante-* as in *ante-natal*, *co-* as in *co-author*, *mal-* as in *maladministration*. See also **clipping compounds**, §191.

(c) **Suffixation**: 'A suffix is a derivative final element which is or formerly was productive in forming words. A sf [suffix] has semantic value, but it does not occur as an independent speech unit' (Marchand, p. 157). There is thus a distinction between suffixes, whose primary value is lexical, e.g., *-hood* as in *fatherhood*, *-ish* as in *youngish*, and inflections, whose primary value is grammatical, e.g. *-s* in *fathers*, *-er* in *younger*. Different types of morpheme-boundary transition may mark this distinction, cf. *youngish* /jʌŋɪʃ/ belonging to WF and *younger* /jʌŋgə/ belonging to grammar. In English, suffixes are rather more numerous than prefixes, having over eighty types, with many sub-varieties. There are also **semi-suffixes**, i.e., elements which 'stand midway between full words and suffixes. Some of them are used only as second-words of *cpds*, though their word character is still clearly recognizable' (Marchand, p. 290). Examples are *-like* in *statesmanlike* and *-monger* in *war-monger*.

(d) **Derivation by zero-morpheme**: 'Its characteristic is that a certain stem is used for the formation of a categorically different

word [sc. a word of different grammatical category] without a derivative element being added. In synchronic terminology, we have
syntagmas whose determinatum is not expressed in the significant
(form). The significate (content) is represented in the syntagma, but
zero-marked (i.e. it has no counterpart in form)' (Marchand, p. 293).
If form is looked at on a wider basis, we may say that the index of
the presence of a grammatical morpheme is patterning in a different
grammatical slot. This type of WF is highly productive, the main
varieties being denominal verbs (e.g. *loan*), deadjectival verbs (e.g.
idle), verbs from particles (e.g. *out*), and deverbal nouns (e.g. *look*).
Where in (a)–(c) we were dealing with sequences of morphemes,
in (d) we have new formations which are not sequences but are new
new syntagmas by virtue of their distinct privileges of grammatical
occurrence.

(e) **Backderivation**: This, too, is not a matter of adding one morpheme to another in a meaningful pattern. It might, in terms of
surface form, be thought of as involving the subtraction of a morpheme, but it can better be interpreted as a means of completing a
proportion. Verbs such as *peddle, televise*, arise from completing
the proportions *writer : write :: peddler/peddlar* : ?; *revision : revise* ::
television : ?. See also §191.

The other varieties account for formations which are not, even in the
special senses of (d) and (e), grammatical syntagmas. Marchand identifies **expressive symbolism** (as in the initial *sp-* of e.g., *spew, spit,
spurn, spout, spattle, spatter, spittle, sputter*); blending, as in *smog,
brunch*; **rhyme-combinations**, as in *fuddy-duddy, ragtag*; **ablaut-
combinations** (i.e., combinations in which the vowel changes within
a stable consonant-framework, the counterpart of rhyme combinations)
as in *pingpong, fiddlefaddle*; **clipping**, with varieties in which the
beginning of a word is retained, as in *lab, pub*, or its end, as in *plane,
phone*, or its middle, as in *flu* (it is normally a main stressed syllable
that is retained, though not in *bus*); and **word-manufacturing**, as
in *radar* (*ra*dio *d*irection *a*nd *ra*nging). This group of varieties
differs from those listed in (a)–(e) in being more relevant to history than
to structure; formations developed in these ways are, or are not, words
in the English language. Formations of types (a)–(e) include well-
established items that we recognise as long-familiar words, but also
many other examples of which we cannot say whether we understand
them by virtue of previous familiarity or because they are new instances
of the use of well-tried formation patterns. As would be expected,
this sentence-like characteristic of the way we use and understand such
formations goes with a strong element of syntactic behaviour in their
formation-rules.

§189. It is time to look more closely at the nature of compounding in English. English is often described as a nominalising language. There are several things this comment can mean. Two relevant and valid senses relate to the manifold and complex potential for expansion in nominal structures and to the extraordinary abundance of nominal WF. In both cases, the implied standard of contrast is the patterning and formation of English verbs. Above all, the profusion of nominal formation is seen in compounding.

Compounds show many lines of resemblance and difference among themselves, so that classification cannot proceed by application of a single set of criteria. Since compounding depends on special relationships between words, which themselves are form-meaning composites, it is useful to begin by distinguishing the two planes of form and meaning. Meaning points the way to a very broad binary division. There are compounds (indeed, they are the most usual kind) in which he determinatum or head is indicated by one element, and delimited or specified by its determinant or modifier; in such cases a structure $x-y$ indicates a y, but a y of the specific variety x (as in *rainbow* above). Thus, at least in a broad sense, a *blackbird* is a kind of bird, and a *kingfisher* is a kind of fisher. Compounds of this kind are called (semantically) **endocentric**. In other compounds the generic meaning lies outside what is expressed in the determinatum; this, a *hunchback* is (usually) a kind of man rather than a kind of back; a *pickpocket* is always a kind of man and not a kind of pocket. Compounds of this kind are (semantically) **exocentric**. Compounds may also be grammatically endocentric, if they belong to the same form-class as their determinatum, and exocentric if they do not (type: *has-been*).

§190. Amongst nouns both endocentric and exocentric compounds are used in great abundance, but the endocentric are more numerous in sub-varieties and in actual numbers of formations. They mirror, in telescoped form, a great variety of semantic and syntactic relations which may be indicated by various devices in discursive syntax. Indeed, some scholars would wish to explain all compounds as terms of the patterns they correspond to in full syntax. Marchand identifies relations of comparison in *blockhead*; compositional substance in *waxwork*; purpose in *gunpowder*; place in *garden-party*; time in *night-club*. He notes five different relations between the determinant *finger* and its determinatum in *finger bowl, fingernail, fingerpost* and *finger wave* (p. 22). Grammatically, we have a contrast between *pork butcher* and *family butcher*. But since a single pattern of formation corresponds to so many contrasted relationships in full syntax distinctions are necessarily blurred, and indeed often seem irrelevant; the contrasts are neutralised. The *gold* in *goldfish* may be descriptive (=*golden*) or comparative (=like *gold*); in full syntax we cannot avoid making the distinction, in compounds we are unable to make it. For such reasons, though it is illuminating to make a comparison with full syntax, it is meaningless to analyse compounds as if they were full syntax.

Note, too, what happens when a compound is well established in the language and has become institutionalised. A *blackbird* was no doubt originally so called by speakers who observed that it was a bird and black; but in course of time blackbirds have come to be identified by zoological properties amongst which colour is not primary; it is still true that *blackbirds* are normally *black birds*, but they are not necessarily so, and the expression *white blackbird* is validly used (cf. *pink bluebells*). Being a compound is a more-less, rather than a yes-no matter; though formally *blackbird* is fully a compound, semantically it is less of compound and more of a word than *night-club*.

Nominal compounds may have nouns as their determinants, as in (additive) *fighter bomber* (appositional), *slave girl*; but they may also have many other kinds of determinant, as in *writing-table, dancing girl, whetstone, blackbird, drawn work, blacksmith, north-east, he-goat, housekeeping, heartburning, earthquake, householder, self-starter, sharpshooter, tomfool.*

Beside this proliferation of varieties can be set just four main types of exocentric nominal compounds:

(i) a predicate-complement structure forms an agent-type noun: *pickpocket*;

(ii) a verb with adverbial complement forms an agent-type noun: *runabout*;

(iii) non-animate nouns are formed with a first element in which noun-verb-adjective contrast is neutralised, plus adverbial particle: *blackout*;

(iv) participle with particle: *dugout*.

Notice, too, the rather unusual de-perfective type, *has-been*.

Note

For the types briefly surveyed in this paragraph see Marchand, pp. 21–45. For an attempt to classify nominal compounds in terms of relations in full syntax, see Lees (1961) and Marchand *Indogermanische Forschungen* (1965), 57–71, 117–145.

§191. Compound adjectives are also highly diversified, both in respect of the internal relations they imply (cf. *headstrong* with *grass-green*) and in respect of the form-classes they exploit, cf. *self-adaptive, icy-cold, deaf-mute, heart-breaking, sea-going, self-advertising, man-made, easy-going, high-born.* This wealth of formation-types contributes, as do the nominal formations, to the extraordinarily high degree of development of nominal structures in English.

Compound verbs are not, on Marchand's definition of compound, very common. The main class is that with locative particles as determinants, e.g., *out-bid*, *over-ride*. But there are secondary formations such as *spotlight* (which is secondary because it is formed from the noun which itself is compound) and *stage-manage* (a back-formation from the noun *stage-manager*).

These last examples serve as warning that in the analysis of compounds we cannot be guided by surface structure alone. Some current developments are of interest in this connection. There is a type of formation called a **clipping compound** (Marchand, p. 98). For example, the prefix *auto-* has long been used in English formations in its Greek sense, corresponding to native *self-*, as in *automobile, auto-hypnosis*; but more recently it has entered into formations with the value of the full formation *automobile*, e.g. *autobus, automania*; cf. the way in which *para-* 'stands for' the whole of *parachute* in such formations as *paratroop*, and *semi-* for *semi-detached* in *semi-villa*. This kind of formation seems to blend the methods of prefixing and compounding. Or again, consider the structure *great train robber*, much used in recent years. Superficially it looks like a standard *-er* formation (but there is no verb **great train rob*), or like an extension of the established nominal form *robber* (but it cannot be analysed as *great-train robber* or as *great train-robber*); despite appearances, its total relationships show that it must be analysed as a back-formation from the total structure *great train robbery*.

§192. Finally, the subject of vogue-words is closely bound up with, though distinct from, innovation. This is another lexical topic that attracts popular notice, as in the following sharp comment:

'The American language, as we all know, is a living, breathing, growing instrument, and it's been living, breathing, growing to such an extent since I've been gone (five years) that I'm not sure I can speak it any more. What brought on this thought is that my friend Peter has just got back from America. "How are things back there?" is what I asked him; "What are people talking about?"'

'He looked pained: "Good God, Crosby, Americans don't *talk* any more. They *communicate*. Or they make communication. Or they break down the barriers of communication. Communication is the biggest single industry in the United States—200 million Americans communicating with one another like telephone wires. Or *not* communicating. There's a lot of non-communication going around, too."

'"Well, what are they communicating about? What's bothering them at the moment?"'

'"Bothered!" he said. "What a word! Americans outgrew that

a long time ago. They also outgrew exasperation, annoyance and vexation. Today they have anxieties. They're anxiety-ridden. It takes a much higher degree of sophistication to be anxiety-ridden than to be simply annoyed. The higher intellects are even above anxiety—thay have *angst*. But you have to be very well educated to have *angst*—a PhD at Columbia University, at least. Arthur Schlesinger has *angst*, President Johnson, a lower intellect, is anxiety-ridden."

"'Well," I said. "what has Arthur Schlesinger got *angst* about? What is the big *angst* at the American dinner tables at this red-hot second?"

"'Ethos. Everybody is anxiety-ridden about the middle-class ethos when they're not having *angst* about the suburban ethos or the Negro ethos or the ethos of intervention or of non-intervention."

"'Did you see any of the old crowd?" I asked. "Old Joe Carter. What's old Joe doing now?"

'He gave me a pitying look. "My, you *have* been away. Americans don't *do* things any more. Peasants do things. In our bright, shiny, affluent Keynesian world, people get *involved*. Involvement is everything in America and anything less than total involvement would be a betrayal of oneself."

"'Well," I asked, "what is Joe's total involvement at the moment?"

"'A girl named Gloria. He's up to his elbows in total involvement with Gloria, but I'm afraid Gloria is not returning the total involement. Our old friend Joe is losing his charisma."

"'His what?"

"'Charisma. That's the hottest property in America—charisma. You either is or you is not got charisma, baby, and if you is not got charisma, you just better leave town. Above all, you better not run for public office. Mayor Lindsay's got charisma. But he's losing it. That's the terrible thing about charisma—the minute anyone gets some, he starts losing it. The Kennedys are losing theirs. Johnson has already lost his."

"'Joe's girl-friends were always neurotic. Is this one?"

"'Nobody is neurotic any more. At least, nobody *we* know. Now everybody has syndromes. Gloria has the Manhattan-Jewish syndrome—a very big syndrome. One of the best. The Manhattan-Jewish syndrome is—well, *everything*, a kind of overall anxiety about being Jewish, about living in Manhattan, about living in the twentieth-century, about being human—big anxieties like that —along with a few small personal anxieties about your face, your figure, your income, and your education. The trouble is poor old

9+

Joe has nothing but the White Anglo-Saxon Protestant syndrome—
and that's a mini-syndrome, if ever there was one."

"'A *mini*-syndrome?'"

"'Everything's gone mini—mini-problems, mini-people, mini-
politicians. You can get through a whole dinner party using 'mini'
along with a judicious sprinkling of 'psychedelic' and 'hallucinogenic'."

"'Oh, yes, *LSD*,' I said.

"'Oh, you must never use 'psychedelic' or 'hallucinogenic' in
connection with LSD," he said, horrified. "You use those words
to describe everything *except* LSD. A department store is psychedelic—or a night club or a party or a dress. Johnson's foreign
policy is hallucinogenic. You must learn to use these words
properly."

"'It all seems down beat to me," I said. "Doesn't anyone talk
about sex any more?"

"'Oh, sex is finished. Dead. Sex is last year. This year it's
love. The hippies love everyone. Johnson loves everyone.
Everything is feeling. That's the true communication now—one
simply radiates love." He looked at me pityingly. "I'm afraid, old
boy, that verbalising has had its day."

"'Verbalising?'"

"'Well, the sort of thing you do for a living with that typewriter—
that's verbalising. Muddying up the truth with a lot of words.
Communication has gone on to higher spheres—feelings, images,
hallucinations, pictures—stuff like that. You might say the hottest
new development in the American language is that words are
finished. One simply doesn't need them any more.'"

John Crosby. *The Observer*, 16th July, 1967.

Exercises

1. Rough out as well as you can the 'families' of the items *molten,
   postage, feather, score, weather.*
2. How far can the peculiarities of the 'sentence' *The molten postage
   feather scored a weather* be accounted for in terms of range? Can a
   better account be given by including grammatical factors?
3. In the *molten postage feather* sentence we may think the grammar is
   deviant, but we are not in any doubt what it is. In the *twenty because
   tomorrow the had a it* sequence we cannot detect any grammar. What
   accounts for the difference between the two?
4. Working, if possible, in pairs, try to find out how far the lexical items
   of the forthcoming issue of the *Sunday Times, Observer* or *Sunday
   Telegraph* are accounted for in the major dictionaries. For an exercise of comfortable length about three pairs are needed per paper.
   Note cases where you have to find a principle for deciding how much

constitutes a lexical item, and cases where you are in doubt whether two things are instances of the same item. Explain the principles on which you decided such difficulties. Attempt to classify the types of innovation you find. Are some kinds particularly common in certain parts of the paper? What form-classes are most represented on your lists? Why?

5. What flavour does the vogue-lexis mocked by Crosby now have? Which items have struck you as vogue-words during the current season? Why do you think vogue-words exist?

6. Work out the linguistic implications of the passages quoted in §183.

7. Work out the reason for distinguishing the noun compound types listed in §190 (list *writing table* to *tomfool*) and the adjective compound types in §191 (list *self-adaptive* to *high-born*); *then* check your analysis with the relevant passages in Marchand.

FURTHER READING

The most relevant works have been cited in the course of the Chapter.

Conclusion

This book is not drawing to a conclusion because it has covered the ground of its title. In a sense it has failed of its purpose if any reader thinks, at this stage, that such an aim could be achieved. Our goal has been more limited—at once more realistic and more worthy: to convey some sense of the role of language in human life, and some notion of how our own language fulfils that role. The tracts of usage left untouched are, I recognise, both ample and important; but I am not so concerned to present all the facts as to inculcate an attitude, with enough facts to explain and justify it. For about this most central human concern the opinions prevalent in English society are as strongly held as they are wrong-headed. On such a matter, radical misconceptions do not simply result in that direct impoverishment of experience consequent on ignorance of any kind; they have in the long run grave social, practical, economic and political consequences. For instance, putting together their feeling for the pre-eminence of RP. as an English accent and their authoritarian and prescriptive notions of linguistic correctness, many English people automatically sort speakers into outsiders and insiders the moment they open their mouths. While there are great advantages in having a standard form of language, there are great disadvantages in having within it a more restricted accent which acts in this litmus-paper kind of way. The fable of *Pygmalion* is about the turning of a statue not into a lady, but into a woman; and Shaw was well aware of this. Eliza Doolittle, being a member of the English-speaking world but lacking an acceptable form of English, was less than human; and if that were not still the case, *My Fair Lady* would not have had so wide an appeal. In that version of the fable, Professor Higgins asks, 'Why can't the English teach their children how to speak?' Of course, it is not a fair question, but if we are prepared to answer the intention of it, we have to point to the fact that a sufficient number of English speakers are more interested in language as a social barrier than as a social bond.

This social fact has practical, economic and political consequences, but such consequences also follow more directly from misconceptions about language. For it can be nothing else that stands in the way of spelling-reform, which would in very short space repay its initial cost by the saving of millions of man-hours for teachers and children, and would lay the foundations of such an attitude towards speech and writing as could in later years, among other things, pay golden dividends in the increased ease of learning foreign languages. Of more direct political concern (though hardly of greater fundamental importance) is that such reform would pave the way for the greater acceptance of English as an international language. Of a world language there is as yet no hope; but over large and divergent areas an international language could come into use, and far the most practicable, in terms of numbers already using it and skilled teachers available (1), is English. But certainly not English as currently spelt. And in fact, as I write, UNESCO. is on the point of giving its support to Esperanto as a first international language. International bodies properly want to take action now; it is at least partly because of our stubbornness about spelling-reform in English that they have been driven to take action which to many professional linguistic scholars seems deplorable. Since the Common Market came into existence, much attention has been given to the question of establishing a European common language, and of late the issue has been considered in this country. Public opinion on such matters is so totally uninstructed that as I write (March, 1962) a Bill is due for second reading in the House of Commons which empowers the Minister of Education to set up a British Academy of Language to work towards this end—but on such terms that no professional linguistic scholar is likely to have any truck with the institution. These things matter; I think they matter so much that the inculcating of more correct attitudes to language is more important than exhaustive coverage of the facts of English structure in this book.

So I hope that readers of this book will be persuaded of several ideas that have for too long been alien to our normal education. They should have some notion of the part language plays in their lives—a notion both of its profound importance and of its essential invulnerability (a language can do what its speakers need it and use it to do, and however it changes as a result of their use it will not fail in this) (2). They should have a just sense of the primacy of speech in language, and should not be taken in by the widespread belief that language is really writing—especially, that writing (or even a particular convention of writing) is needed to stabilise or give range or even adequacy to a language (3). They should understand properly the expression *linguistic correctness*, taking it to refer to conformity to the usage required by one's speech-community in relation to a given medium, 'style' and register. And they should not be brow-beaten by those who claim authority outside usage for the imposition of some forms of expression and the exclusion of others (4). They will envisage a standard language as that form of a language shared by its educated speakers, and they will recognise that what actually goes under this designation in English is very far from being uniform.

Along with these more humane, sensible and scholarly attitudes to language will go an awareness of the scope of our ignorance about our own language and of the ever-present danger of assuming we have analytical knowledge when we have no more than impressions gained introspectively. If this book has brought about in some of its readers such reversals of deep-ingrained assumptions and misconceptions, it will have achieved a great deal. It has also aimed at giving such an introduction to the facts of English structure as will embody the new attitude to language in a fairly coherent picture of what the reader's own language is like. But it would take at least another book of this scope to make that picture accurate and exhaustive in detail—and by the time that book was written, there would already be quite considerable alterations in usage. It is considerations such as these that have determined the balance between exposition of theory and exposition of facts in this book. Breaking off where I do, I have to hope the book has created a sufficient momentum of interest to carry forward the reader's attention, so that each observes for himself the larger mechanisms whereby his language holds him enmeshed in that intricate pattern of personal and social life wherein we have our being.

Notes

1. There are far too few qualified teachers of English as a foreign language, but more proportionately than for any other language proposed for international use.

2. In other words, the very common complaints that English is declining or being corrupted simply do not make sense. Three recent examples from people making what appear to be professional judgements are: 'In the following pages we shall see good words, or good senses of words, losing their edge, or, more rarely, recovering it or getting a new edge that serves some different purpose. I have tried not to obtrude the moral, but I should be glad if I sent any reader away with a new sense of responsibility to the language. It is unnecessary defeatism to believe that we can do nothing about it. Our conversation will have little effect; but if we get into print . . . we can help to strengthen or weaken some disastrous vogue word; can encourage a good, and resist a bad, gallicism or Americanism. . . . I am not suggesting that we can by an archaising purism repair any of the losses that have already occurred. It may not, however, be entirely useless to resolve that we ourselves will never commit verbicide' (C. S. Lewis, 'Studies in Words,' Cambridge University Press, London, 1960, pp. 6–8); 'Let us not blame them [sc. the translators of *The New English Bible*] because the English language is not in better shape, or because in other centuries it was richer than it is now' (Gordon Rupp in *The Listener*, 16 March, 1961); 'Various other changes [sc. in addition to the increasing prominence given to the teaching of English in schools and universities] have been blunting and enfeebling our language.' (Raymond Mortimer, in the *Sunday Times*, 1 April, 1962, p. 30, col. 1.)

3. One aspect of how wrong, under the present system, people can be about the relationship between speech and writing is shown by the following extract from a letter to the *Sunday Times*; and that the misconception is not confined to a few individuals is shown by the fact that the editor of a leading paper should have been prepared to print it:

'I have been pondering for some time on the vagaries of the English language and its illogical pronunciation.   For instance, there are six ways of pronouncing "ough", involving at least fifteen words . . .' (*Sunday Times*, 1 April, 1962, p. 43, col. 1).

4. For a survey of such views and an examination of educated usage in relation to the shibboleths, cf. Fries (1940).

Bibliography

ABERCROMBIE, DAVID (1953), 'English Accents', *English Language Teaching*, VII, 113–123.

—— (1958), 'The Department of Phonetics', *University of Edinburgh Gazette*, 20.

—— (1964₁), 'Syllable Quantity and Enclitics in English', *In Honour of Daniel Jones*, edited by David Abercrombie et al., London, 216–222. (Now also in Abercrombie [1965].)

—— (1964₂), 'A Phonetician's View of Verse Structure', *Linguistics*, 6, 5–13. (Now also in Abercrombie [1965].)

—— (1965), 'Studies in Phonetics and Linguistics', London.

—— (1967), 'Elements of General Phonetics', Edinburgh.

ALLEN, HAROLD B. (ed.) (1958), 'Readings in Applied English Linguistics', New York.

ARNOLD, G. F. (1957), 'Stress in English Words', *Lingua*, VI, 221–267, 397–441.

BAZELL, C. E. (1953), 'Linguistic Form', Istanbul.

—— (et al., edd.) (1966), 'In Memory of J. R. Firth', London.

BEHRE, FRANK (1955), 'Meditative-polemic "should" in modern English "that"-clauses'. Stockholm.

BLOCH, BERNARD (1947), 'English Verb Inflection', *Language*, 23, 399–418.

—— and TRAGER, GEORGE L. (1942), 'Outline of Linguistic Analysis'. Baltimore.

BLOOMFIELD, LEONARD (1935), 'Language' (British edition). London.

BOLINGER, DWIGHT L. (1957), 'The Interrogative Structures of American English', *Proceedings of the American Dialect Society*, No. 28. Alabama.

—— (1961), 'Generality, Gradience, and the All-or-None'. The Hague.

BRADLEY, HENRY (1913), 'On the Relations between Spoken and Written Language with Special Reference to English', Proceedings of the British Academy, VI.

BROWN, ROGER (1958), 'Words and Things'. Glencoe, Illinois.

BRYANT, MARGARET M. (1962), 'Modern English and its Heritage'. New York. Second edition.

CARROLL, JOHN B. (1953), 'The Study of Language'. Cambridge, Massachusetts. (Also 1954, London.)

CARVELL, H. T. and SVARTVIK, J. (1966), 'Linguistic Classification and Numerical Taxonomy'. The Hague.

CHOMSKY, NOAM (1957), 'Syntactic Structures'. The Hague.

—— (1964), 'Current Issues in Linguistic Theory'. The Hague. (Also in Fodor and Katz [1964].)

—— (1965), 'Aspects of the Theory of Syntax'. Cambridge, Massachusetts.

—— (1966), 'Cartesian Linguistics'. New York.

CHRISTOPHERSEN, PAUL (1939), 'The Articles: a study of their theory and use in English'. Copenhagen.

COHEN, A. (1952). 'The Phonemes of English'. The Hague.

CRYSTAL, DAVID (1966), 'Specification and English Tenses', *Journal of Linguistics*, 2, 1–34.

—— and QUIRK, RANDOLPH (1964), 'Systems of Prosodic and Paralinguistic Features in English'. The Hague.

CURME, G. O. (1935, 1931), 'A Grammar of the English Language. Volume 2: Parts of Speech, Accidence. Volume 3: Syntax'. New York.

FILLMORE, C. (1965), 'Indirect Object Constructions in English'. The Hague.

FIRTH, J. R. (1948), 'Sounds and Prosodies', *Transactions of the Philological Society*, 127–152. (Also in 1957_2.)

—— (1957_1), 'Introduction' and 'A Synopsis of Linguistic Theory, 1930–1955' in *Studies in Linguistic Analysis*. Philological Society, Oxford.

—— (1957_2), 'Papers in Linguistics, 1934–1951'. London.

—— (1964), 'The Tongues of Men *and* Speech' (originally 1937 and 1930 respectively). London.

FODOR, JERRY A. and KATZ, JERROLD J. (1964), 'The Structure of Language'. Englewood Cliffs, New Jersey.

FRANCIS, W. N. (1958), 'The Structure of American English. With a chapter on American English Dialects by Raven I McDavid, Jr.' New York.

FRIES, CHARLES C. (1925), 'The Periphrastic Future with *Shall* and *Will* in Modern English', *Publications of the Modern Language Association of America*, 40, 963–1024.

—— (1926), 'The Expression of the Future', *Language*, 3, 87–95.

—— (1940), 'American English Grammar'. New York.

—— (1952), 'The Structure of English'. New York (English cheap edition, London, 1958).

FRY, D. B. (1947), 'The Frequency of Occurrence of Speech Sounds

9*

in Southern English', *Archives Néérlandaises de Phonetique Experimentale*, XX, 103–106.

FRY, D. B. (1955), 'Duration and Intensity as Physical Correlates of Linguistic Stress', *Journal of the Acoustical Society of America*, 27, 765–768.

GELB, I. J. (1952), 'Writing'. Chicago. (Also as Phoenix Paperback.)

GIMSON, A. C. (1962), 'An Introduction to the Pronunciation of English'. London.

GLEASON, HENRY A., Jr. (1961), 'An Introduction to Descriptive Linguistics'. Second edition. New York. To be used with the same author's 'Workbook in Descriptive Linguistics'.

—— (1965), 'Linguistics and English Grammar'. New York.

HALL, ROBERT A., Jr. (1943), 'Melanesian Pidgin English'. Linguistic Society of America, Baltimore.

—— (1950), 'Leave Your Language Alone'. Ithaca. (A second, revised edition is available under the title 'Linguistics and your Language' in paperback, New York, 1960.)

HALLIDAY, M. A. K. (1961), 'Categories of the Theory of Grammar', *Word*, 17, 241–292.

—— (1963_1), 'The Tones of English', *Archivum Linguisticum*, 15, 1–28 (see also 1967_3 and McIntosh and Halliday).

—— (1963_2), 'Intonation in English Grammar', *Transactions of the Philological Society*, 143–169 (see also 1967_3 and McIntosh and Halliday).

—— (1963_3), 'Class in Relation to the Axes of Chain and Choice', *Linguistics*, 2, 5–15.

—— (1966), 'Some Notes on "Deep" Grammar', *Journal of Linguistics*, 2, 57–67.

—— (1967_1), 'Notes on Transitivity and Theme', *Journal of Linguistics*, 3, 37–81 (with two further articles to follow on the subject in the same journal).

—— (1967_2), 'Grammar, Society and the Noun'. University College, London.

—— (1967_3), 'Intonation and Grammar in British English'. The Hague.

HALLIDAY, M. A. K., McINTOSH, A., and STREVENS, P. (1964), 'The Linguistic Sciences and Language Teaching'. London.

HAMP, Eric, et al. (1965); Readings in Linguistics'. Chicago.

HARRIS, Z. S. (1951), 'Methods in Structural Linguistics'. Chicago. (Also 1952, Cambridge, England, and as a Phoenix Paperback under the title, 'Structural Linguistics', 1960.)

—— (1952), 'Discourse Analysis', *Language*, 28, 1–30.

HERDAN, GUSTAV (1960), 'Type-Token Mathematics'. The Hague.

HILL, A. A. (1958), 'An Introduction to Linguistic Structures'. New York.

HJELMSLEV, LOUIS (1953), 'Prolegomena to a Theory of Language', translated by F. J. Whitfield. Baltimore' (The Danish original was published in 1943.)

HOCKETT, C. F. (1958), 'A Course in Modern Linguistics'. New York.

—— (1961), 'Linguistic Elements and their Relations', *Language*, 37, 29–53.

HUDDLESTON, R. D. (1965), 'Rank and Depth', *Language*, 41, 574–586.

—— (1967), 'More on the English Comparative', *Journal of Linguistics*, 3, 91–102.

HUDSON, R. A. (1967), 'Constituency in a Systemic Description of the English Clause'. *Lingua*, 17.

INTERNATIONAL PHONETIC ASSOCIATION, The Principles of the, (1949). London. The Association's journal, *Le Maitre Phonétique*, carries the recommended alphabet of symbols inside its back cover.

JACOBSON, S. (1964), 'Adverbial Positions in English'. Stockholm.

JAKOBSON, ROMAN (1956), 'For Roman Jakobson', ed. M. Halle, et al. The Hague.

—— (1961), 'Linguistics and Communication Theory', *Proceedings of Symposia in Applied Mathematics*, Providence, 12.

—— R., FANT, C. G. M. and HALLE, M. (1952), 'Preliminaries to Speech Analysis'. Cambridge, Massachusetts.

—— and HALLE, M. (1956), 'Fundamentals of Language'. The Hague.

JENSEN, A. M. (1961). 'Language and Society' (essays presented to A. M. J.). Copenhagen.

JESPERSEN, OTTO (1909–1949), 'A Modern English Grammar on Historical Principles'. Parts 1–7. Heidelberg.

—— (1933), 'Essentials of English Grammar'. London.

JONES, DANIEL (1950), 'The Phoneme: Its Nature and Use'. Cambridge, England.

—— (1956₁), 'An Outline of English Phonetics'. Eighth edition. Cambridge, England.

—— (1956₂), 'The Pronunciation of English'. Fourth edition. London.

JOOS, MARTIN (1948), 'Acoustic Phonetics'. Language Monograph, 23, Baltimore.

—— (1957), ed., 'Readings in Linguistics'. Washington. (Second edition, with revised Preface, 1958; also in paperback.)

—— (1962), 'The Five Clocks'. Bloomington.

KATZ, J. J. and POSTAL, P. M. (1964), 'An Integrated Theory of Linguistic Descriptions'. Research Monograph 26, M.I.T., Cambridge, Massachusetts.

KELLER, HELEN (1903), 'The Story of my Life'. New York. (Reprinted many times in hard cover and paperback.)

KENNEDY, A. G. (1920), 'The Modern English Verb-Adverb Combination', University Series, *Language and Literature*, I, 1, Stanford.

KINGDON, R. (1951, reprinted 1957), 'The Irregular Verbs', *English Language Teaching*, XI, 123–133 (1957).

—— (1958₁), 'The Groundwork of English Intonation'. London.

—— (1958₂), 'The Groundwork of English Stress'. London.

KRUISINGA, E. and READES, P. A. (1953, 1960), 'An English Grammar', I, Parts 1 and 2. Groningen.

LADEFOGED, PETER (1962), 'Elements of Acoustic Phonetics'. Edinburgh.

—— and BROADBENT, D. E. (1957), 'Information Conveyed by Vowels', *Journal of the Acoustical Society of America*, 29, 98–104.

LAMB, SYDNEY M. (1964), 'On Alteration, Transformation, Realization and Stratification'. *Georgetown Monograph Series on Languages and Linguistics*, 17, 105–122. Washington, D.C.

LEES, R. B. (1961), 'The Grammar of English Nominalizations'. Bloomington.

—— and KLIMA, E. S. (1963), 'Rules for English Pronominalization', *Language*, 39, 17–28.

LENNEBERG, E. H. (1964), ed., 'New Directions in the Study of Language'. Cambridge, Massachusetts (now also as an M.I.T. Press paperback).

LEECH, G. N. (1966), 'English in Advertising'. London.

LORENZ, KONRAD (1952), 'King Solomon's Ring', translated by Marjorie Kerr Wilson. London. (Also in paperback.)

McINTOSH, A. and HALLIDAY, M. A. K. (1966), 'Patterns of Language'. London.

MALINOWSKI, BRONISLAV (1923), Supplement I, 'The Problem of Meaning in Primitive Languages', in Ogden and Richards, q.v.

—— (1935), 'Coral Gardens and their Magic'. London.

MARCHAND, HANS (1960), 'The Categories and Types of Present-Day English Word-Formation'. Wiesbaden.

—— (1966), 'Attributive and Predicative Derived Adjectives', *Anglia*, 84, 131–149.

MARTINET, ANDRÉ (1962), 'A Functional View of Language'. Oxford.

—— (1964), 'Elements of General Linguistics' (translated by E. Palmer from 'Elements de Linguistique Générale', which first appeared in 1960). London.

MARTINET, ANDRÉ and WEINREICH, URIEL (1954), 'Linguistics Today', *Publications of the Linguistic Circle of New York, 2.* New York.

MILLER, G. A. (1951), 'Language and Communication'. New York. (Also in paperback.)

MITCHELL, T. F. (1958), 'Syntagmatic Relations in Linguistic Analysis', *Transactions of the Philological Society,* 101–118.

NIDA, EUGENE (1949), 'Morphology'. Second edition. *University of Michigan Publications, Linguistics, 2.* Ann Arbor.

—— (1966), A Synopsis of English Syntax'. Second edition, revised. The Hague.

O'CONNOR, D. and ARNOLD, G. F. (1961), 'Intonation of Colloquial English'. London.

OGDEN, C. K. and RICHARDS, I. A. (1923), 'The Meaning of Meaning' (cf. MALINOWSKI, 1923). London (tenth edition 1949, reprinted 1960; also in paperback).

OLSSON, YNGVE (1961), 'On the Syntax of the English Verb with special reference to HAVE A LOOK and Similar Complex Structures' Gothenburg.

O'NEIL, WAYNE (1965), 'Kernels and Transformations'. New York.

OXFORD ENGLISH DICTIONARY (1933). 13 volumes. Oxford.

PALMER, H. E. (1928), 'A Grammar of Spoken English on a Strictly Phonetic Basis'. Cambridge, England.

PALMER, F. R. (1965), 'A Linguistic Study of the English Verb'. London.

PEIRCE, C. S. (1931–), 'Collected Papers'. Volumes 1–8 continuing. Cambridge, Massachusetts.

PERMANENT INTERNATIONAL COMMITTEE OF LINGUISTS (1939–), 'Linguistic Bibliography'. (The first issue was a two-volume bibliography covering the years 1939–1947; thereafter one volume appears for each year.)

PICKETT, VELMA (1956), 'An Introduction to the Study of Grammatical Structure'. Glendale, California.

PIKE, K. L. (1943), 'Phonetics'. *University of Michigan Publications in Language and Literature,* 21. Ann Arbor.

—— (1945), 'The Intonation of American English'. *University of Michigan Publications, Linguistics,* 1. Ann Arbor.

—— (1947), 'Phonemics'. *University of Michigan Publications, Linguistics,* 3. Ann Arbor.

—— (1967), 'Language in Relation to a Unified Theory of the Structure of Human Behavior'. Second edition, revised. The Hague.

POTTER, RALPH K., KOPP, GEORGE A. and GREEN, HARRIET C. (1947), 'Visible Speech'. Bell Telephone Laboratories Series. New York.

POUTSMA, H. (1926–1929), 'A Grammar of Late Modern English'. Parts I, 1–2; II, 2. Groningen.

QUIRK, RANDOLPH (1955), 'Colloquial English and Communication'. *Studies in Communication*, University College, London, 169–182.

—— (1957), 'Relative Clauses in Educated Spoken English', *English Studies*, XXXVIII, 97–109.

—— (1958), 'Substitutions and Syntactical Research', *Archivum Linguisticum*, X, 37–42.

—— (1960), 'Towards a Description of English Usage'. *Transactions of the Philological Society*, 40–61.

—— (1965), 'Descriptive Statement and Serial Relationship', *Language*, 41, 205–217.

—— (1966₁), 'Acceptability in Language', *Proceedings of the University of Newcastle upon Tyne Philosophical Society*, I, 7, 79–92.

—— (1966₂), 'On English Usage', *Journal of the Royal Society of Arts*, 114, 837–851.

—— (1967), 'Our Knowledge of English', *The Incorporated Linguist*, 6, I, 1–6.

—— (1968), 'The Use of English'. Second edition, revised. London.

—— et al. (1964), 'Studies in the Correspondence of Prosodic to Grammatical Features in English', *Proceedings of the Ninth International Congress of Linguists*, 1962, 679–691. The Hague.

—— and MULHOLLAND, J. (1964), 'Complex Prepositions and Related Sequences', English Studies, 44, 64–73 (Zandvoort volume).

—— and SVARTVIK, JAN (1966), 'Investigating Linguistic Acceptability'. The Hague.

ROBERTS, PAUL (1964), 'English Syntax'. New York.

ROBINS, R. H. (1957), 'Aspects of Prosodic Analysis', *Proceedings of the University of Durham Philosophical Society*, I, B, 1.

—— (1959), 'In Defence of WP', *Transactions of the Philological Society*, 116–144.

—— (1964), 'General Linguistics: An Introductory Survey'. London.

ROGET, P. M. (1962), 'Thesaurus', ed. R. A. Dutch. London.

ROSENBAUM, P. S. (1967), 'Phrase Structure Principles of English Complex Sentence Formation', *Journal of Linguistics*, 3, 103–118.

RYLE, G. (1949), 'The Concept of Mind'. London.

SAPIR, E. (1921), 'Language, an Introduction to the Study of Speech'. New York. (Also in paperback).

—— (1949), 'Selected Writings', ed. David G. Mandelbaum. Berkeley. (Also as a paperback, 1956, under the title 'Culture, Language and Personality', Cambridge, England.)

SAUSSURE, FERDINAND DE (1916), 'Cours de Linguistique Générale'. Paris.

—— (1961), 'Course in General Linguistics', translated by Wade Baskin. London.

—— (1967), 'Cours de Linguistique Générale', édition critique. Wiesbaden.

SCHEURWEGHS, G. (1959), 'Present-day English Syntax'. London.

SCHUBIGER, MARIA (1958), 'English Intonation'. Tübingen.

SHARP, A. E. (1960), 'The Analysis of Stress and Juncture in English', Transactions of the Philological Society, 104–135.

SLEDD, JAMES (1959), 'A Short Introduction to English Grammar'. Chicago.

SMITH, A. H. and QUIRK, RANDOLPH (1954), 'Some Problems of Verbal Communication', Transactions of the Yorkshire Dialect Society, Part LIV, IX (1955 for 1954), 10–20.

SQUIRE, J. C. (1966), ed. 'A Common Purpose'. Champaign, Illinois. (Paper by Quirk.)

STETSON, R. H. (1945), 'Bases of Phonology'. Oberlin.

—— (1951), 'Motor Phonetics'. Second edition. Amsterdam.

STRANG, BARBARA M. H. (1958), 'Types and Tokens in Language', Proceedings of the University of Durham Philosophical Society, I, B, 3.

—— (1964), 'Theory and Practice in Morpheme Identification', Proceedings of the Ninth International Congress of Linguistics, 1962, 358–365. The Hague.

—— (1965), 'Metaphors and Models'. Newcastle upon Tyne.

—— (1966), 'Some Features of S–V Concord in Present-Day English', in English Studies Today (Proceedings of the Sixth I.A.U.P.E. Congress), 73–87. Rome.

STREVENS, PETER (1956), 'Spoken Language'. London.

—— (1964), 'Varieties of English', English Studies, 45, 20–30.

SWEET, HENRY (1891–1898), 'A New English Grammar, Logical and Historical'. Oxford (now reprinted, 1955–60).

SVARTVIK, JAN (1966), 'On Voice in the English Verb'. The Hague.

THOMAS, OWEN P. (1966), 'Transformational Grammar and the Teacher of English'. New York.

THORNE, J. P. (1966), 'English Imperative Sentences', Journal of Linguistics, 2, 69–78.

TRAGER, G. L. and SMITH, HENRY LEE, Jr. (1951), 'An Outline of Linguistic Structure'. Studies in Linguistics, Occasional Papers, 3. Norman.

TWADDELL, W. F. (1960), 'The English Verb Auxiliaries'. Providence, Rhode Island.

VENDRYES, J. (1925), 'Language'. London.

WARD, IDA C. (1948). 'The Phonetics of English'. Fourth edition (1945) reprinted with minor corrections. Cambridge, England.

WEBSTER, NOAH (1961), 'Third New International Dictionary of the English Language'. Springfield, Massachusetts.

WHITEHALL, HAROLD B. (1956), 'Structural Essentials of English'. New York.

WHORF, BENJAMIN LEE (1956), 'Language, Thought and Reality', ed. John B. Carroll. Cambridge, Massachusetts. (Also in paperback.)

WITTGENSTEIN, LUDWIG (1953), 'Philosophical Investigations', translated by G. E. M. Anscombe, Oxford.

YULE, GEORGE U. (1944), 'The Statistical Study of Literary Vocabulary'. London.

ZANDVOORT, R. W. (1965), 'A Handbook of English Grammar'. Third unilingual English edition. London.

ZIMMER, K. E. (1964), 'Affixal negation in English and other Languages', Monograph 5, Supplement to *Word*, 20.

Index

The Index is designed to be the fullest of three guides to the material of the book—the others being the analytical contents and the running titles of the pages. It can best achieve its end by being something of a subject-index and something of a word-index, but not uniformly one or the other. Items are included whenever they have a remotely technical or linguistic sense; different senses of the same term are distinguished if they seem likely to cause confusion, but minor differences (for instance, if an author quoted uses a different definition from my own) are not indicated. References are by page-number, and are given in bold type when they are of central importance for the definition or application of a term. There is naturally considerable, but not total, correspondence between the use of bold in the text and its use in the Index. In deciding whether to enter separately closely related words, such as *phonemic*, *phonemically*, I have been less concerned with narrow consistency than with achieving what I thought the greatest measure of clarity without cumbersomeness; but words whose attributive is formed differently from the base, such as *noun*, *nominal*, do have separate entries. Where a straightforward derivative, such as *verbal*, *adverbial*, has a separate entry, this is normally a sign that the derived form has achieved independent status as a technical term, and does not simply mean 'having the character of a [*verb, adverb* . . .]'.

The order is alphabetical across the entry, even if interrupted by word-boundary. But some entries contain supplementary material, which does not enter into the alphabetical ordering—abbreviations, synonyms and cross-references are thus added in brackets, and so, if necessary, are nouns commonly associated with certain attributive entries; glosses distinguishing variant meanings are in square brackets.

The Index is somewhat swollen by entries for terms not adopted by me but quoted or referred to in the work of other scholars; cross-reference is meant to guide readers through such terminological problems. On the other hand, the Index would have been more cumbersome if I had not omitted the material of the Exercises, Further Reading, Bibliography and plates. Privative terms (e.g., formations in *de-, non-, un-*) are not entered separately from their positive partners unless they have an independent function. Where an entry would require over forty references evenly distributed throughout the text it may be said to occur *passim*; in such cases I have not thought it meaningful to include an entry unless attention has to be called to a bold-type treatment in the text. The absence of entries for e.g., *contrast, pattern* and *speech*, and the brevity of entries for *form, function, structure* and *system*, therefore suggest the lines of my treatment of the subject as clearly as the number of entries beginning with *non-*.